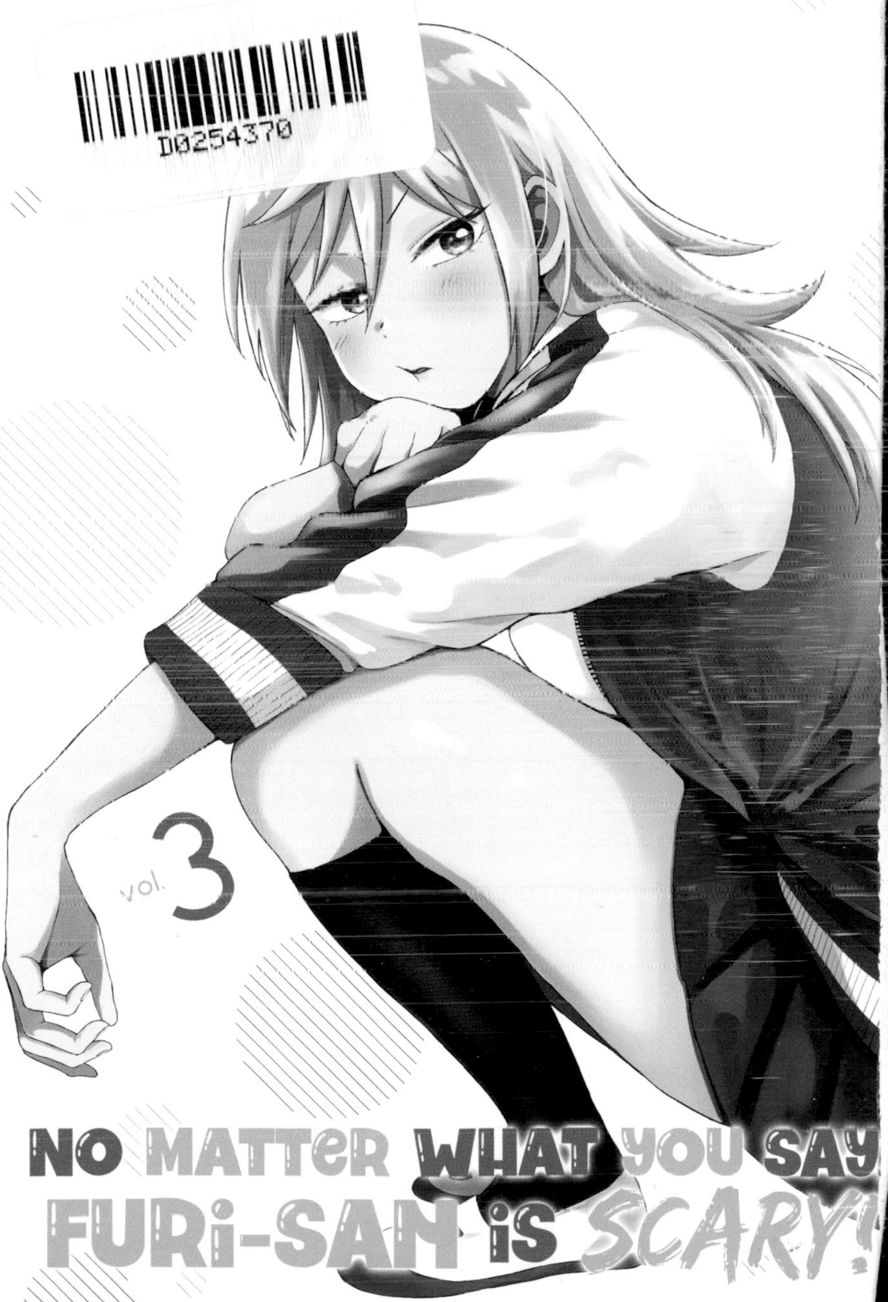
vol. 3

NO MATTER WHAT YOU SAY FURi-SAN iS SCARY!

Contents

Chapter 18 ———— 003

Chapter 19 ———— 009

Chapter 20 ———— 025

Chapter 21 ———— 041

Chapter 22 ———— 057

Chapter 23 ———— 073

Chapter 24 ———— 089

Chapter 25 ———— 105

Chapter 26 ———— 115

Bonus Chapter (24.5) — 130

Chapter 18

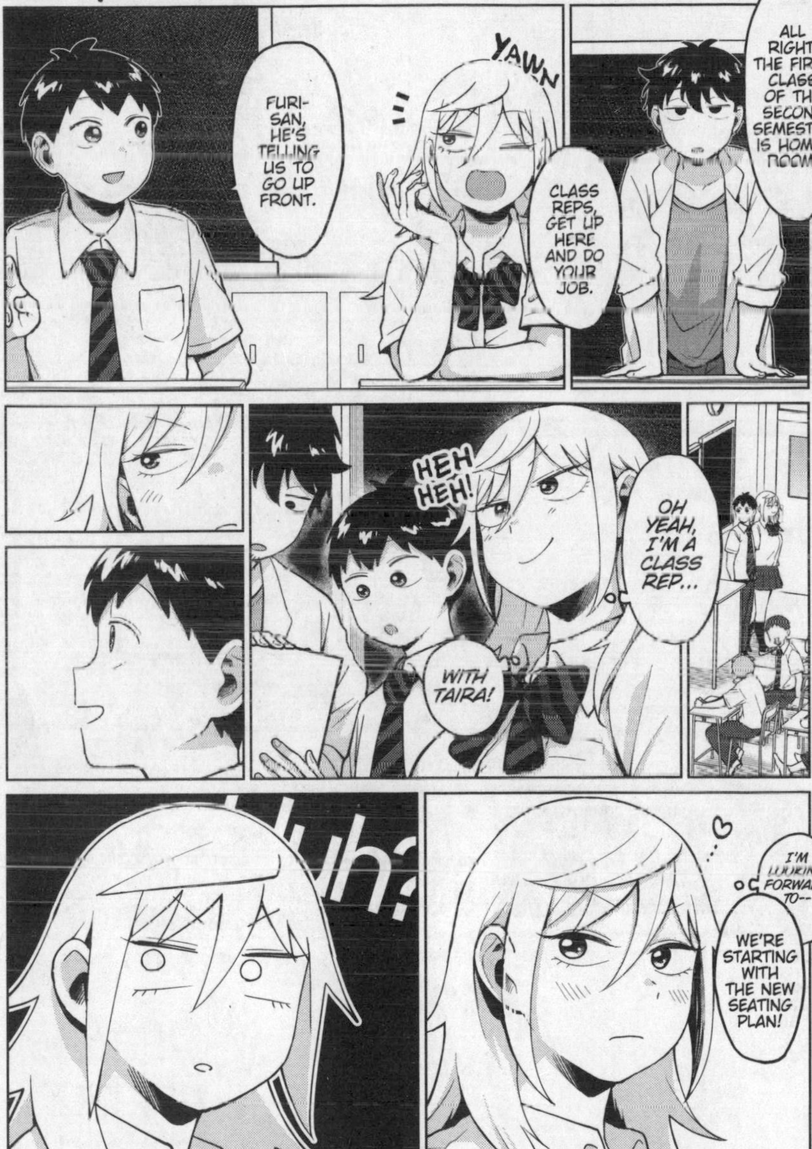
ALL RIGHT, THE FIRST CLASS OF THE SECOND SEMESTER IS HOMEROOM.
YAWN
CLASS REPS, GET UP HERE AND DO YOUR JOB.
FURI-SAN, HE'S TELLING US TO GO UP FRONT.
OH YEAH, I'M A CLASS REP...
HEH HEH!
WITH TAIRA!
I'M LOOKING FORWARD TO--
WE'RE STARTING WITH THE NEW SEATING PLAN!
Huh?

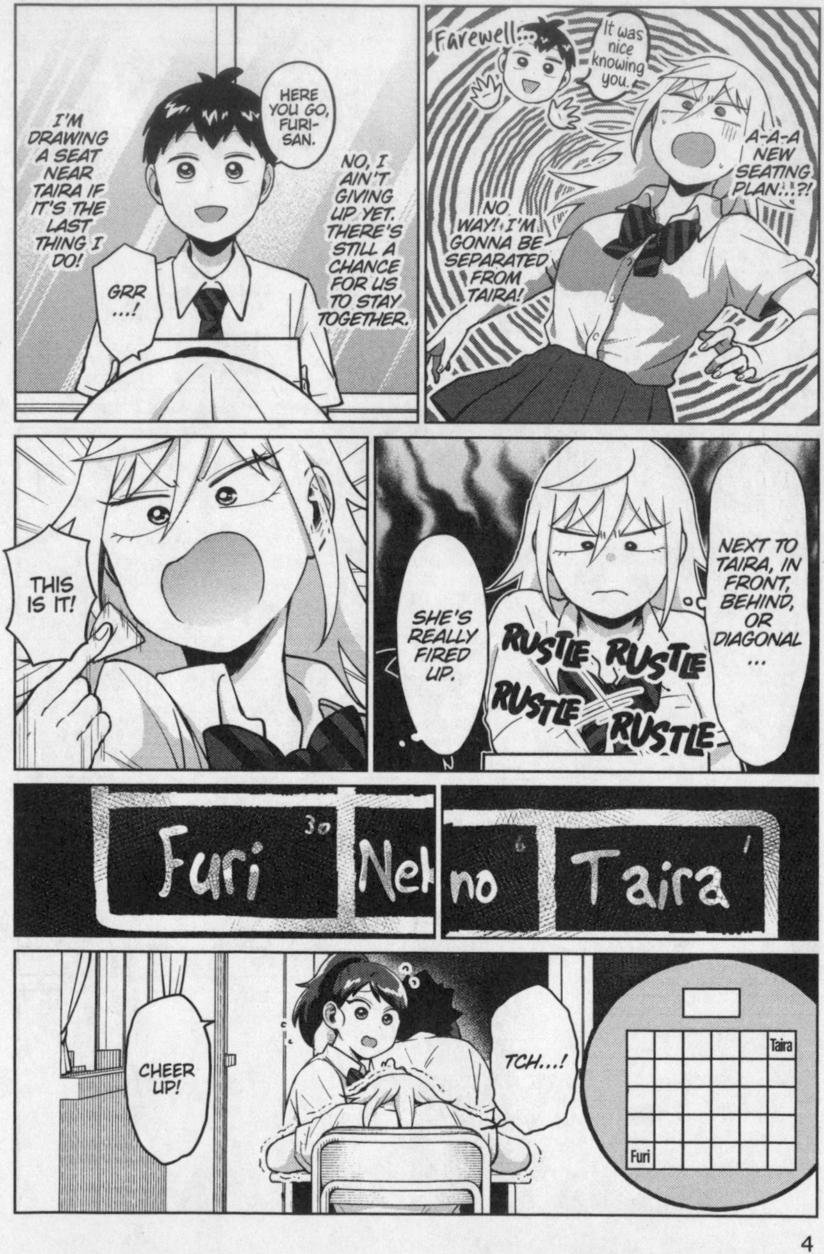
Farewell...
It was nice knowing you.
A-A-A NEW SEATING PLAN...?!
NO WAY! I'M GONNA BE SEPARATED FROM TAIRA!
HERE YOU GO, FURI-SAN.
NO, I AIN'T GIVING UP YET. THERE'S STILL A CHANCE FOR US TO STAY TOGETHER.
I'M DRAWING A SEAT NEAR TAIRA IF IT'S THE LAST THING I DO!
GRR ...!
NEXT TO TAIRA, IN FRONT, BEHIND, OR DIAGONAL ...
RUSTLE RUSTLE
RUSTLE RUSTLE
SHE'S REALLY FIRED UP.
THIS IS IT!
no Taira
Furi Nek
Taira
Furi
TCH...!
CHEER UP!

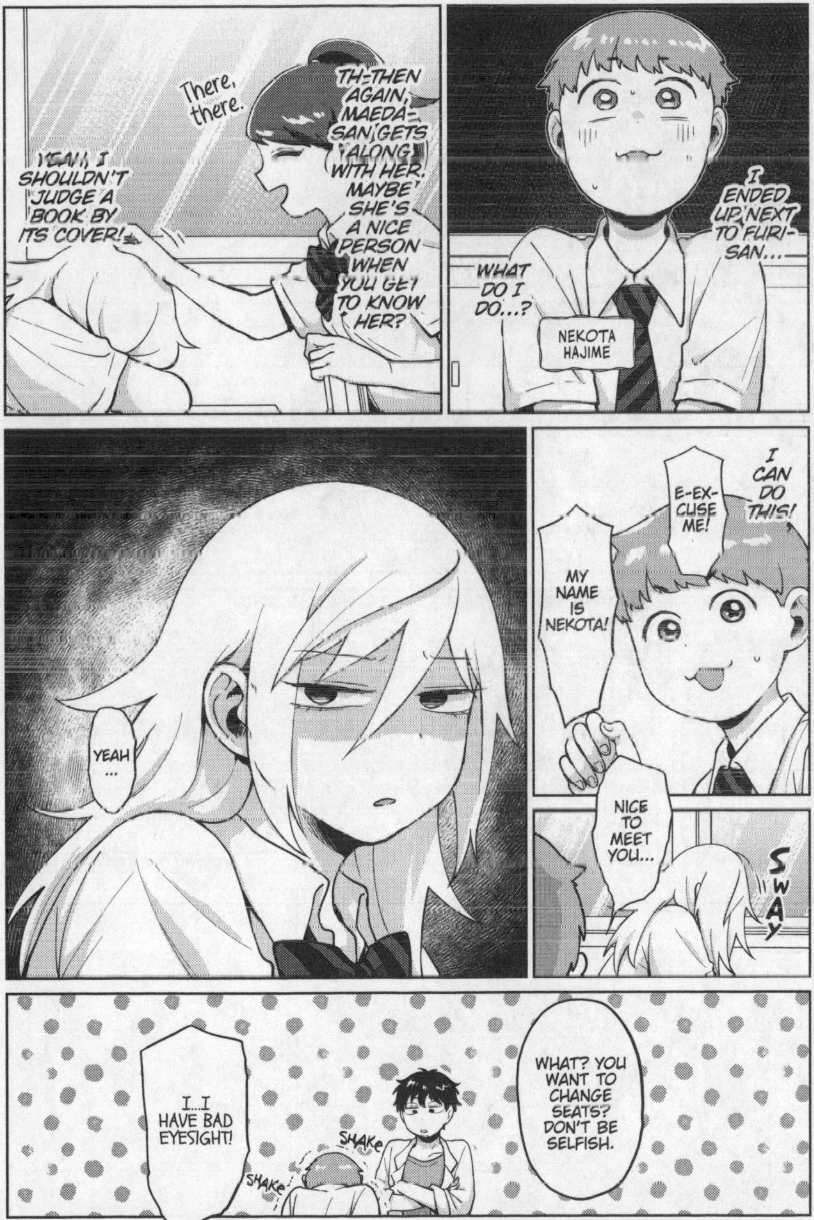
I ENDED UP NEXT TO FURI-SAN...
WHAT DO I DO...?
NEKOTA HAJIME
TH-THEN AGAIN, MAEDA-SAN GETS ALONG WITH HER. MAYBE SHE'S A NICE PERSON WHEN YOU GET TO KNOW HER?
There, there.
YEAH, I SHOULDN'T JUDGE A BOOK BY ITS COVER!
I CAN DO THIS!
E-EXCUSE ME!
MY NAME IS NEKOTA!
NICE TO MEET YOU...
SWAY
YEAH ...
WHAT? YOU WANT TO CHANGE SEATS? DON'T BE SELFISH.
SHAKE
SHAKE
I...I HAVE BAD EYESIGHT!

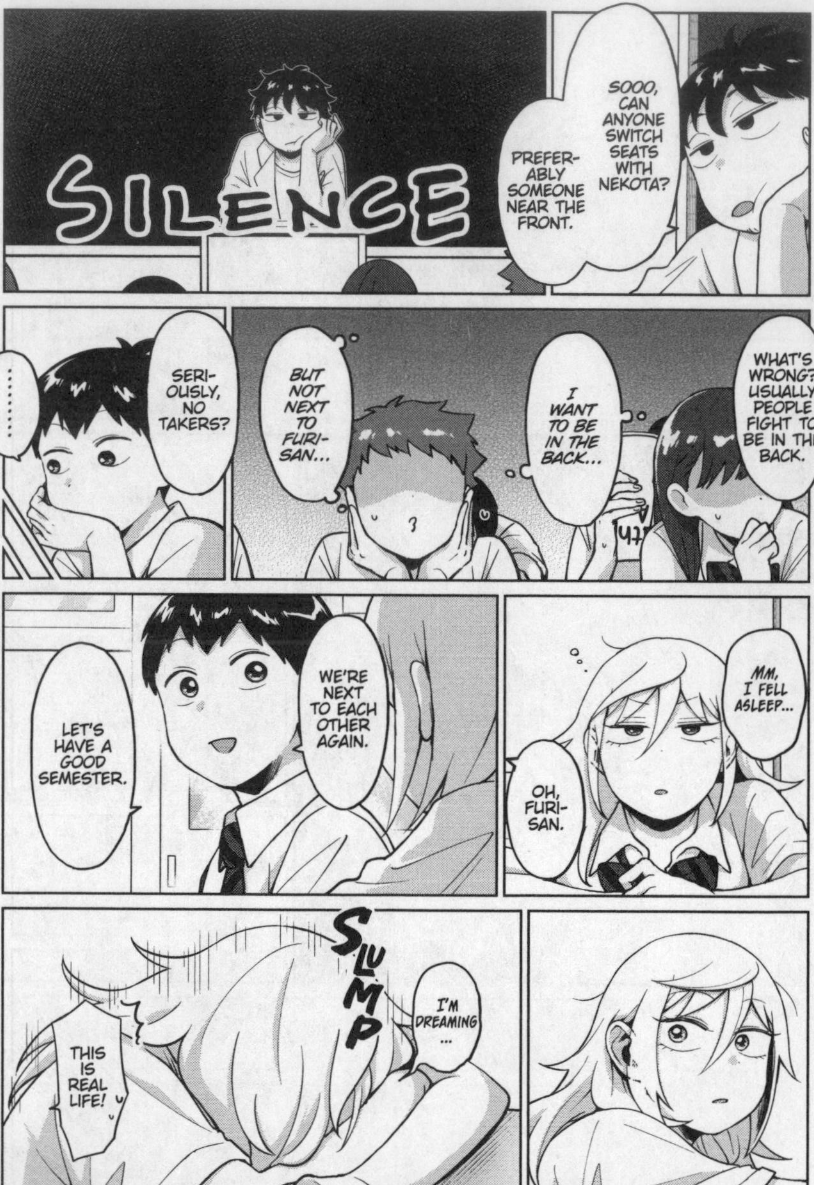
SOOO, CAN ANYONE SWITCH SEATS WITH NEKOTA?
PREFERABLY SOMEONE NEAR THE FRONT.
SILENCE
WHAT'S WRONG? USUALLY PEOPLE FIGHT TO BE IN THE BACK.
I WANT TO BE IN THE BACK...
BUT NOT NEXT TO FURI-SAN...
SERIOUSLY, NO TAKERS?
......
MM, I FELL ASLEEP...
OH, FURI-SAN.
WE'RE NEXT TO EACH OTHER AGAIN.
LET'S HAVE A GOOD SEMESTER.
SLUMP
I'M DREAMING...
THIS IS REAL LIFE!

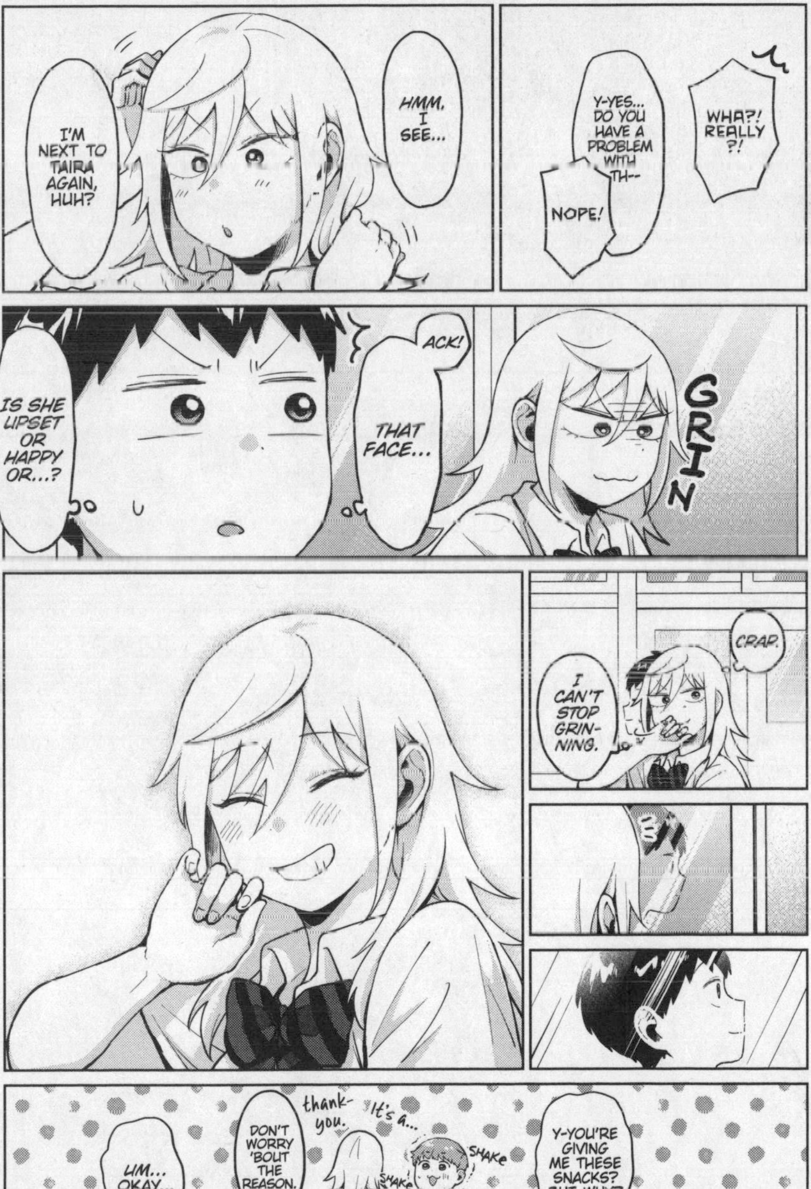
WHA?! REALLY ?!
Y-YES... DO YOU HAVE A PROBLEM WITH TH--
NOPE!
HMM, I SEE...
I'M NEXT TO TAIRA AGAIN, HUH?
GRIN
ACK!
THAT FACE...
IS SHE UPSET OR HAPPY OR...?
CRAP.
I CAN'T STOP GRIN-NING.
Y-YOU'RE GIVING ME THESE SNACKS? BUT WHY?
SHAKE
SHAKE
It's a...
thank-you.
DON'T WORRY 'BOUT THE REASON.
UM... OKAY...

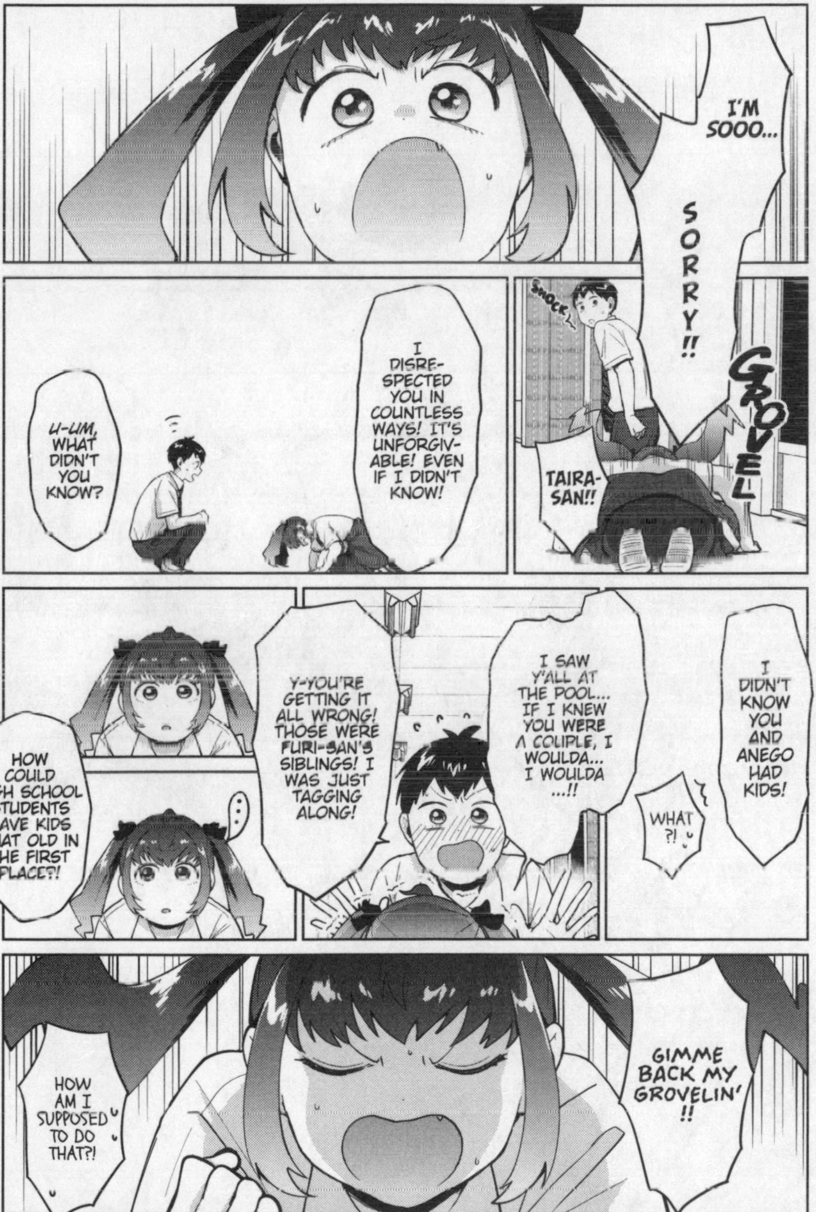
I'M SOOO...
SORRY!!
SHOCK
GROVEL
TAIRA-SAN!!
I DISRESPECTED YOU IN COUNTLESS WAYS! IT'S UNFORGIVABLE! EVEN IF I DIDN'T KNOW!
U-UM, WHAT DIDN'T YOU KNOW?
I DIDN'T KNOW YOU AND ANEGO HAD KIDS!
WHAT?!
I SAW Y'ALL AT THE POOL... IF I KNEW YOU WERE A COUPLE, I WOULDA... I WOULDA ...!!
Y-YOU'RE GETTING IT ALL WRONG! THOSE WERE FURI-SAN'S SIBLINGS! I WAS JUST TAGGING ALONG!
HOW COULD HIGH SCHOOL STUDENTS HAVE KIDS THAT OLD IN THE FIRST PLACE?!
...
GIMME BACK MY GROVELIN'!!
HOW AM I SUPPOSED TO DO THAT?!

Chapter 19

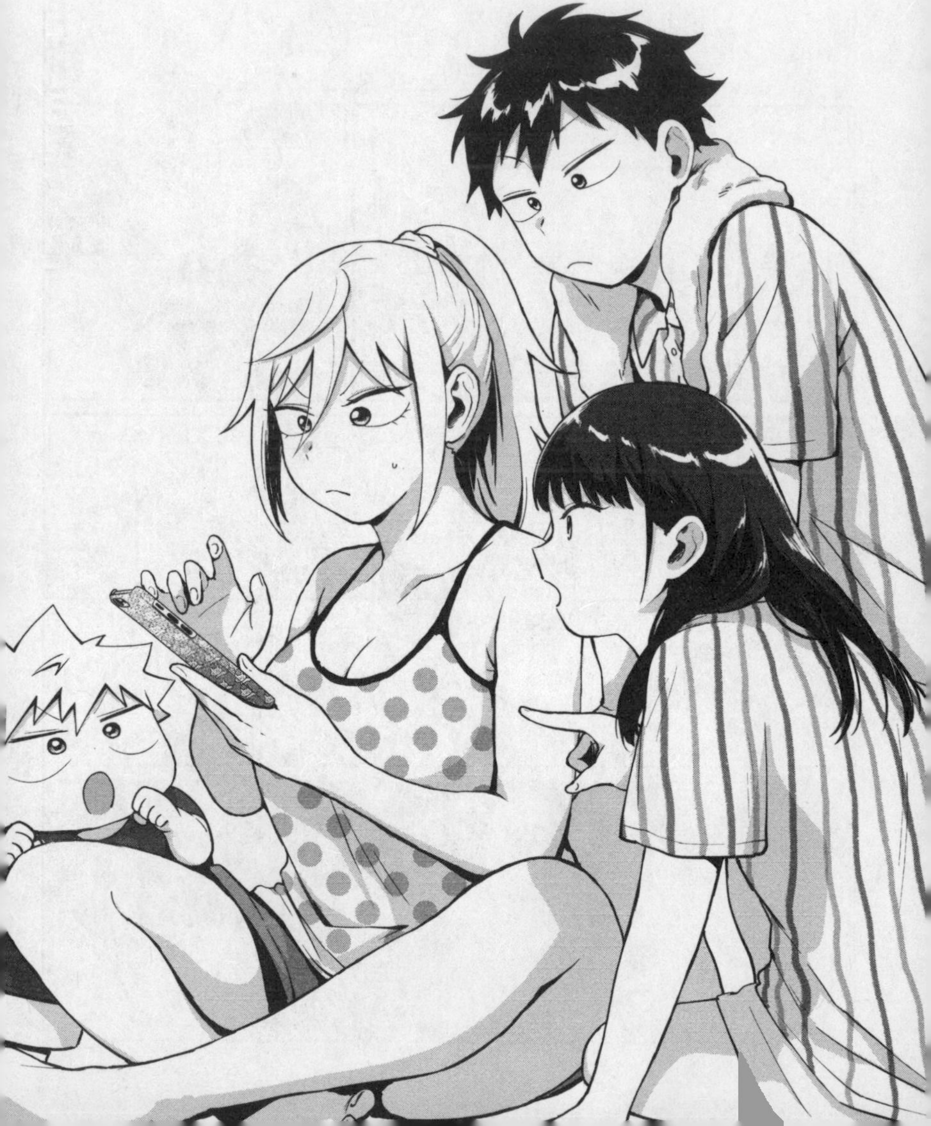

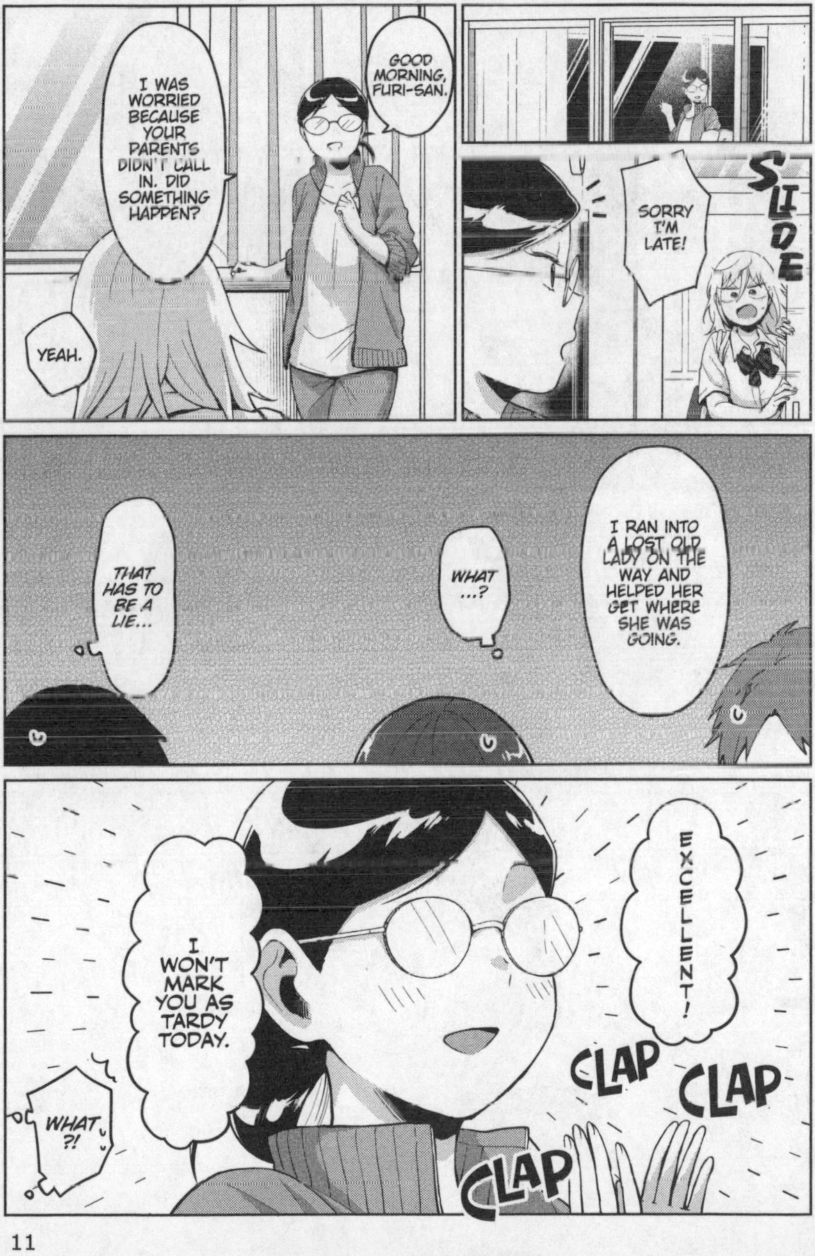
SLIDE
SORRY I'M LATE!
GOOD MORNING, FURI-SAN.
I WAS WORRIED BECAUSE YOUR PARENTS DIDN'T CALL IN. DID SOMETHING HAPPEN?
YEAH.
I RAN INTO A LOST OLD LADY ON THE WAY AND HELPED HER GET WHERE SHE WAS GOING.
WHAT ...?
THAT HAS TO BE A LIE...
EXCELLENT!
I WON'T MARK YOU AS TARDY TODAY.
CLAP
CLAP
CLAP
WHAT ?!

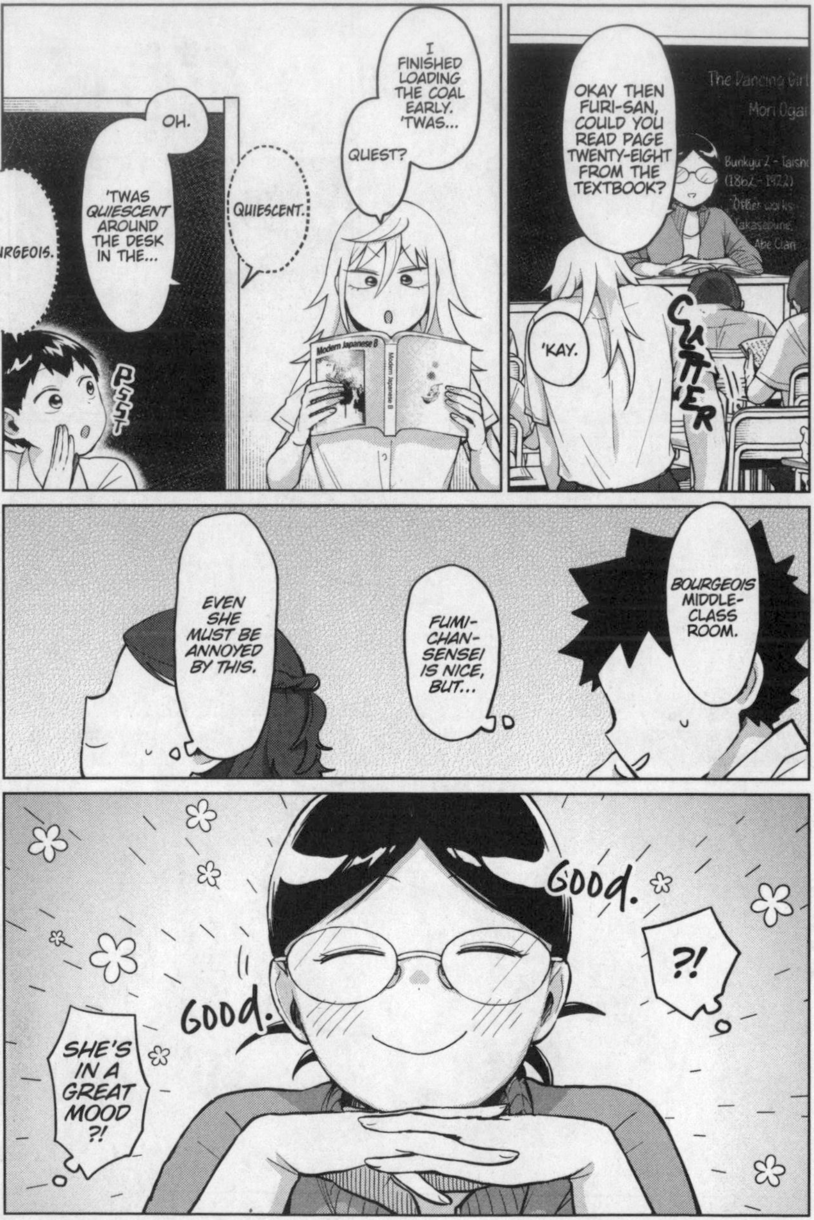
OKAY THEN FURI-SAN, COULD YOU READ PAGE TWENTY-EIGHT FROM THE TEXTBOOK?
'KAY.
CLATTER
I FINISHED LOADING THE COAL EARLY. 'TWAS...
QUEST?
QUIESCENT.
Modern Japanese B
OH.
'TWAS QUIESCENT AROUND THE DESK IN THE...
BOURGEOIS.
PSST
BOURGEOIS MIDDLE-CLASS ROOM.
FUMI-CHAN-SENSEI IS NICE, BUT...
EVEN SHE MUST BE ANNOYED BY THIS.
GOOD.
?!
GOOD.
SHE'S IN A GREAT MOOD?!

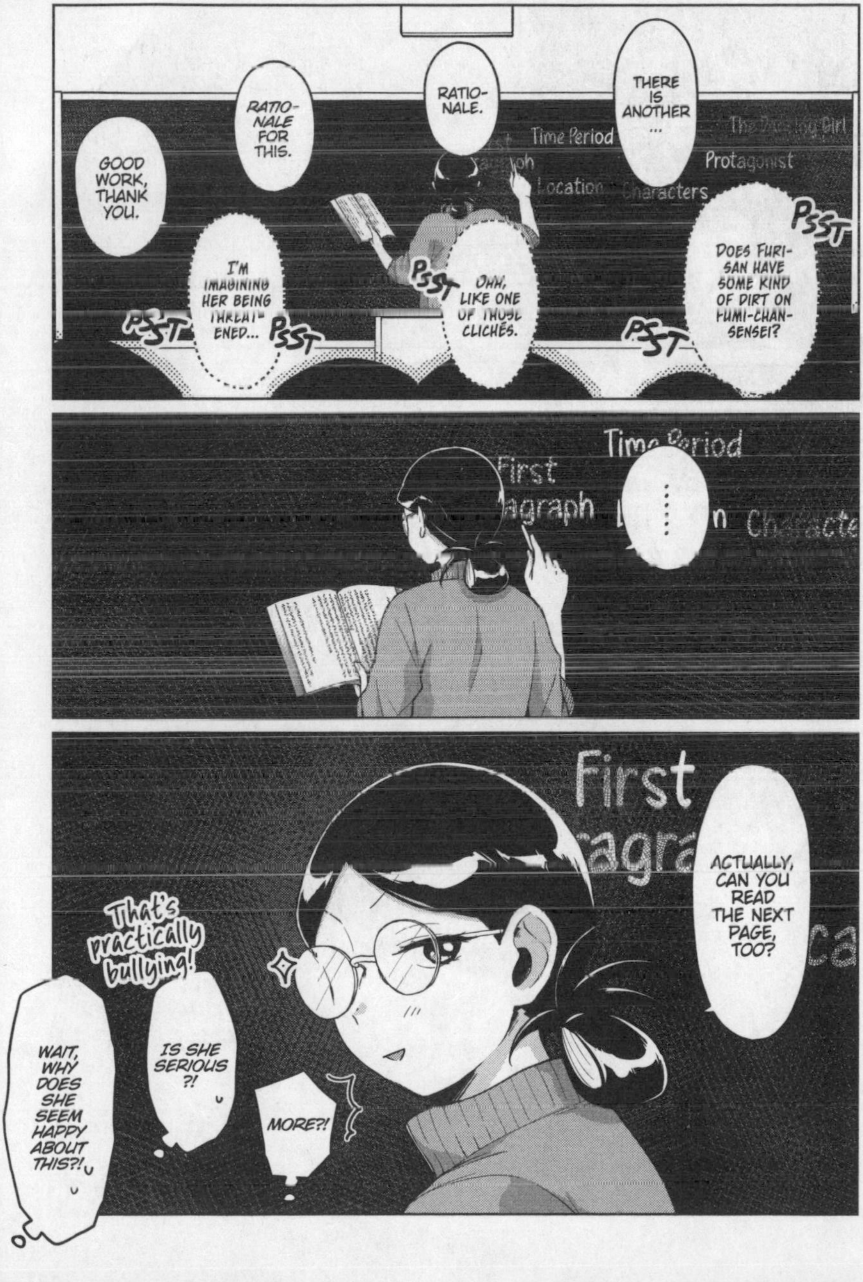
THERE IS ANOTHER ...
RATIONALE.
RATIONALE FOR THIS.
GOOD WORK, THANK YOU.
Protagonist
Characters
Time Period
Location
PSST
DOES FURI-SAN HAVE SOME KIND OF DIRT ON FUMI-CHAN-SENSEI?
PSST
OHH, LIKE ONE OF THOSE CLICHÉS.
PSST
I'M IMAGINING HER BEING THREATENED...
PSST
Time Period
First
......
ACTUALLY, CAN YOU READ THE NEXT PAGE, TOO?
First
MORE?!
IS SHE SERIOUS?!
That's practically bullying!
WAIT, WHY DOES SHE SEEM HAPPY ABOUT THIS?!

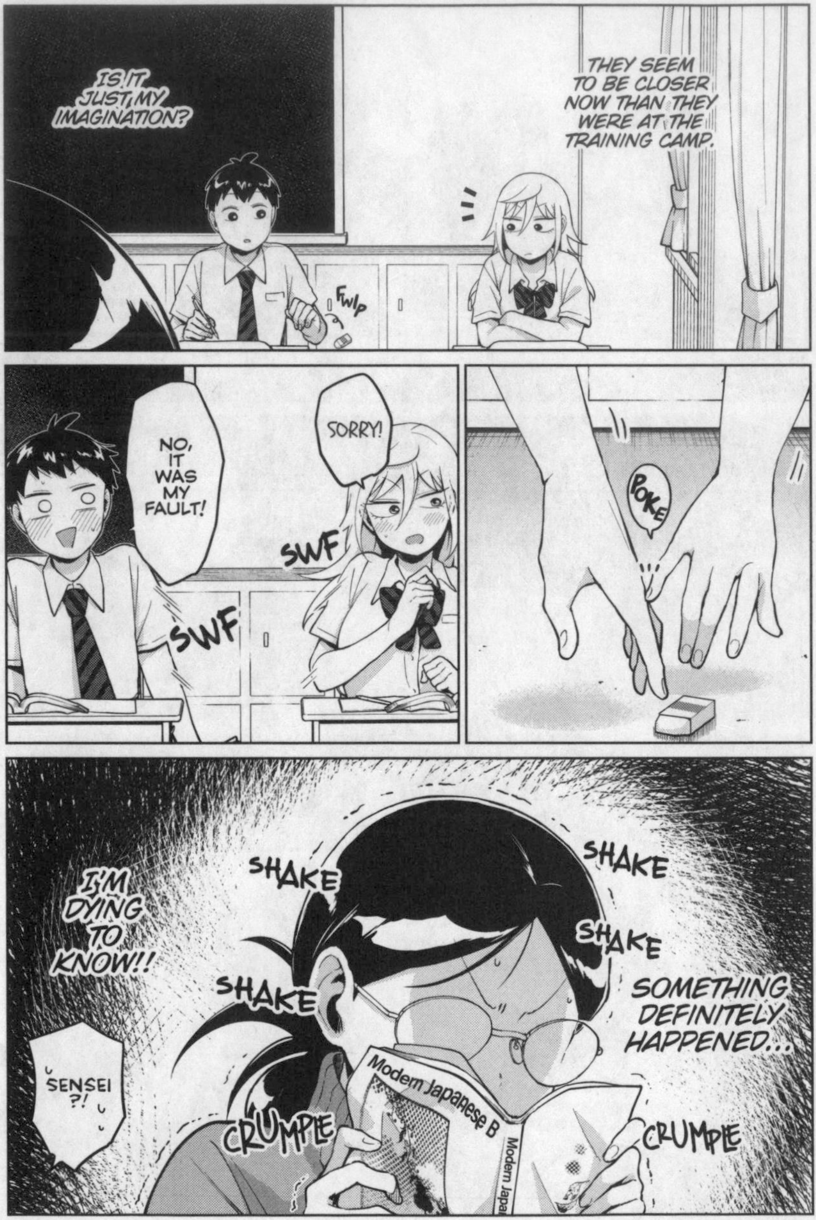
THEY SEEM TO BE CLOSER NOW THAN THEY WERE AT THE TRAINING CAMP.
IS IT JUST MY IMAGINATION?
FWIP
POKE
SORRY!
NO, IT WAS MY FAULT!
SWF
SWF
SHAKE
SHAKE
SOMETHING DEFINITELY HAPPENED...
SHAKE
I'M DYING TO KNOW!!
CRUMPLE
Modern Japanese B
CRUMPLE
SENSEI ?!

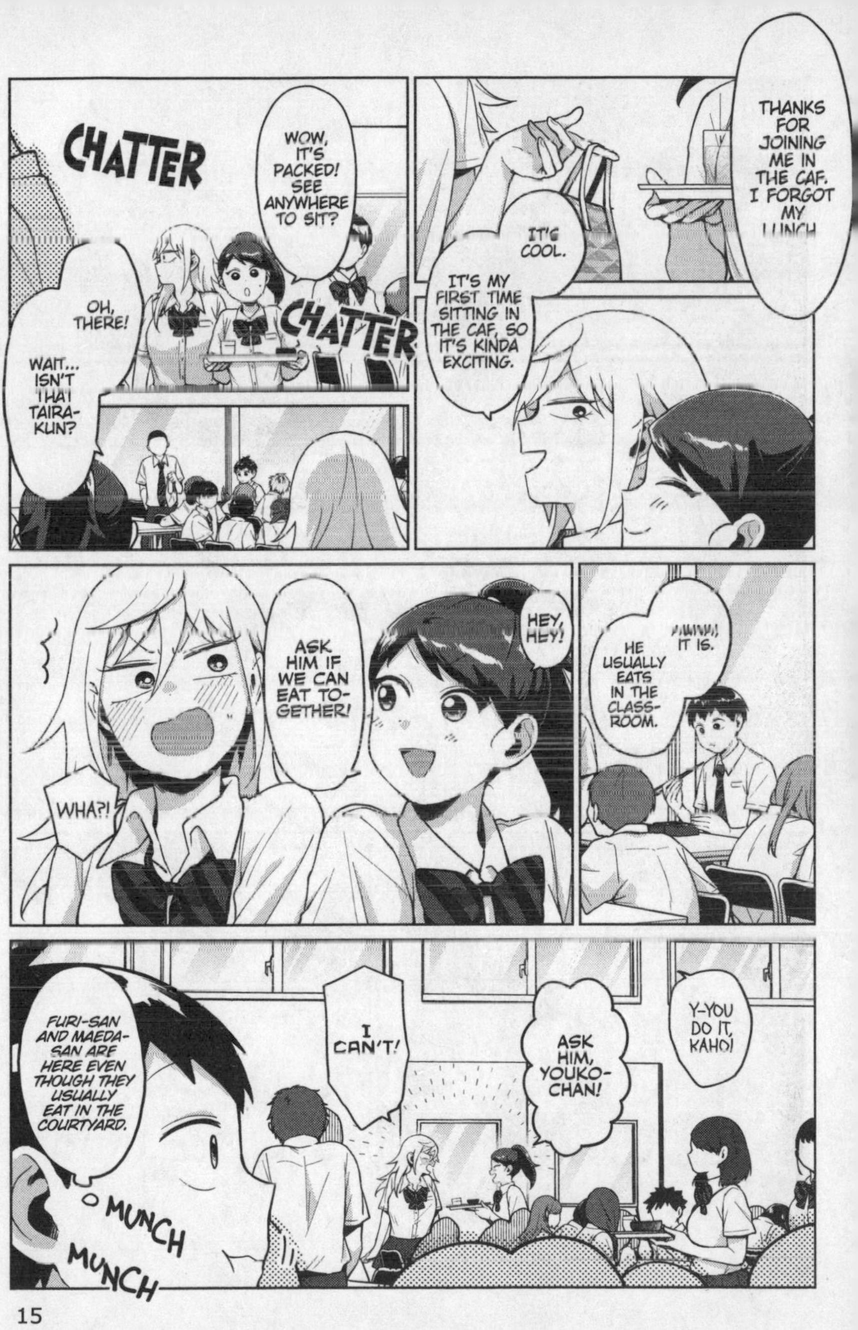
THANKS FOR JOINING ME IN THE CAF. I FORGOT MY LUNCH
IT'S COOL.
IT'S MY FIRST TIME SITTING IN THE CAF, SO IT'S KINDA EXCITING.
CHATTER
WOW, IT'S PACKED! SEE ANYWHERE TO SIT?
CHATTER
OH, THERE!
WAIT... ISN'T THAT TAIRA-KUN?
IT IS.
HE USUALLY EATS IN THE CLASS-ROOM.
HEY, HEY!
ASK HIM IF WE CAN EAT TO-GETHER!
WHA?!
Y-YOU DO IT, KAHO!
ASK HIM, YOUKO-CHAN!
I CAN'T!
FURI-SAN AND MAEDA-SAN ARE HERE EVEN THOUGH THEY USUALLY EAT IN THE COURTYARD.
MUNCH
MUNCH

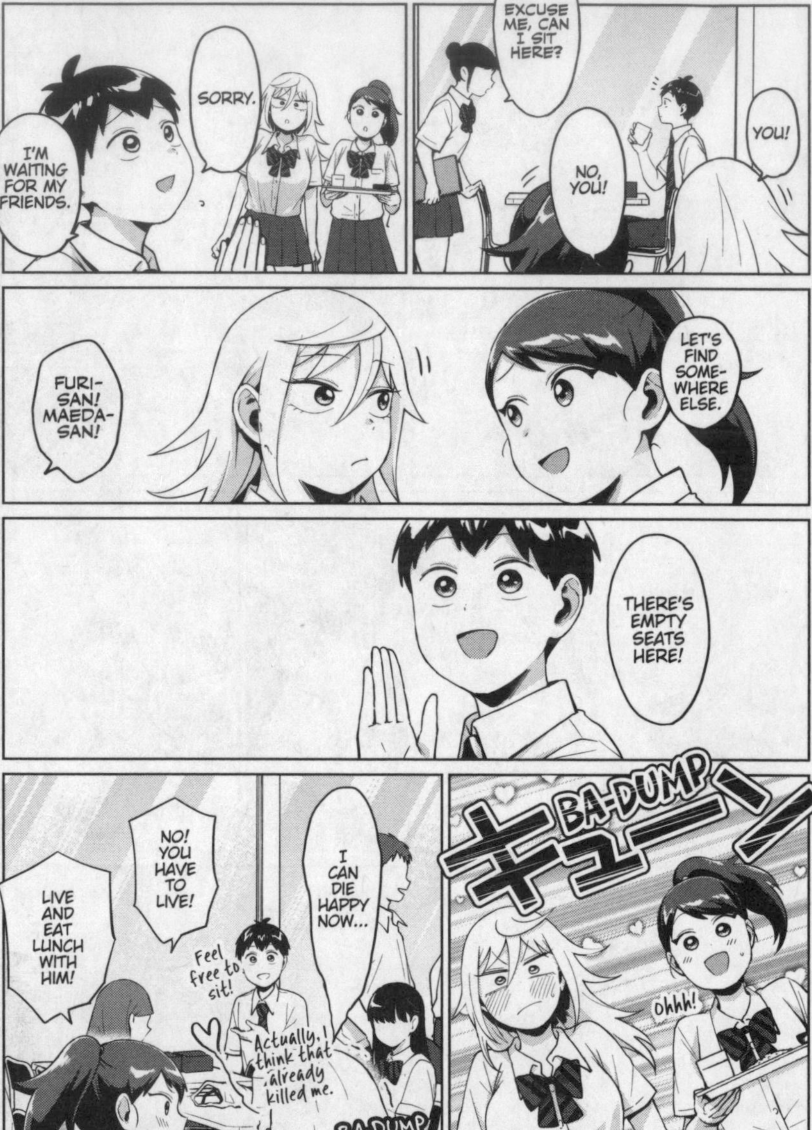
EXCUSE ME, CAN I SIT HERE?
YOU!
NO, YOU!
SORRY.
I'M WAITING FOR MY FRIENDS.
LET'S FIND SOMEWHERE ELSE.
FURI-SAN! MAEDA-SAN!
THERE'S EMPTY SEATS HERE!
BA-DUMP
キュー
Ohhh!
I CAN DIE HAPPY NOW...
NO! YOU HAVE TO LIVE!
LIVE AND EAT LUNCH WITH HIM!
Feel free to sit!
Actually, I think that already killed me.
BA-DUMP
BA-DUMP

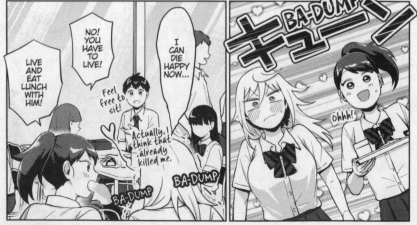

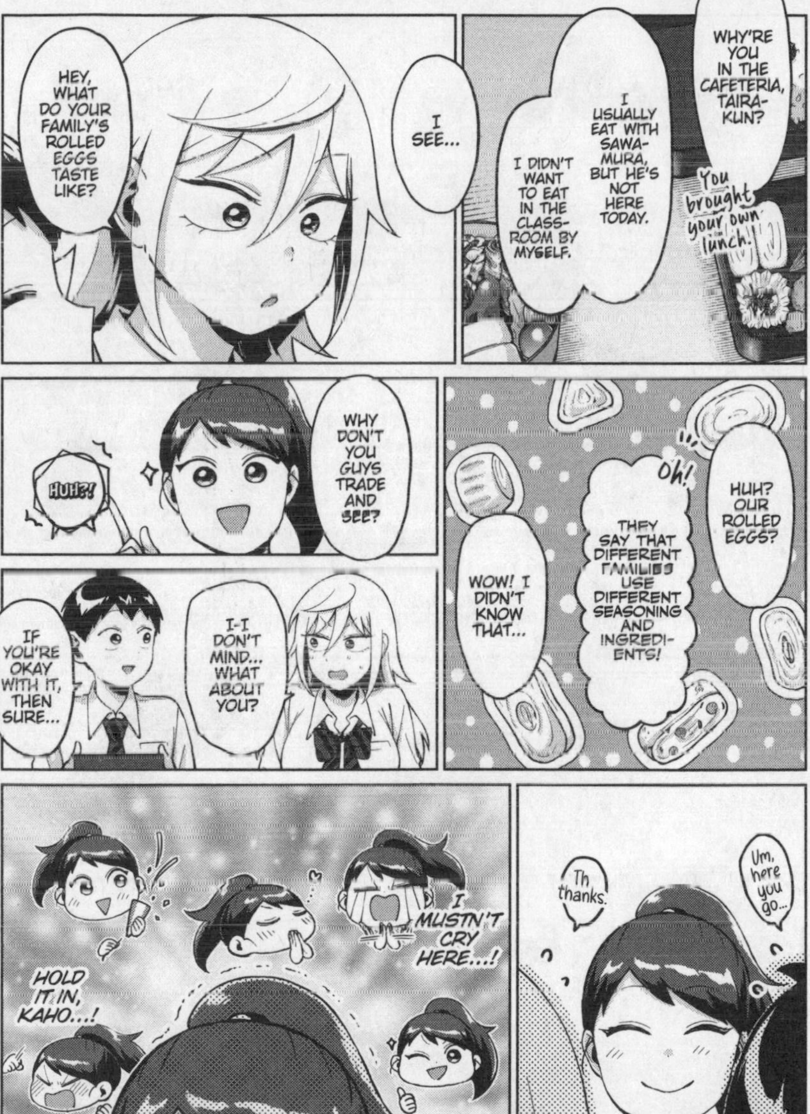
WHY'RE YOU IN THE CAFETERIA, TAIRA-KUN?
You brought your own lunch!
I USUALLY EAT WITH SAWAMURA, BUT HE'S NOT HERE TODAY.
I DIDN'T WANT TO EAT IN THE CLASSROOM BY MYSELF.
I SEE...
HEY, WHAT DO YOUR FAMILY'S ROLLED EGGS TASTE LIKE?
HUH? OUR ROLLED EGGS?
Oh!
THEY SAY THAT DIFFERENT FAMILIES USE DIFFERENT SEASONING AND INGREDIENTS!
WOW! I DIDN'T KNOW THAT...
WHY DON'T YOU GUYS TRADE AND SEE?
HUH?!
I-I DON'T MIND... WHAT ABOUT YOU?
IF YOU'RE OKAY WITH IT, THEN SURE...
Um, here you go...
Th thanks.
I MUSTN'T CRY HERE...!
HOLD IT IN, KAHO...!

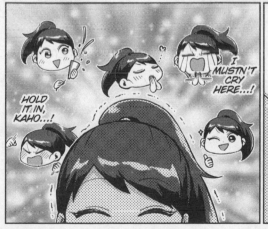

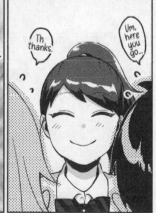

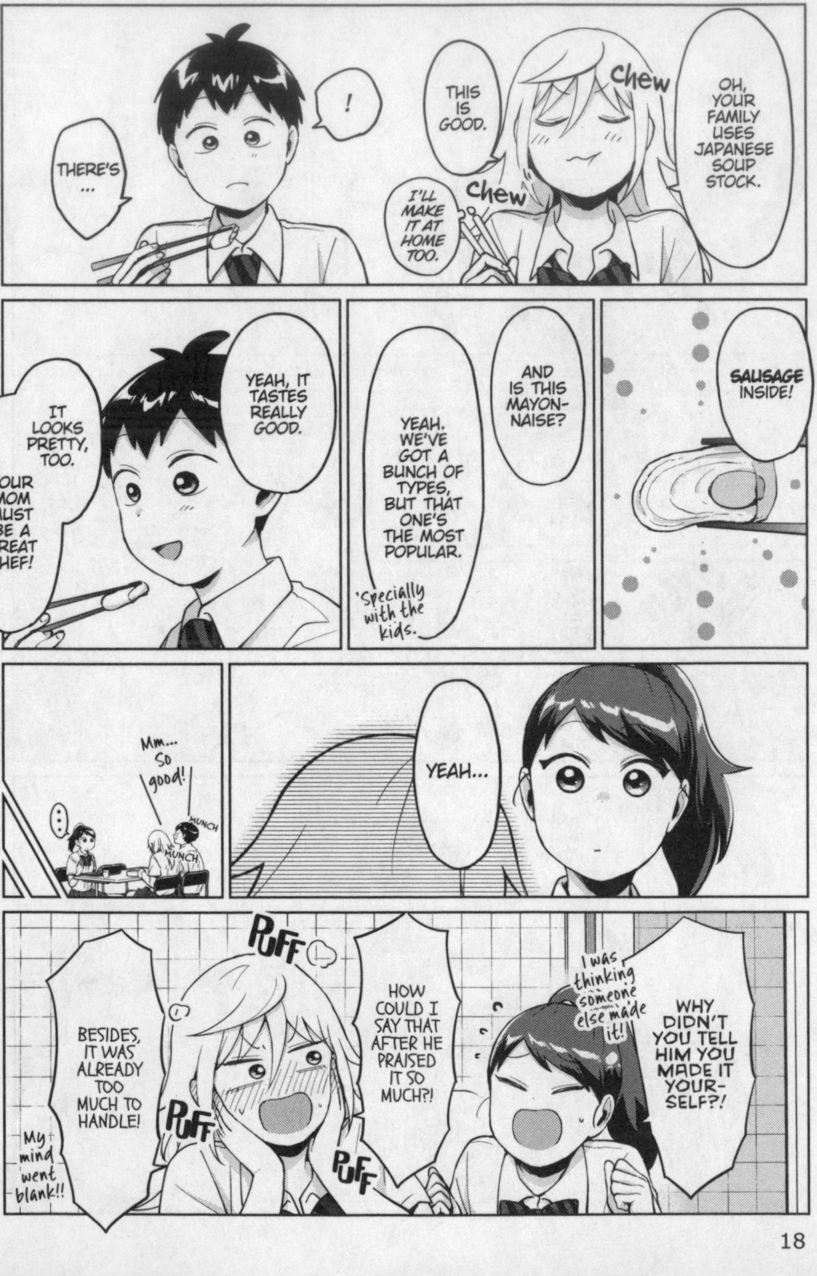
OH, YOUR FAMILY USES JAPANESE SOUP STOCK.
Chew
THIS IS GOOD.
I'LL MAKE IT AT HOME TOO.
Chew
!
THERE'S...
SAUSAGE INSIDE!
AND IS THIS MAYON-NAISE?
YEAH. WE'VE GOT A BUNCH OF TYPES, BUT THAT ONE'S THE MOST POPULAR.
'Specially with the kids.
YEAH, IT TASTES REALLY GOOD.
IT LOOKS PRETTY, TOO.
YOUR MOM MUST BE A GREAT CHEF!
YEAH...
Mm... So good!
MUNCH
MUNCH
...
WHY DIDN'T YOU TELL HIM YOU MADE IT YOUR-SELF?!
I was thinking someone else made it!
HOW COULD I SAY THAT AFTER HE PRAISED IT SO MUCH?!
PUFF
BESIDES, IT WAS ALREADY TOO MUCH TO HANDLE!
PUFF
PUFF
My mind went blank!!

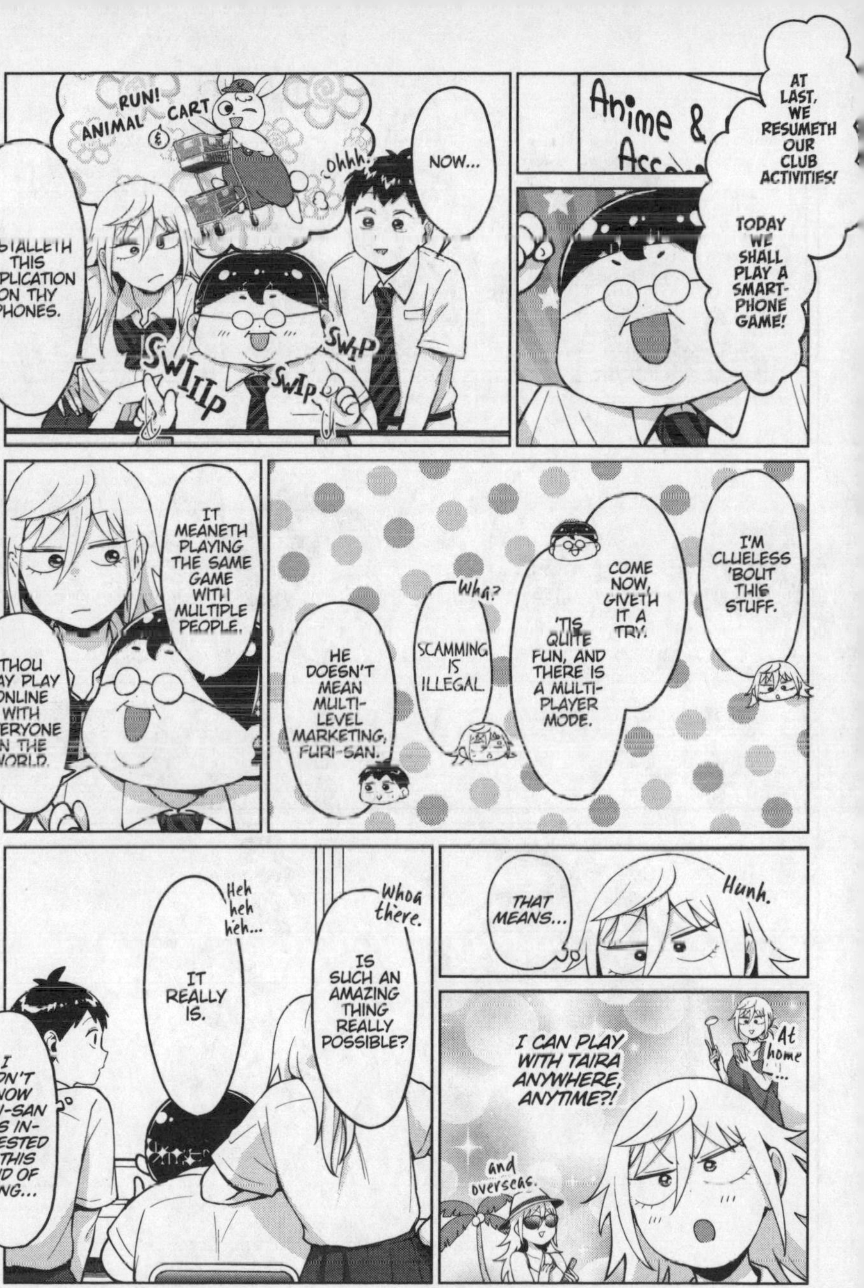
Anime &
AT LAST, WE RESUMETH OUR CLUB ACTIVITIES!
TODAY WE SHALL PLAY A SMARTPHONE GAME!
NOW...
ohhh.
RUN! ANIMAL CART
INSTALLETH THIS APPLICATION ON THY PHONES.
SWIP
SWIP
SWIIIP
I'M CLUELESS 'BOUT THIS STUFF.
COME NOW, GIVETH IT A TRY.
'TIS QUITE FUN, AND THERE IS A MULTI-PLAYER MODE.
Wha?
SCAMMING IS ILLEGAL.
HE DOESN'T MEAN MULTI-LEVEL MARKETING, FURI-SAN.
IT MEANETH PLAYING THE SAME GAME WITH MULTIPLE PEOPLE.
THOU MAY PLAY ONLINE WITH EVERYONE IN THE WORLD.
Hunh.
THAT MEANS...
I CAN PLAY WITH TAIRA ANYWHERE, ANYTIME?!
At home...
and overseas.
Whoa there.
IS SUCH AN AMAZING THING REALLY POSSIBLE?
Heh heh heh...
IT REALLY IS.
I DIDN'T KNOW FURI-SAN WAS INTERESTED IN THIS KIND OF THING...

I LOST AGAIN!!
our rank is...
Last Place
You incurred a fine of 5000 pells for going in reverse.
THIS IS TOO HARD FOR ME.
FLOP
I'M TIRED.
I GIVE UP.
TAIRA AND I SHALL DUEL, THEN.
WHOEVER LOSETH NEXT MUST LISTEN TO THE WINNER'S COMMAND. DOTH THOU ACCEPT?
THERE YOU GO AGAIN WITH THAT RULE...
NEVER MIND, I'LL PLAY.
FWIP

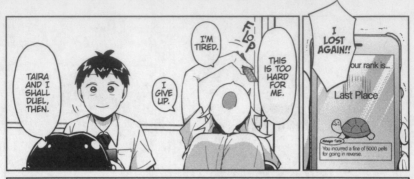

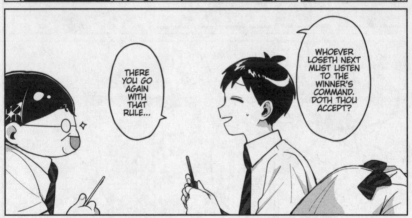

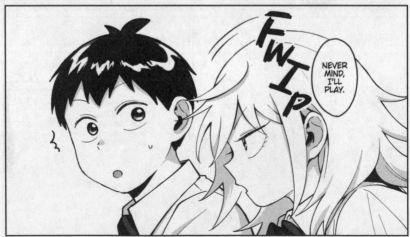

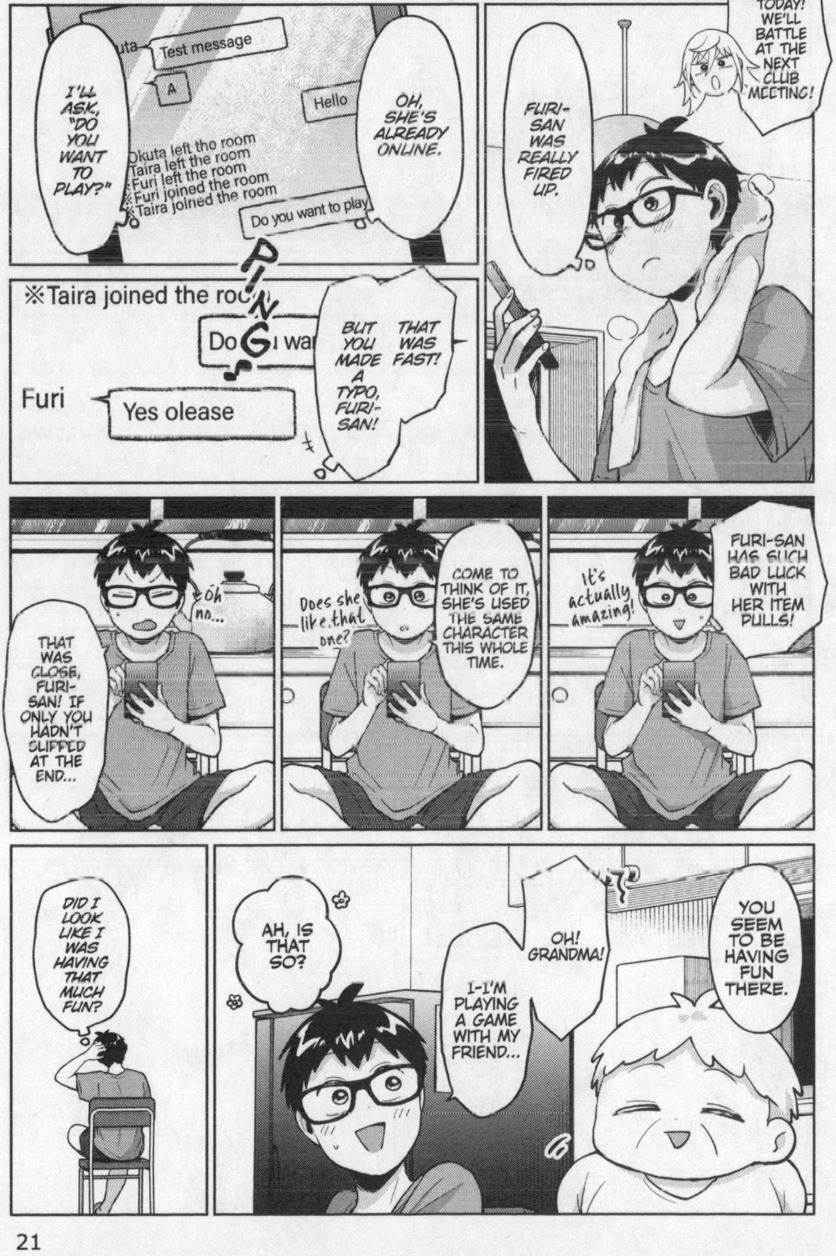
BUT NOT TODAY! WE'LL BATTLE AT THE NEXT CLUB MEETING!
FURI-SAN WAS REALLY FIRED UP.
OH, SHE'S ALREADY ONLINE.
I'LL ASK, "DO YOU WANT TO PLAY?"
Test message
A
Hello
Okuta left tho room
Taira left the room
※Furi left the room
※Furi joined the room
※Taira joined the room
Do you want to play
THAT WAS FAST!
BUT YOU MADE A TYPO, FURI-SAN!
PING
※Taira joined the roo
Furi
Yes olease
FURI-SAN HAS SUCH BAD LUCK WITH HER ITEM PULLS!
It's actually amazing!
COME TO THINK OF IT, SHE'S USED THE SAME CHARACTER THIS WHOLE TIME.
Does she like that one?
Oh no...
THAT WAS CLOSE, FURI-SAN! IF ONLY YOU HADN'T SLIPPED AT THE END...
YOU SEEM TO BE HAVING FUN THERE.
OH! GRANDMA!
I-I'M PLAYING A GAME WITH MY FRIEND...
AH, IS THAT SO?
DID I LOOK LIKE I WAS HAVING THAT MUCH FUN?

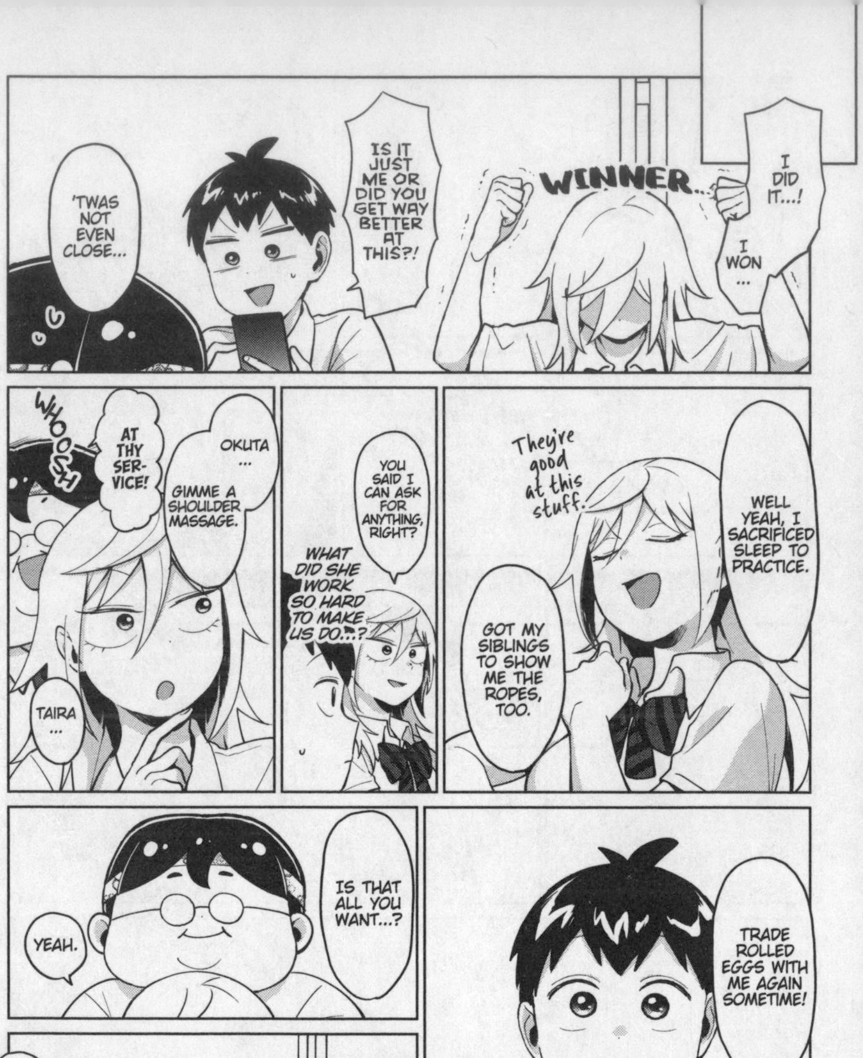
I DID IT...!
I WON ...
WINNER...
IS IT JUST ME OR DID YOU GET WAY BETTER AT THIS?!
'TWAS NOT EVEN CLOSE...
WELL YEAH, I SACRIFICED SLEEP TO PRACTICE.
They're good at this stuff.
GOT MY SIBLINGS TO SHOW ME THE ROPES, TOO.
YOU SAID I CAN ASK FOR ANYTHING, RIGHT?
WHAT DID SHE WORK SO HARD TO MAKE US DO...?
OKUTA ... GIMME A SHOULDER MASSAGE.
AT THY SERVICE!
WHOOSH
TAIRA ...
TRADE ROLLED EGGS WITH ME AGAIN SOMETIME!
IS THAT ALL YOU WANT...?
YEAH.
NOW I'LL BE ABLE TO EAT LUNCH WITH HIM AGAIN...
Ahhh, that's the spot.
Your shoulders are quite stiff, miss.
DID SHE LIKE MY FAMILY'S ROLLED EGGS?

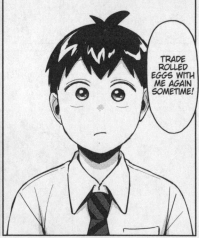

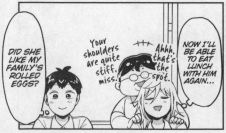

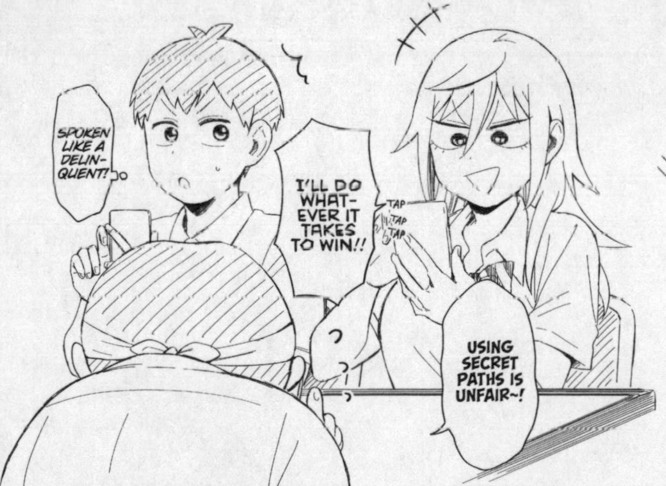
USING SECRET PATHS IS UNFAIR~!
TAP TAP TAP
I'LL DO WHATEVER IT TAKES TO WIN!!
SPOKEN LIKE A DELINQUENT!

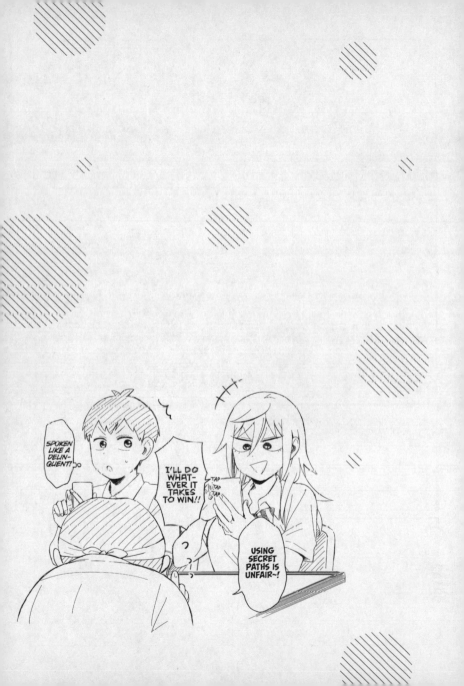

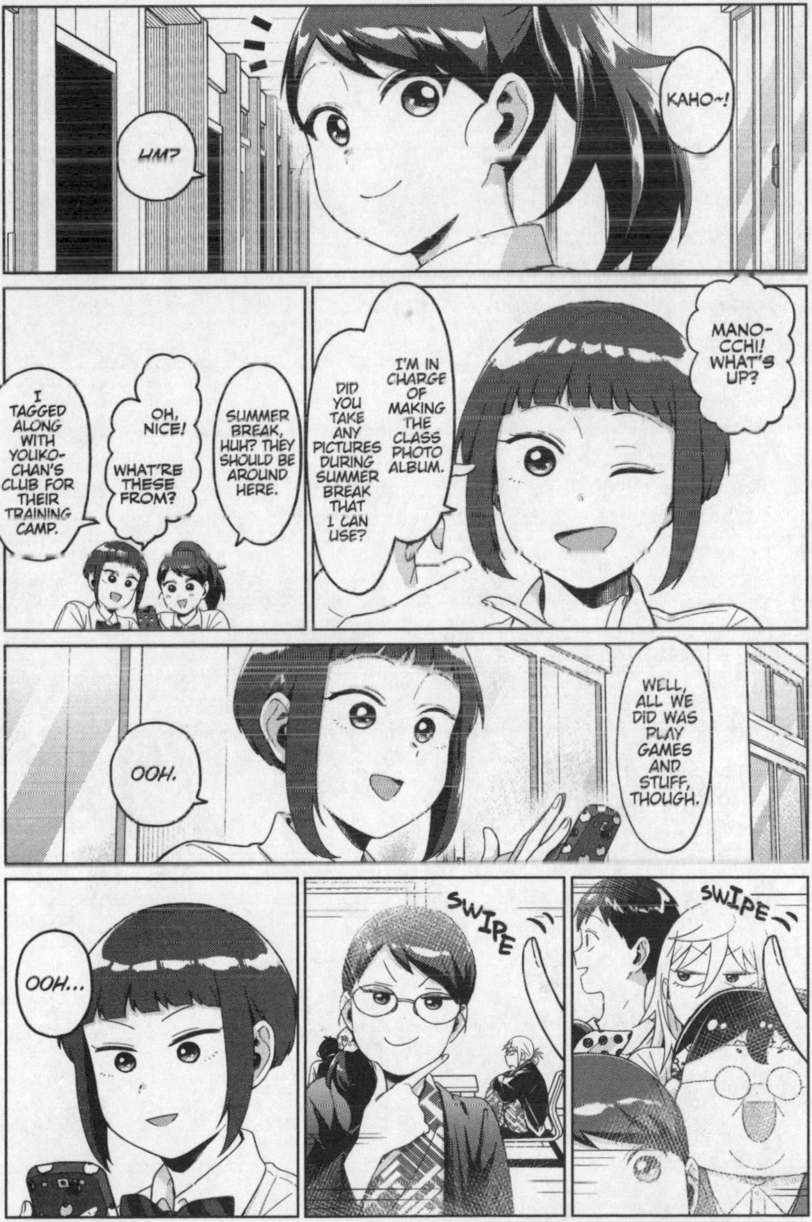
KAHO~!
HM?
MANO-CCHI! WHAT'S UP?
I'M IN CHARGE OF MAKING THE CLASS PHOTO ALBUM.
DID YOU TAKE ANY PICTURES DURING SUMMER BREAK THAT I CAN USE?
SUMMER BREAK, HUH? THEY SHOULD BE AROUND HERE.
OH, NICE!
WHAT'RE THESE FROM?
I TAGGED ALONG WITH YOUKO-CHAN'S CLUB FOR THEIR TRAINING CAMP.
WELL, ALL WE DID WAS PLAY GAMES AND STUFF, THOUGH.
OOH.
SWIPE
SWIPE
OOH...

Chapter 20

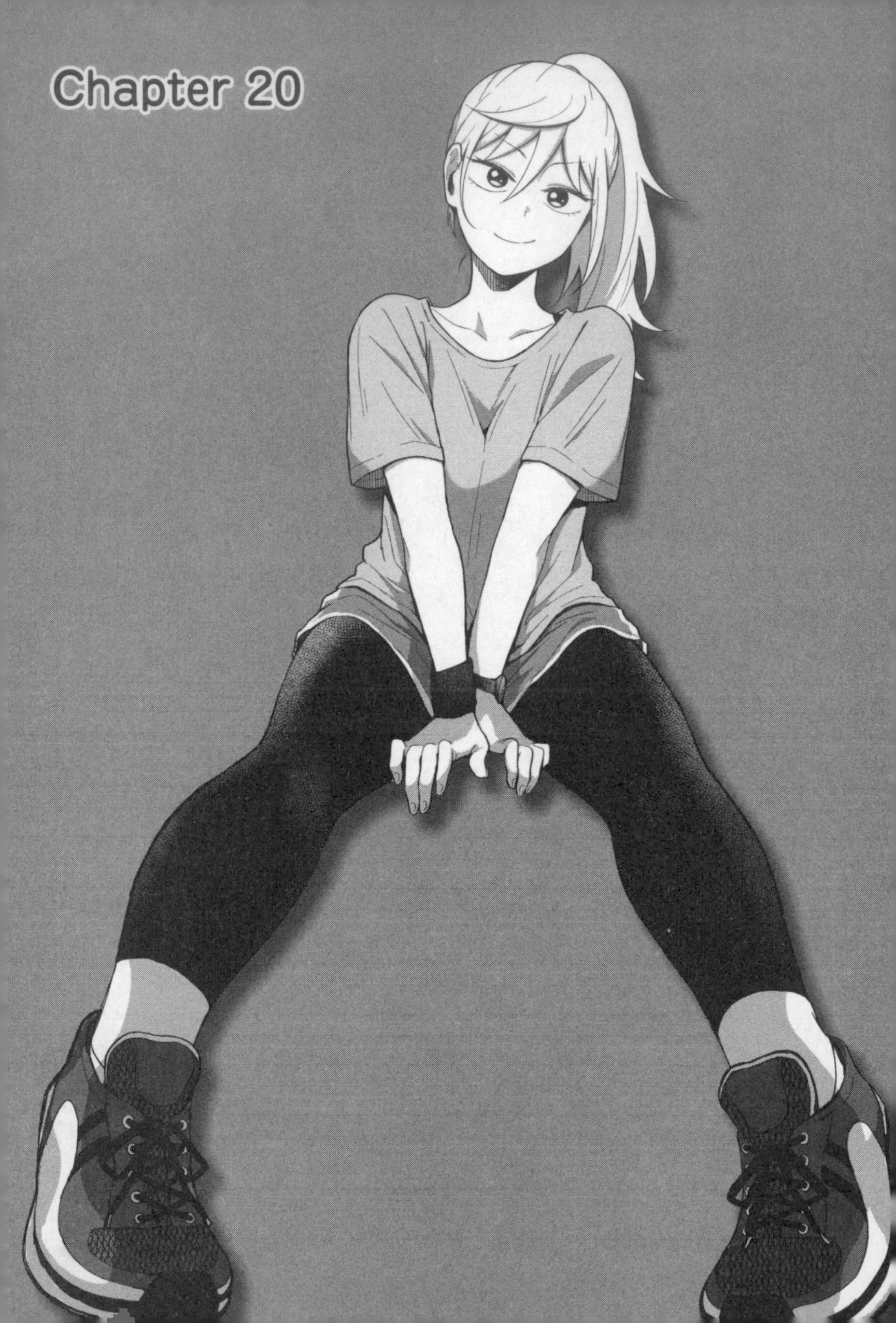

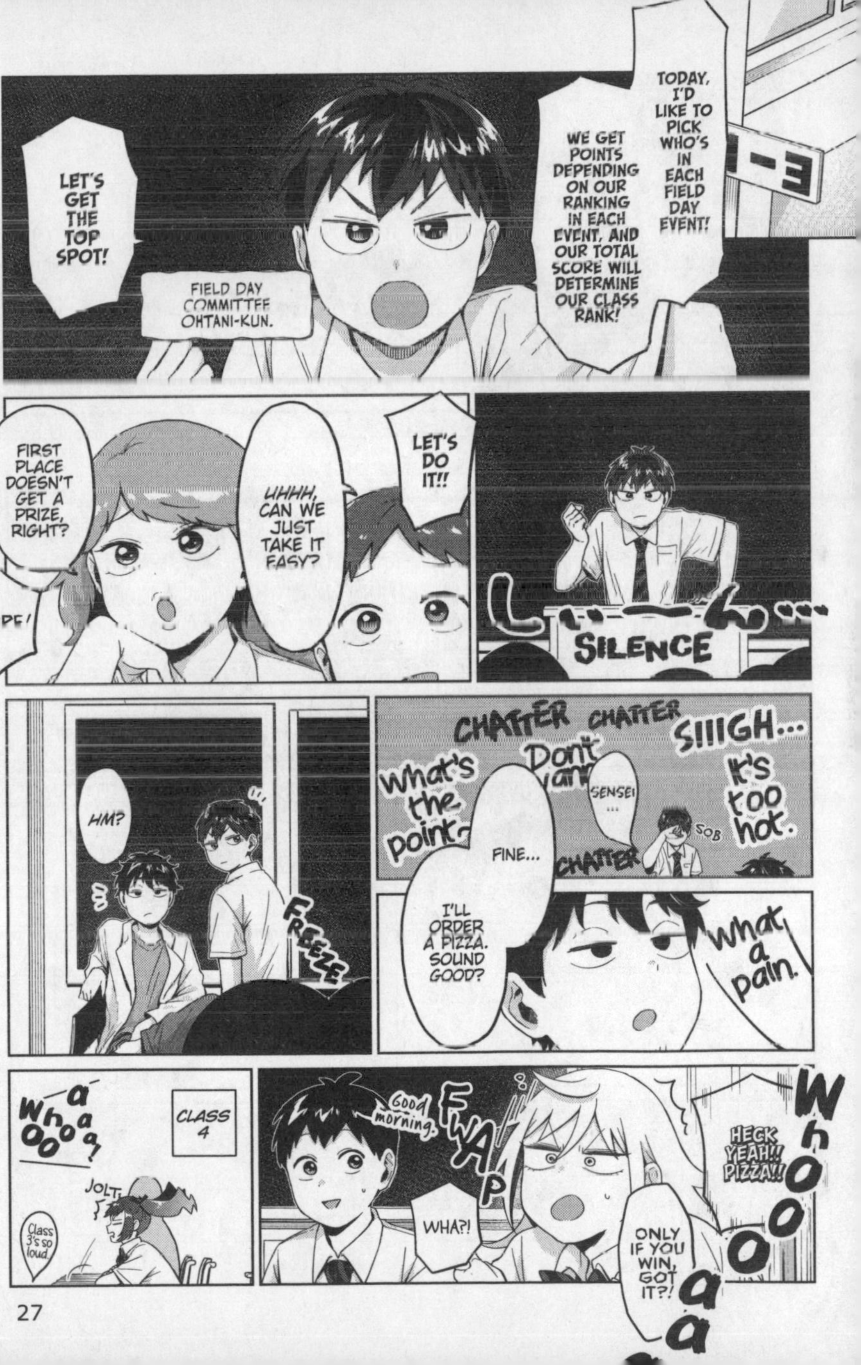
1-3
TODAY, I'D LIKE TO PICK WHO'S IN EACH FIELD DAY EVENT!
WE GET POINTS DEPENDING ON OUR RANKING IN EACH EVENT, AND OUR TOTAL SCORE WILL DETERMINE OUR CLASS RANK!
LET'S GET THE TOP SPOT!
FIELD DAY COMMITTEE OHTANI-KUN.
SILENCE
LET'S DO IT!!
UHHH, CAN WE JUST TAKE IT EASY?
FIRST PLACE DOESN'T GET A PRIZE, RIGHT?
NOPE!
CHATTER CHATTER
SIIIGH...
It's too hot.
What's the point?
SENSEI...
SOB
CHATTER
What a pain.
FINE...
I'LL ORDER A PIZZA. SOUND GOOD?
FREEZE
HM?
Whoooooaaa
HECK YEAH!! PIZZA!!
ONLY IF YOU WIN, GOT IT?!
FWAP
WHA?!
Good morning.
CLASS 4
Whoooaaa
JOLT
Class 3's so loud.

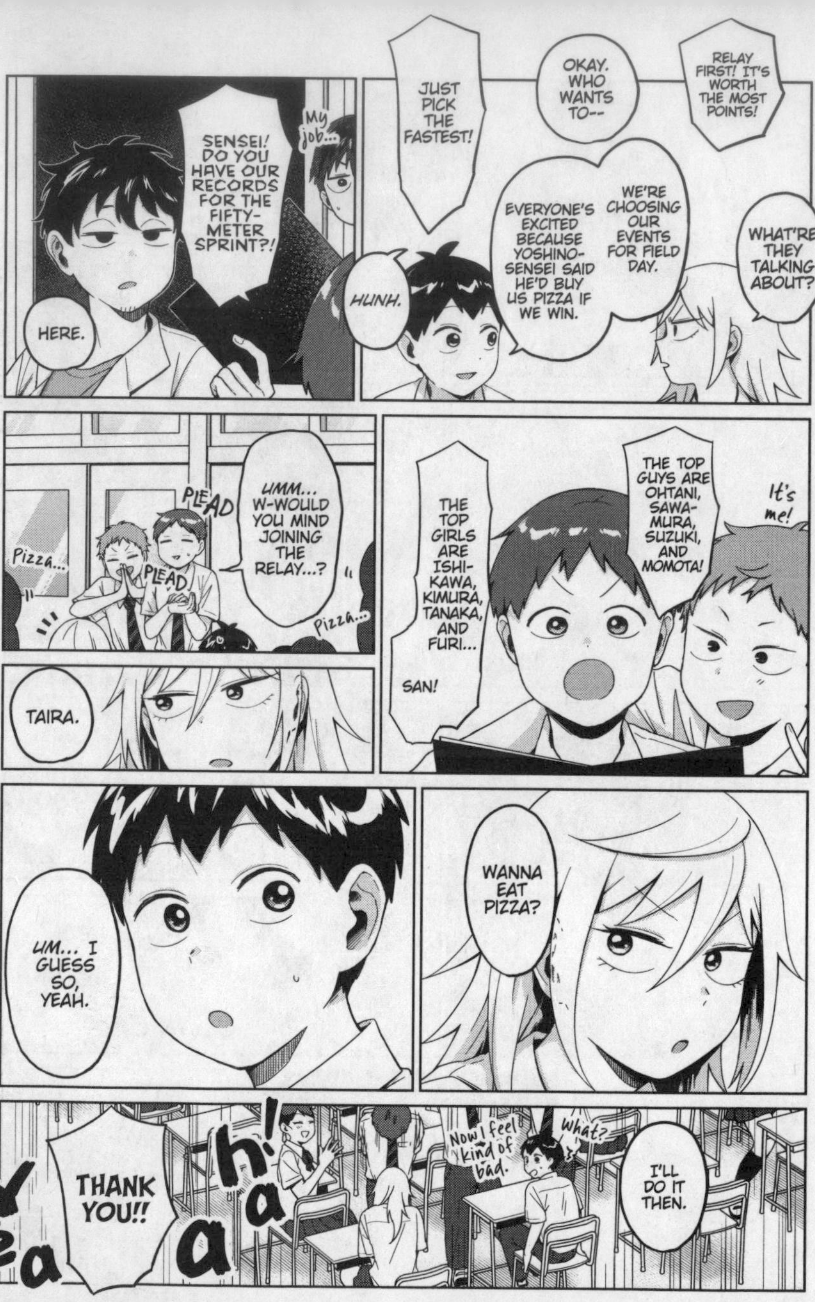

RELAY FIRST! IT'S WORTH THE MOST POINTS!
OKAY. WHO WANTS TO--
JUST PICK THE FASTEST!
WHAT'RE THEY TALKING ABOUT?
WE'RE CHOOSING OUR EVENTS FOR FIELD DAY.
EVERYONE'S EXCITED BECAUSE YOSHINO-SENSEI SAID HE'D BUY US PIZZA IF WE WIN.
HUNH.
My job...
SENSEI! DO YOU HAVE OUR RECORDS FOR THE FIFTY-METER SPRINT?!
HERE.
It's me!
THE TOP GUYS ARE OHTANI, SAWAMURA, SUZUKI, AND MOMOTA!
THE TOP GIRLS ARE ISHIKAWA, KIMURA, TANAKA, AND FURI...
SAN!
UMM... W-WOULD YOU MIND JOINING THE RELAY...?
PLEAD
PLEAD
Pizza...
Pizza...
TAIRA.
WANNA EAT PIZZA?
UM... I GUESS SO, YEAH.
I'LL DO IT THEN.
What?
Now I feel kind of bad.
THANK YOU!!
Yeaaah!

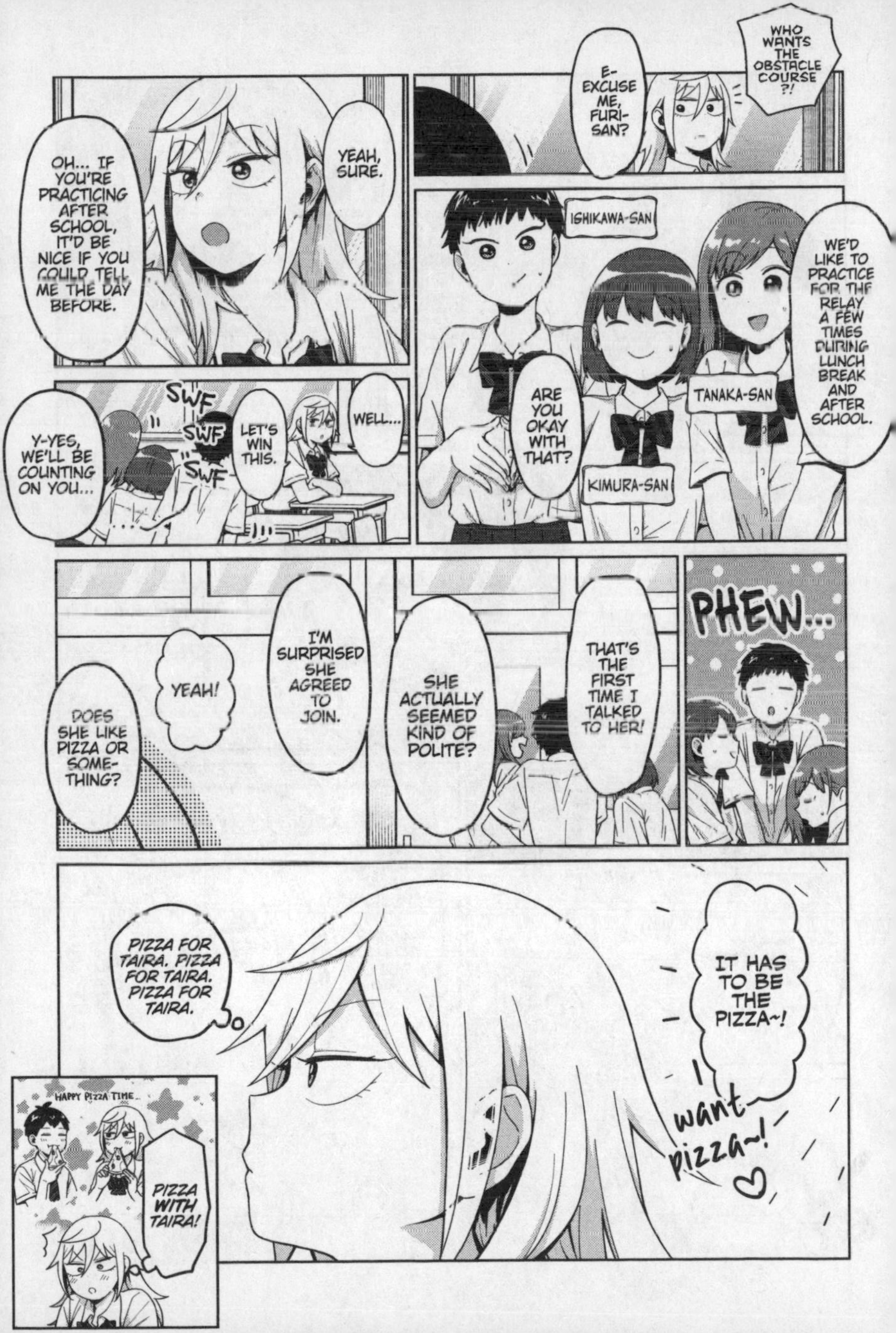
WHO WANTS THE OBSTACLE COURSE ?!
E-EXCUSE ME, FURI-SAN?
WE'D LIKE TO PRACTICE FOR THE RELAY A FEW TIMES DURING LUNCH BREAK AND AFTER SCHOOL.
TANAKA-SAN
ISHIKAWA-SAN
ARE YOU OKAY WITH THAT?
KIMURA-SAN
YEAH, SURE.
OH... IF YOU'RE PRACTICING AFTER SCHOOL, IT'D BE NICE IF YOU COULD TELL ME THE DAY BEFORE.
WELL...
LET'S WIN THIS.
SWF
SWF
SWF
Y-YES, WE'LL BE COUNTING ON YOU...
PHEW...
THAT'S THE FIRST TIME I TALKED TO HER!
SHE ACTUALLY SEEMED KIND OF POLITE?
I'M SURPRISED SHE AGREED TO JOIN.
YEAH!
DOES SHE LIKE PIZZA OR SOME-THING?
IT HAS TO BE THE PIZZA~!
I want pizza~! ♥
PIZZA FOR TAIRA. PIZZA FOR TAIRA. PIZZA FOR TAIRA.
HAPPY PIZZA TIME...
PIZZA WITH TAIRA!

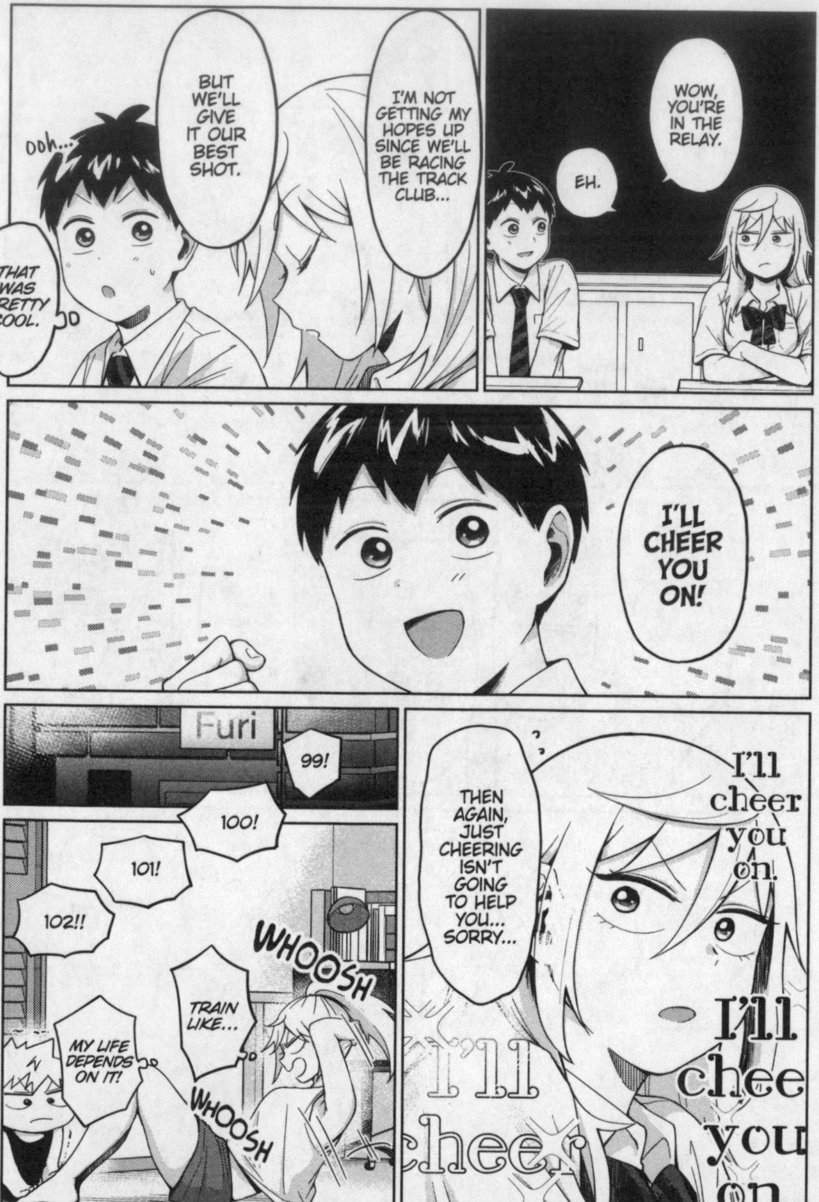
WOW, YOU'RE IN THE RELAY.
EH.
I'M NOT GETTING MY HOPES UP SINCE WE'LL BE RACING THE TRACK CLUB...
BUT WE'LL GIVE IT OUR BEST SHOT.
ooh...
THAT WAS PRETTY COOL.
I'LL CHEER YOU ON!
I'll cheer you on.
THEN AGAIN, JUST CHEERING ISN'T GOING TO HELP YOU... SORRY...
I'll chee you on.
I'll cheer
Furi
99!
100!
101!
102!!
WHOOSH
TRAIN LIKE...
MY LIFE DEPENDS ON IT!
WHOOSH

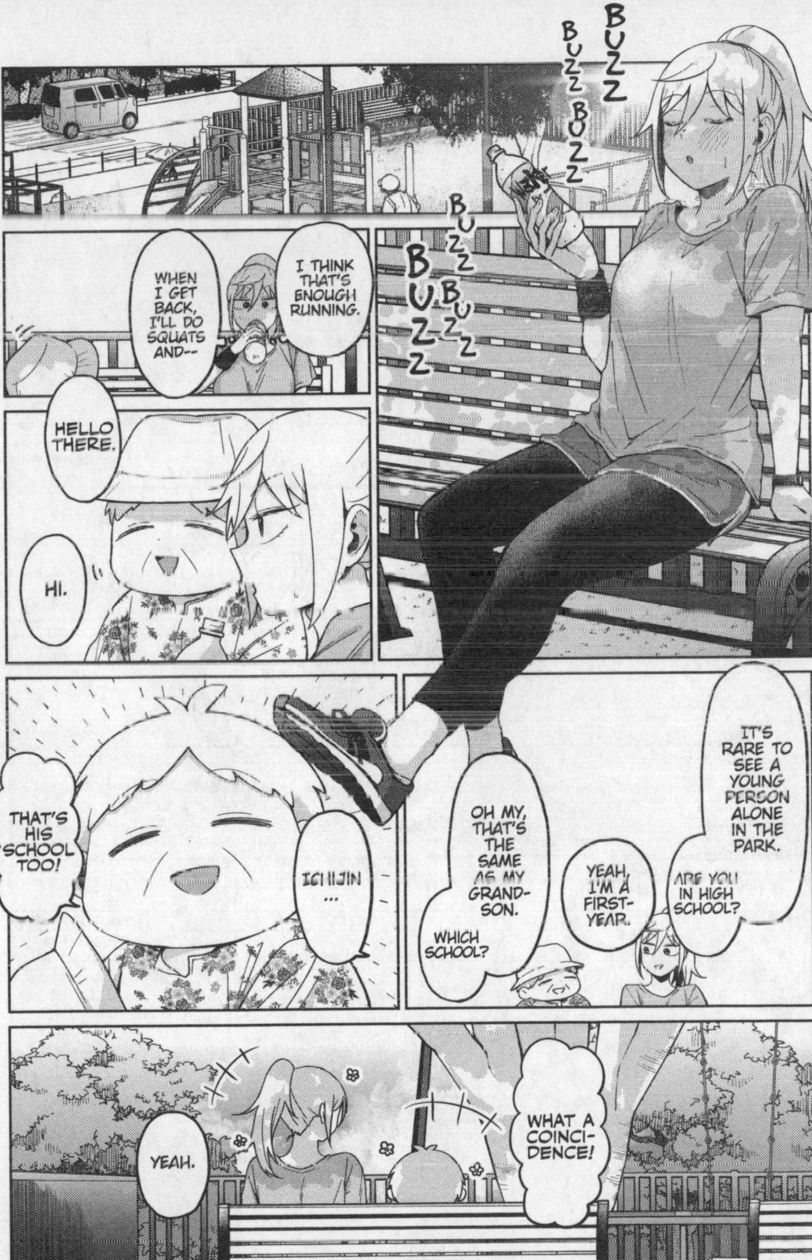
BUZZ BUZZ BUZZ BUZZ
BUZZ BUZZ BUZZ BUZZ
I THINK THAT'S ENOUGH RUNNING.
WHEN I GET BACK, I'LL DO SQUATS AND--
HELLO THERE.
HI.
IT'S RARE TO SEE A YOUNG PERSON ALONE IN THE PARK.
ARE YOU IN HIGH SCHOOL?
YEAH, I'M A FIRST-YEAR.
OH MY, THAT'S THE SAME AS MY GRAND-SON.
WHICH SCHOOL?
ICHIJIN ...
THAT'S HIS SCHOOL TOO!
WHAT A COINCI-DENCE!
YEAH.

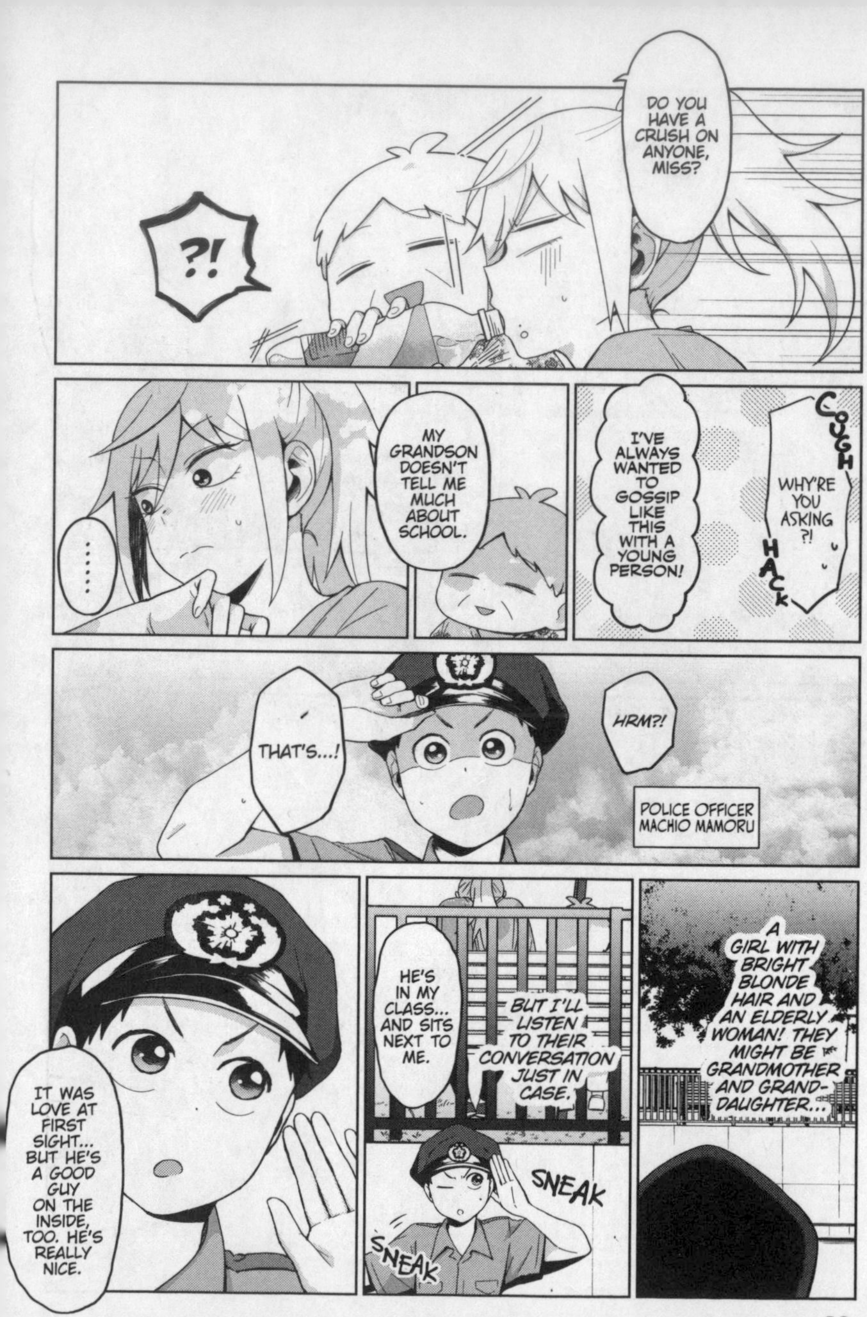
DO YOU HAVE A CRUSH ON ANYONE, MISS?
?!
COUGH
WHY'RE YOU ASKING?!
HACK
I'VE ALWAYS WANTED TO GOSSIP LIKE THIS WITH A YOUNG PERSON!
MY GRANDSON DOESN'T TELL ME MUCH ABOUT SCHOOL.
......
HRM?!
POLICE OFFICER MACHIO MAMORU
THAT'S...!
A GIRL WITH BRIGHT BLONDE HAIR AND AN ELDERLY WOMAN! THEY MIGHT BE GRANDMOTHER AND GRAND-DAUGHTER...
BUT I'LL LISTEN TO THEIR CONVERSATION JUST IN CASE.
HE'S IN MY CLASS... AND SITS NEXT TO ME.
SNEAK
SNEAK
IT WAS LOVE AT FIRST SIGHT... BUT HE'S A GOOD GUY ON THE INSIDE, TOO. HE'S REALLY NICE.

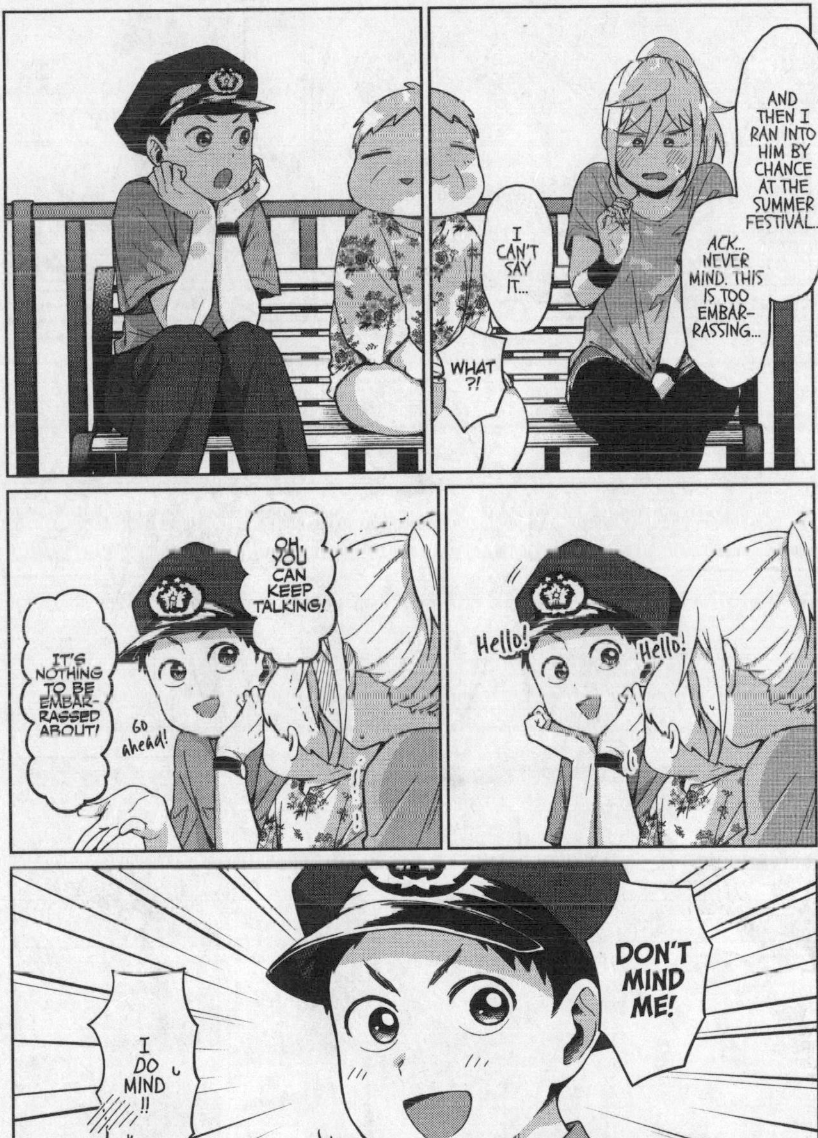
AND THEN I RAN INTO HIM BY CHANCE AT THE SUMMER FESTIVAL...
ACK... NEVER MIND. THIS IS TOO EMBARRASSING...
I CAN'T SAY IT...
WHAT?!
Hello!
Hello!
OH, YOU CAN KEEP TALKING!
IT'S NOTHING TO BE EMBARRASSED ABOUT!
Go ahead!
DON'T MIND ME!
I DO MIND!!

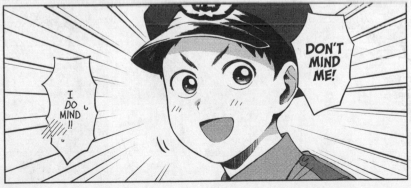

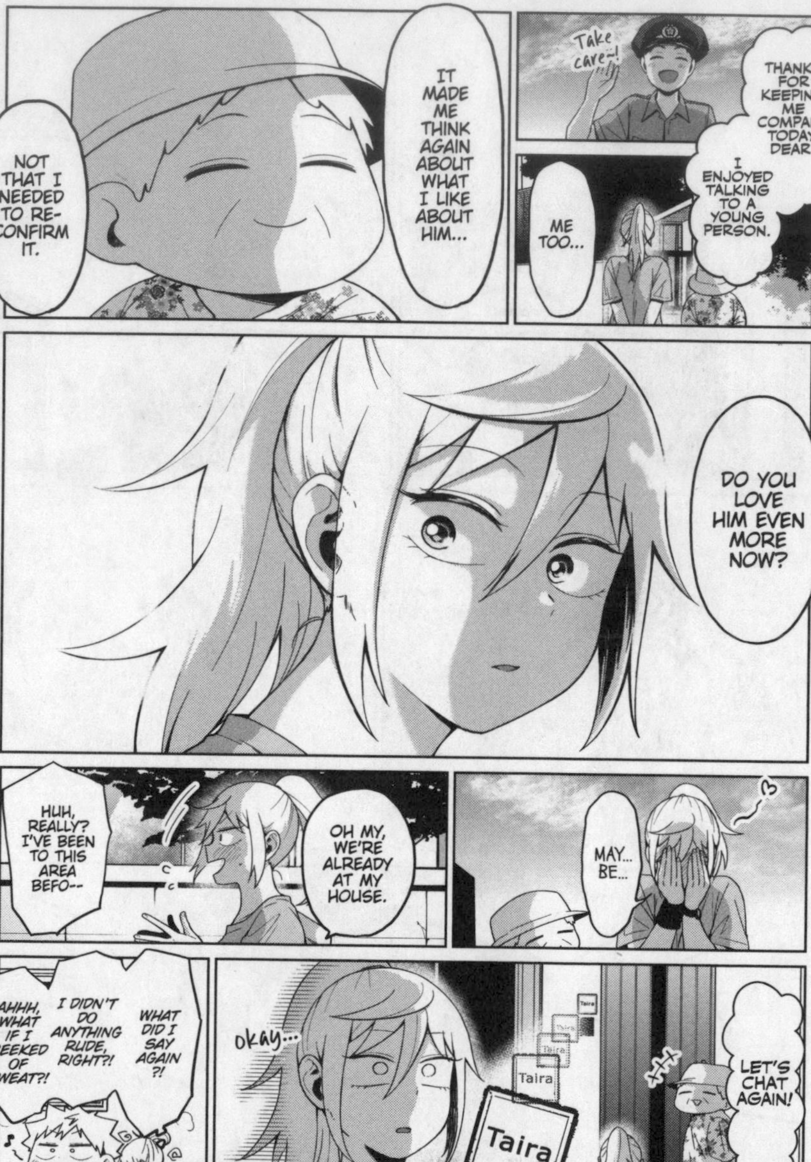
Take care~!
THANKS FOR KEEPING ME COMPANY TODAY, DEAR.
I ENJOYED TALKING TO A YOUNG PERSON.
ME TOO...
IT MADE ME THINK AGAIN ABOUT WHAT I LIKE ABOUT HIM...
NOT THAT I NEEDED TO RE-CONFIRM IT.
DO YOU LOVE HIM EVEN MORE NOW?
MAY... BE...
OH MY, WE'RE ALREADY AT MY HOUSE.
HUH, REALLY? I'VE BEEN TO THIS AREA BEFO--
LET'S CHAT AGAIN!
Taira
okay...
WHAT DID I SAY AGAIN?!
I DIDN'T DO ANYTHING RUDE, RIGHT?!
AHHH, WHAT IF I REEKED OF SWEAT?!

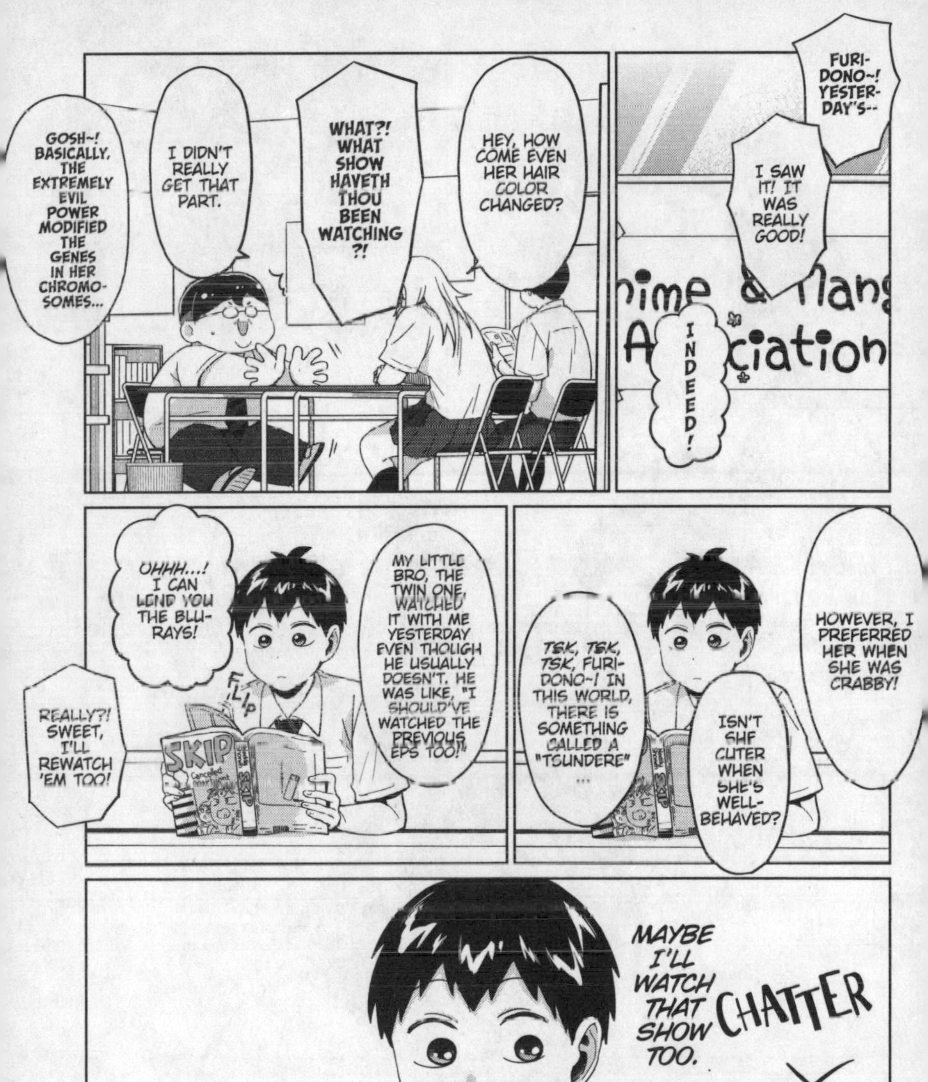
FURI-DONO~! YESTERDAY'S--
I SAW IT! IT WAS REALLY GOOD!
INDEED!
HEY, HOW COME EVEN HER HAIR COLOR CHANGED?
WHAT?! WHAT SHOW HAVETH THOU BEEN WATCHING?!
I DIDN'T REALLY GET THAT PART.
GOSH~! BASICALLY, THE EXTREMELY EVIL POWER MODIFIED THE GENES IN HER CHROMOSOMES...
HOWEVER, I PREFERRED HER WHEN SHE WAS CRABBY!
ISN'T SHE CUTER WHEN SHE'S WELL-BEHAVED?
TSK, TSK, TSK, FURI-DONO~! IN THIS WORLD, THERE IS SOMETHING CALLED A "TSUNDERE"...
MY LITTLE BRO, THE TWIN ONE, WATCHED IT WITH ME YESTERDAY EVEN THOUGH HE USUALLY DOESN'T. HE WAS LIKE, "I SHOULD'VE WATCHED THE PREVIOUS EPS TOO!"
OHHH...! I CAN LEND YOU THE BLU-RAYS!
FLIP
SKIP
REALLY?! SWEET, I'LL REWATCH 'EM TOO!
MAYBE I'LL WATCH THAT SHOW TOO.
CHATTER
CHATTER
LEFT OUT.

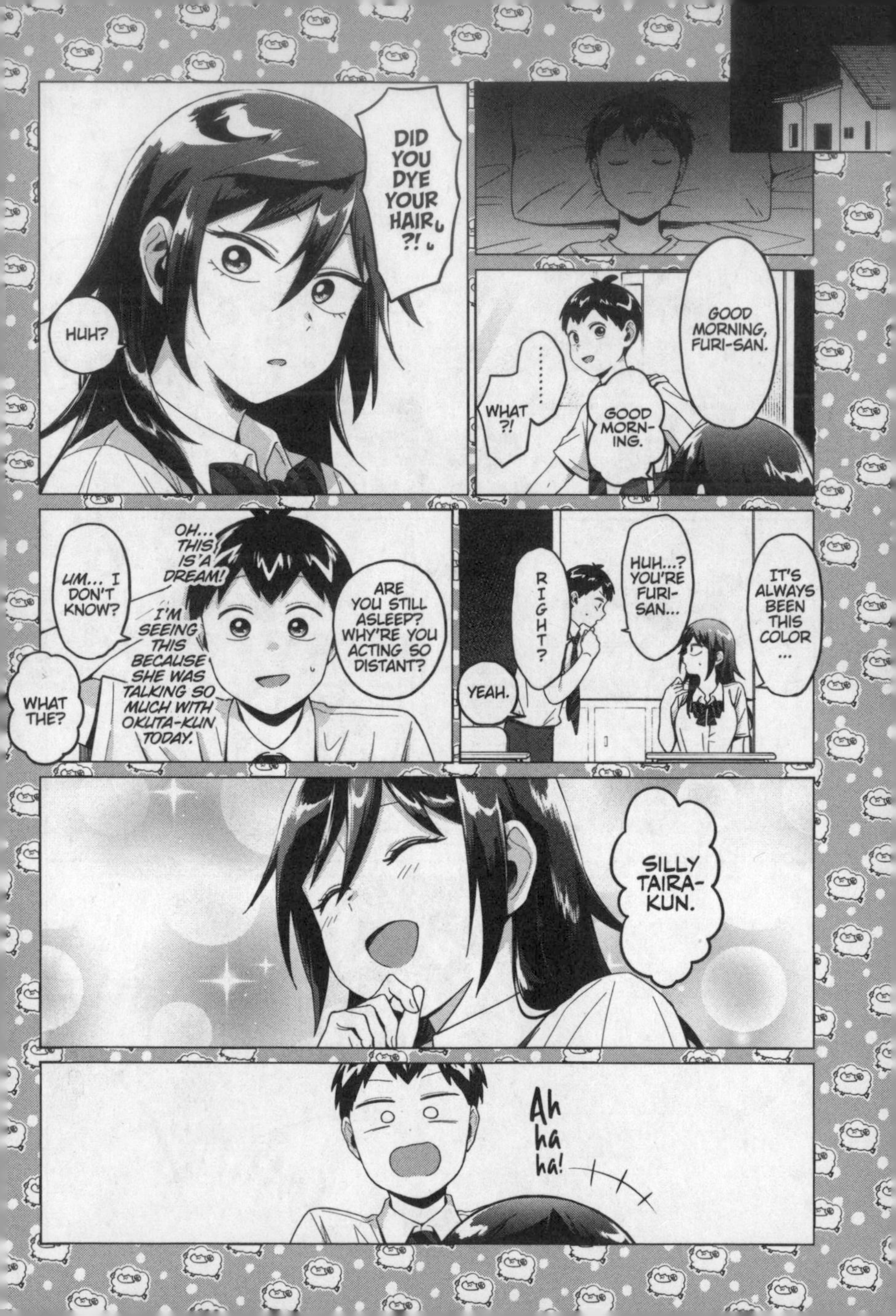
GOOD MORNING, FURI-SAN.
......
GOOD MORNING.
WHAT?!
DID YOU DYE YOUR HAIR?!
HUH?
IT'S ALWAYS BEEN THIS COLOR ...
HUH...? YOU'RE FURI-SAN...
RIGHT?
YEAH.
ARE YOU STILL ASLEEP? WHY'RE YOU ACTING SO DISTANT?
OH... THIS IS A DREAM!
I'M SEEING THIS BECAUSE SHE WAS TALKING SO MUCH WITH OKUTA-KUN TODAY.
UM... I DON'T KNOW?
WHAT THE?
SILLY TAIRA-KUN.
Ah ha ha!

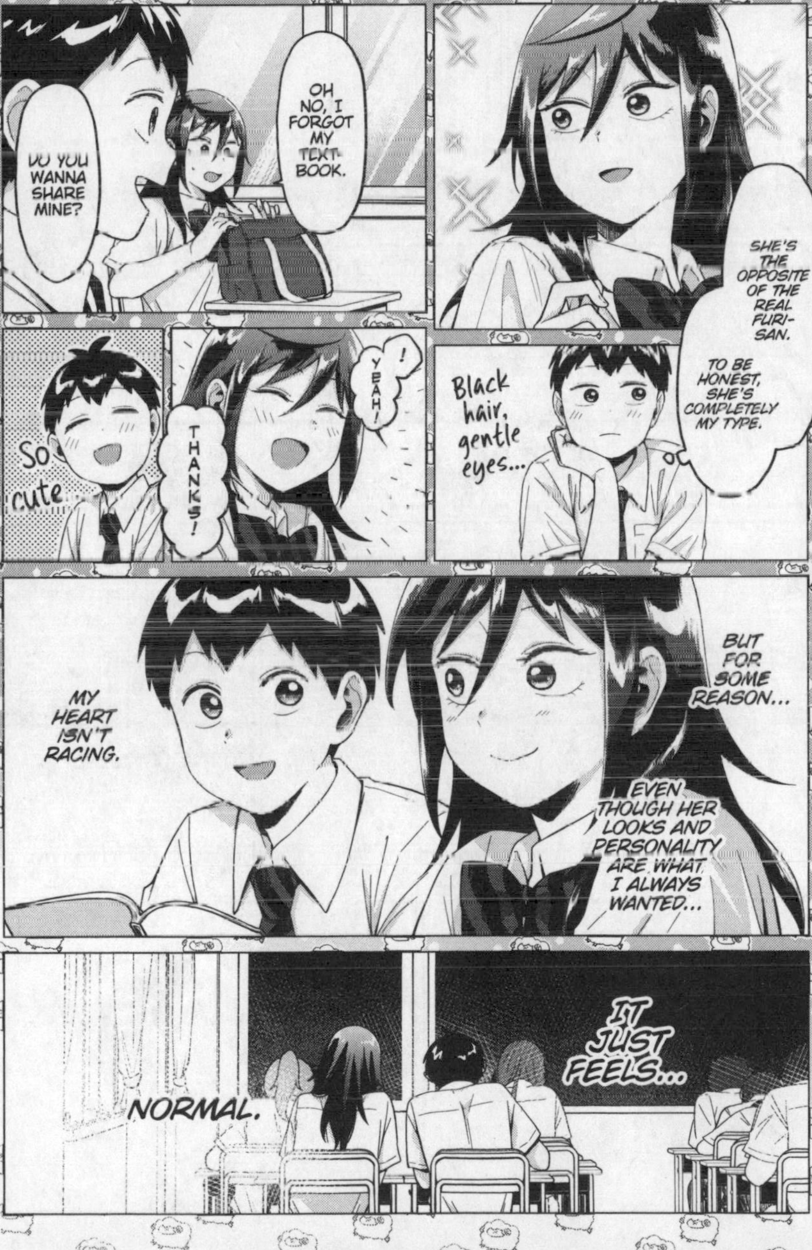
SHE'S THE OPPOSITE OF THE REAL FURI-SAN.
OH NO, I FORGOT MY TEXTBOOK.
DO YOU WANNA SHARE MINE?
TO BE HONEST, SHE'S COMPLETELY MY TYPE.
Black hair, gentle eyes...
YEAH!
!
THANKS!
So cute
BUT FOR SOME REASON...
EVEN THOUGH HER LOOKS AND PERSONALITY ARE WHAT I ALWAYS WANTED...
MY HEART ISN'T RACING.
IT JUST FEELS...
NORMAL.

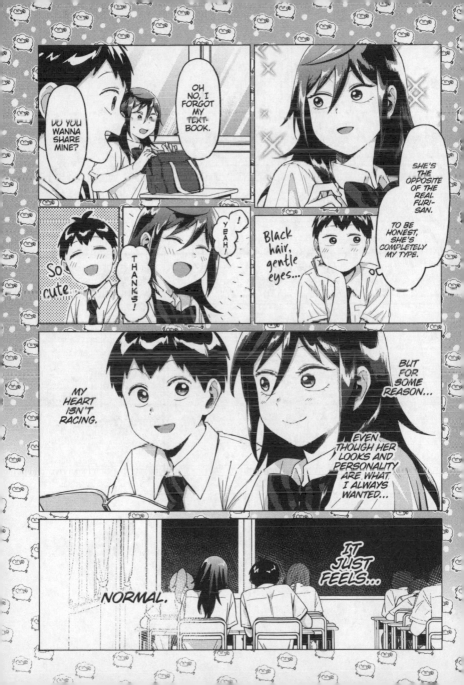

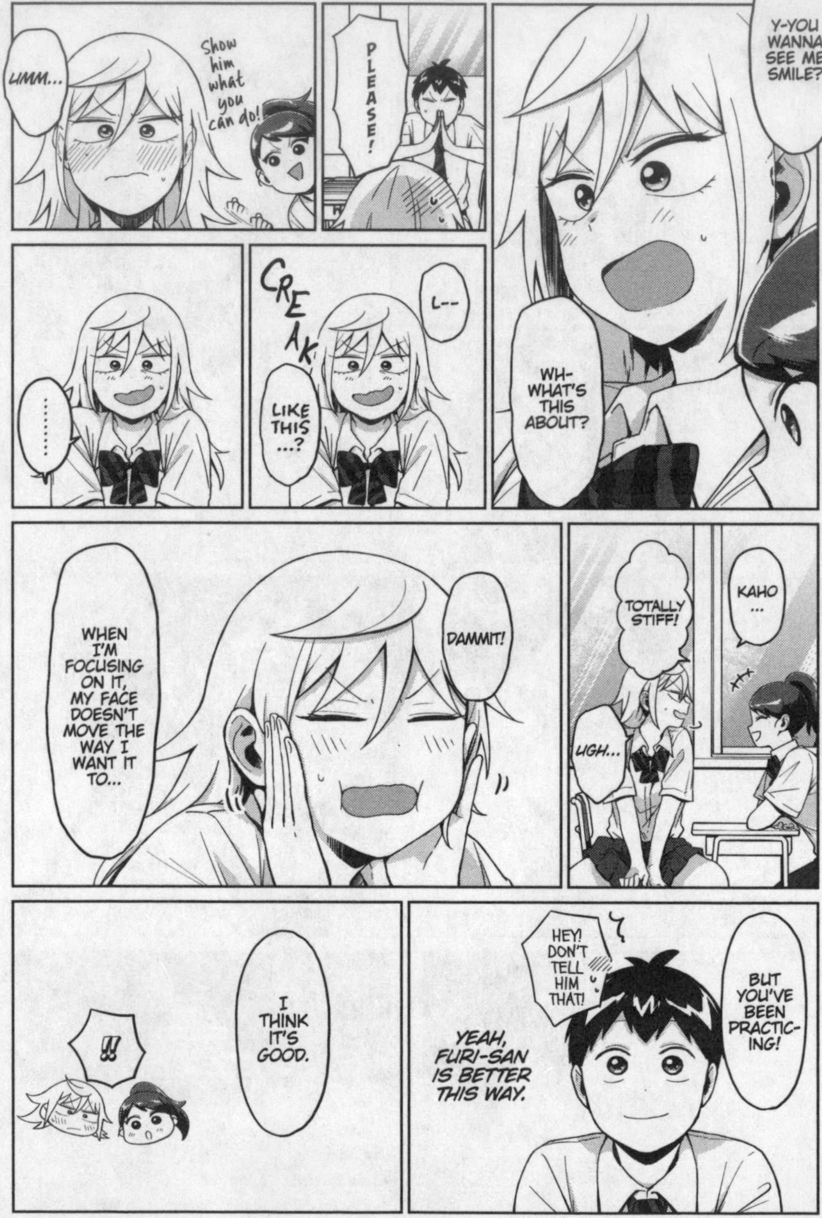
Y-YOU WANNA SEE ME SMILE?
WH-WHAT'S THIS ABOUT?
PLEASE!
Show him what you can do!
UMM...
CREAK
L--
LIKE THIS ...?
......
KAHO ...
TOTALLY STIFF!
UGH...
DAMMIT!
WHEN I'M FOCUSING ON IT, MY FACE DOESN'T MOVE THE WAY I WANT IT TO...
BUT YOU'VE BEEN PRACTIC-ING!
HEY! DON'T TELL HIM THAT!
YEAH, FURI-SAN IS BETTER THIS WAY.
I THINK IT'S GOOD.
!!

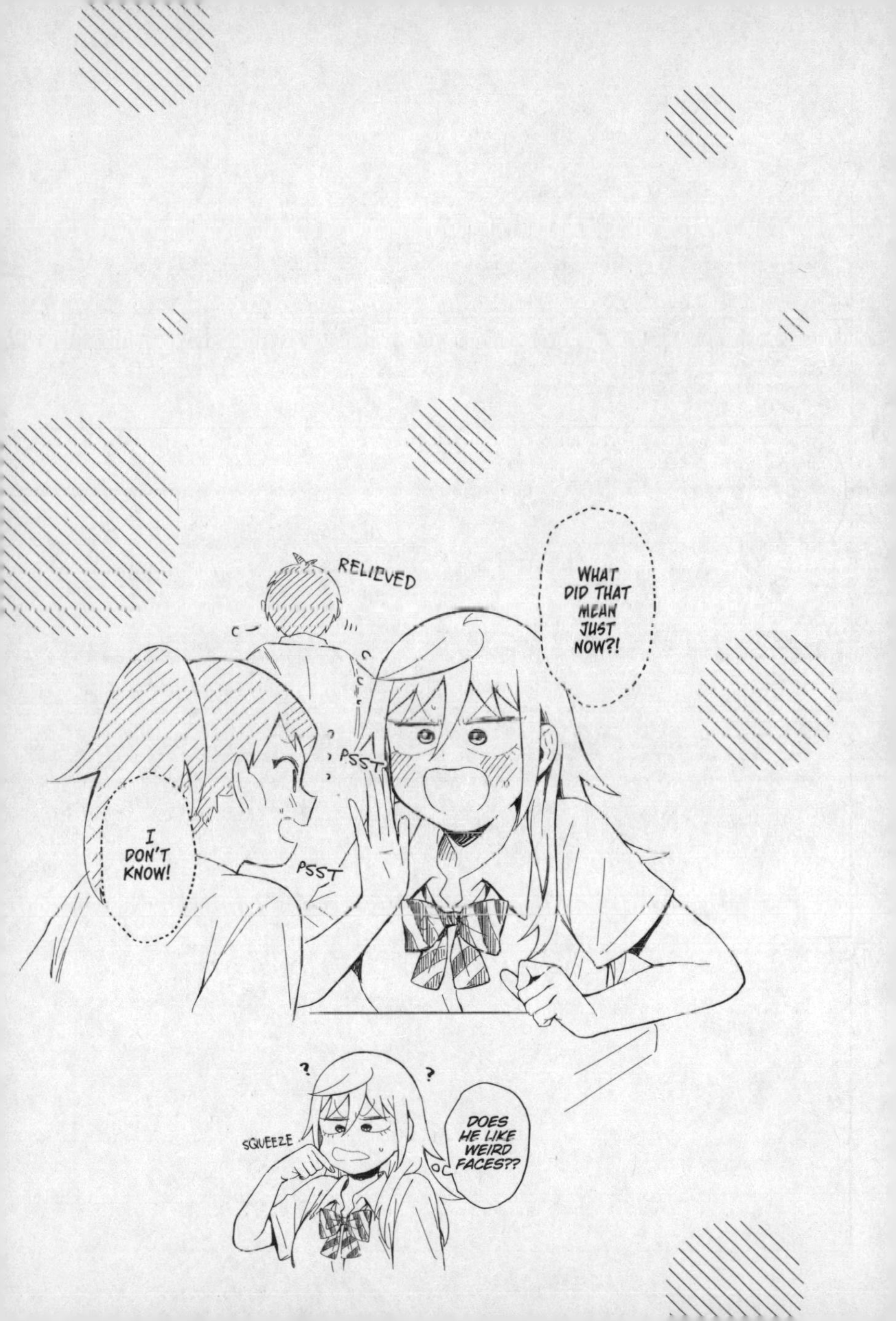
WHAT DID THAT MEAN JUST NOW?!
RELIEVED
PSST
PSST
I DON'T KNOW!
DOES HE LIKE WEIRD FACES??
SQUEEZE

Chapter 21

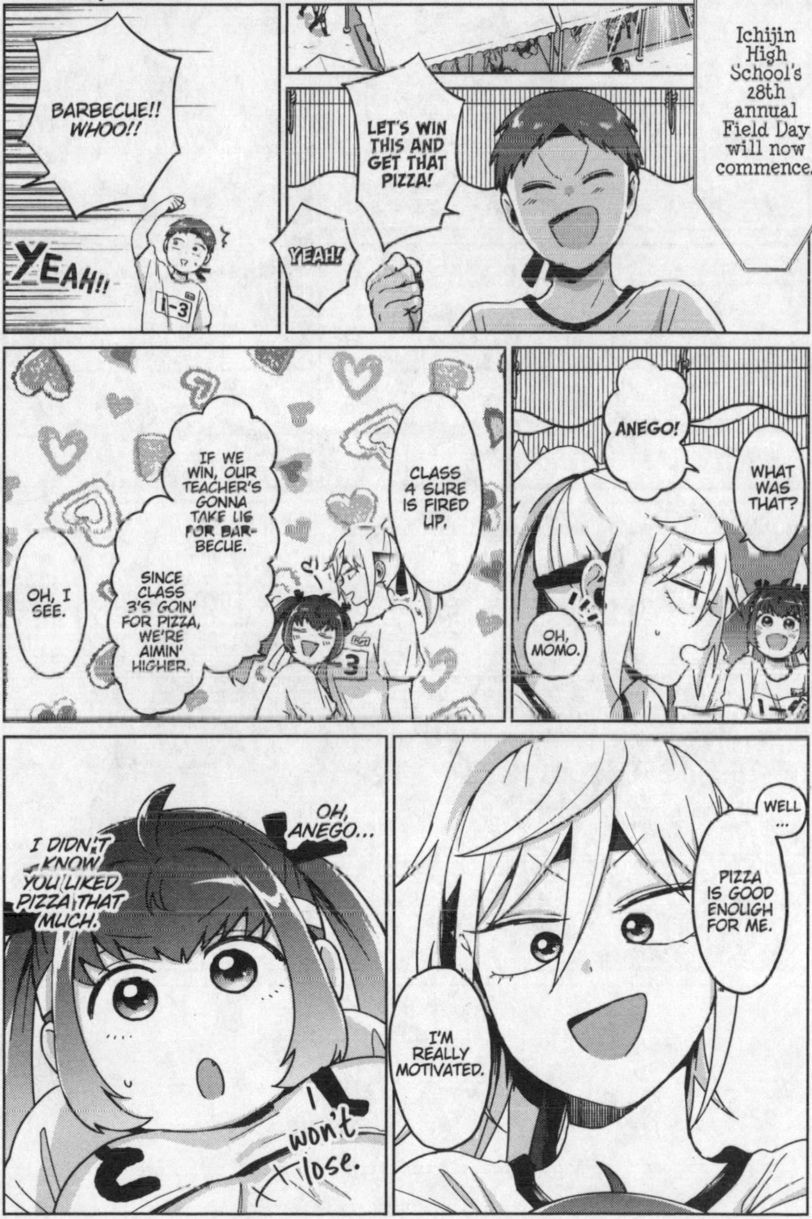
Ichijin High School's 28th annual Field Day will now commence.
LET'S WIN THIS AND GET THAT PIZZA!
YEAH!
BARBECUE!! WHOO!!
YEAH!!
ANEGO!
WHAT WAS THAT?
OH, MOMO.
CLASS 4 SURE IS FIRED UP.
IF WE WIN, OUR TEACHER'S GONNA TAKE US FOR BARBECUE.
SINCE CLASS 3'S GOIN' FOR PIZZA, WE'RE AIMIN' HIGHER.
OH, I SEE.
WELL ...
PIZZA IS GOOD ENOUGH FOR ME.
I'M REALLY MOTIVATED.
OH, ANEGO...
I DIDN'T KNOW YOU LIKED PIZZA THAT MUCH.
I won't lose.

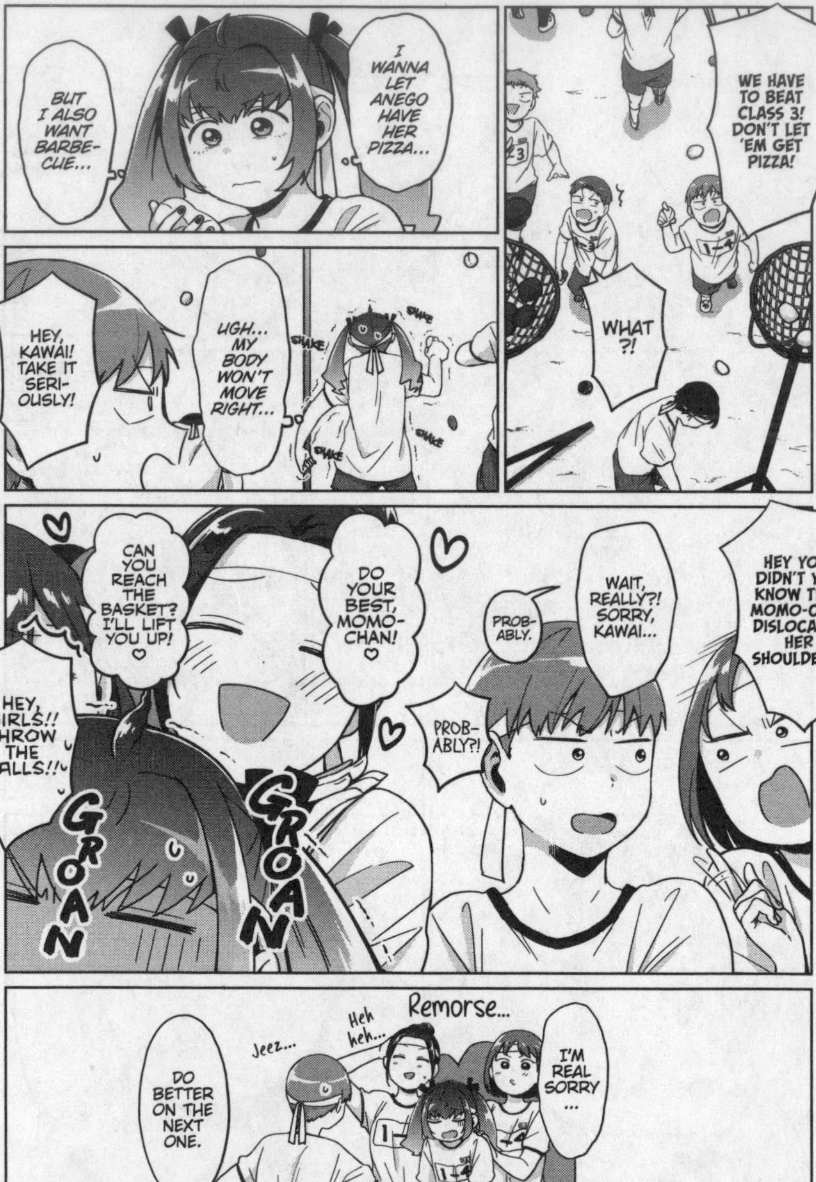
WE HAVE TO BEAT CLASS 3! DON'T LET 'EM GET PIZZA!
WHAT?!
I WANNA LET ANEGO HAVE HER PIZZA...
BUT I ALSO WANT BARBECUE...
UGH... MY BODY WON'T MOVE RIGHT...
SHAKE
SHAKE
SHAKE
SHAKE
HEY, KAWAI! TAKE IT SERIOUSLY!
HEY YOU! DIDN'T YOU KNOW THAT MOMO-CHAN DISLOCATED HER SHOULDER?!
WAIT, REALLY?! SORRY, KAWAI...
PROBABLY.
PROBABLY?!
DO YOUR BEST, MOMO-CHAN! ♡
CAN YOU REACH THE BASKET? I'LL LIFT YOU UP! ♡
HEY, GIRLS!! THROW THE BALLS!!
GROAN
GROAN
Remorse...
I'M REAL SORRY...
Heh heh...
Jeez...
DO BETTER ON THE NEXT ONE.

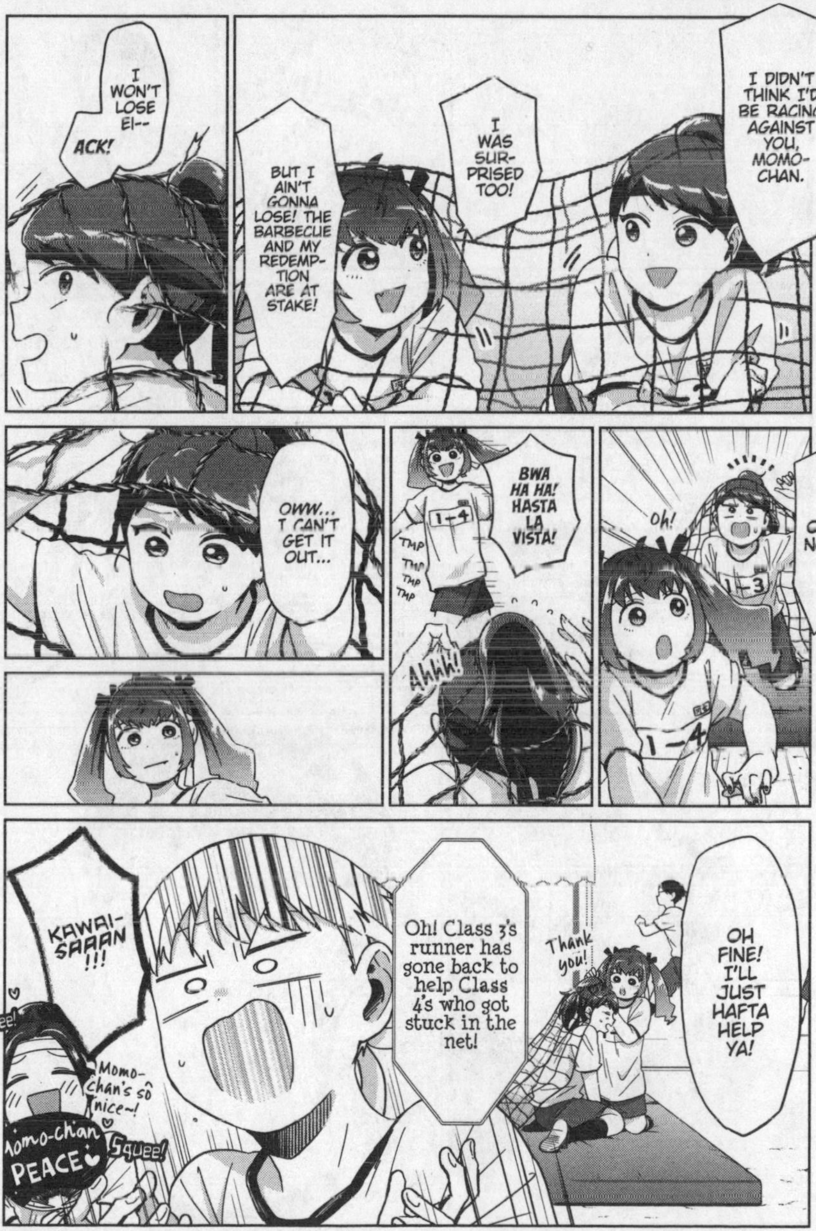
I DIDN'T THINK I'D BE RACING AGAINST YOU, MOMO-CHAN.
I WAS SUR-PRISED TOO!
BUT I AIN'T GONNA LOSE! THE BARBECUE AND MY REDEMP-TION ARE AT STAKE!
I WON'T LOSE EI--
ACK!
OH NO!
Oh!
BWA HA HA! HASTA LA VISTA!
TMP TMP TMP TMP
AHHH!
OWW... I CAN'T GET IT OUT...
OH FINE! I'LL JUST HAFTA HELP YA!
Thank you!
Oh! Class 3's runner has gone back to help Class 4's who got stuck in the net!
KAWAI-SAAAN!!!
Squee!
Momo-chan's so nice~!
Momo-chan PEACE
Squee!

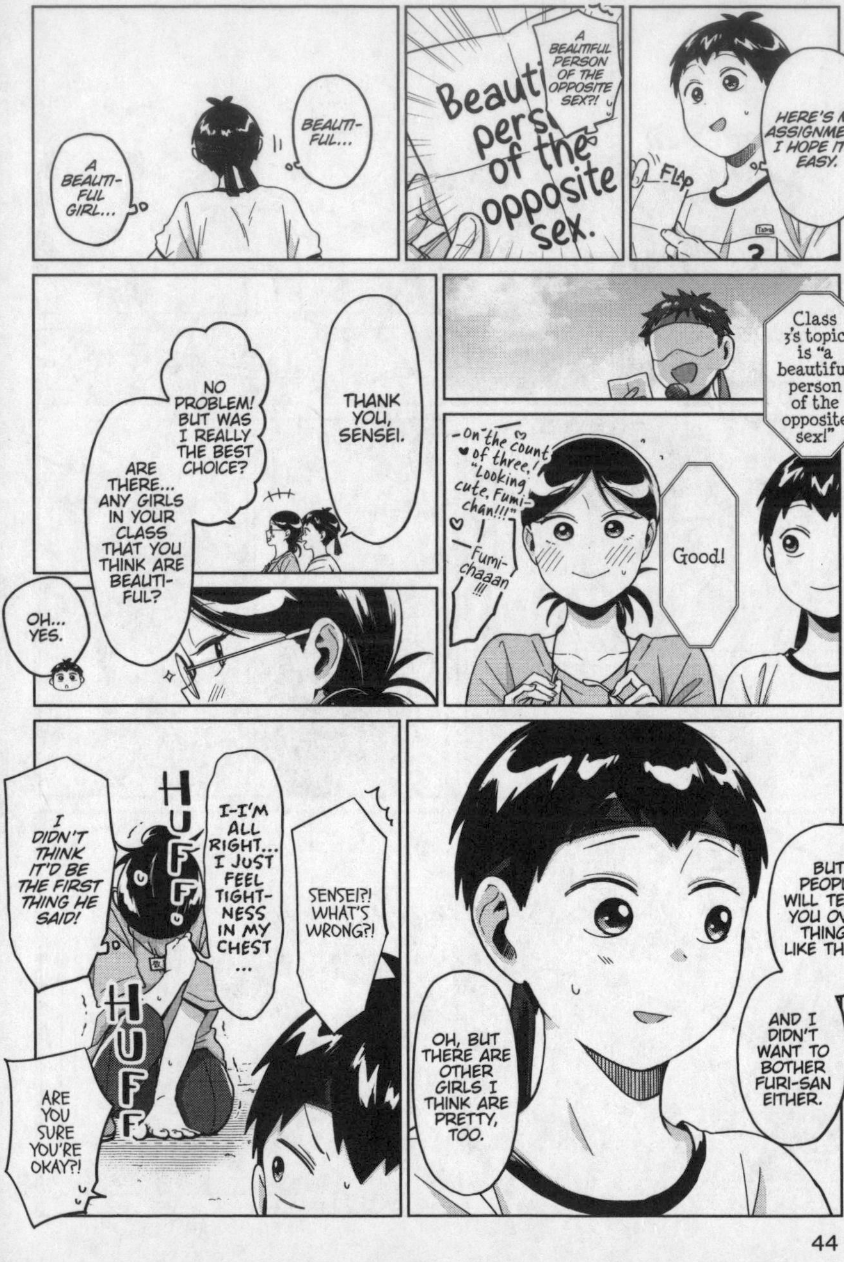
HERE'S MY ASSIGNMENT. I HOPE IT'S EASY.
FLAP
A BEAUTIFUL PERSON OF THE OPPOSITE SEX?!
Beautiful person of the opposite sex.
BEAUTIFUL...
A BEAUTIFUL GIRL...
Class 3's topic is "a beautiful person of the opposite sex!"
Good!
—On the count of three! "Looking cute, Fumi-chan!!!"
—Fumi-chaaan!!!
THANK YOU, SENSEI.
NO PROBLEM! BUT WAS I REALLY THE BEST CHOICE?
ARE THERE... ANY GIRLS IN YOUR CLASS THAT YOU THINK ARE BEAUTIFUL?
OH... YES.
BUT PEOPLE WILL TEASE YOU OVER THINGS LIKE THIS...
AND I DIDN'T WANT TO BOTHER FURI-SAN EITHER.
OH, BUT THERE ARE OTHER GIRLS I THINK ARE PRETTY, TOO.
SENSEI!?! WHAT'S WRONG?!
I-I'M ALL RIGHT... I JUST FEEL TIGHTNESS IN MY CHEST...
HUFF
HUFF
I DIDN'T THINK IT'D BE THE FIRST THING HE SAID!
ARE YOU SURE YOU'RE OKAY?!

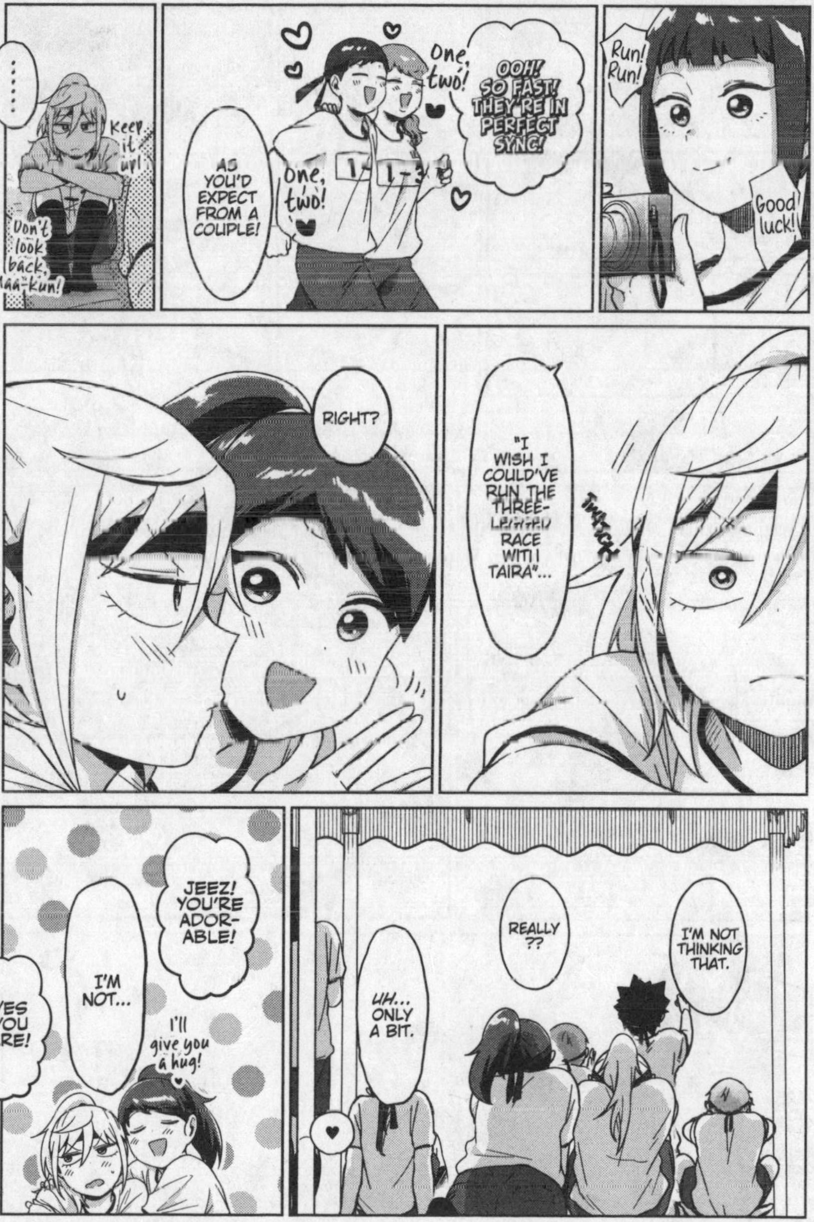
Run! Run!
Good luck!
OOH! SO FAST! THEY'RE IN PERFECT SYNC!
One, two!
One, two!
AS YOU'D EXPECT FROM A COUPLE!
......
Keep it up!
Don't look back, Maa-kun!
"I WISH I COULD'VE RUN THE THREE-LEGGED RACE WITH TAIRA"...
TWITCH!
RIGHT?
I'M NOT THINKING THAT.
REALLY ??
UH... ONLY A BIT.
JEEZ! YOU'RE ADORABLE!
I'M NOT...
I'll give you a hug!
YES YOU ARE!

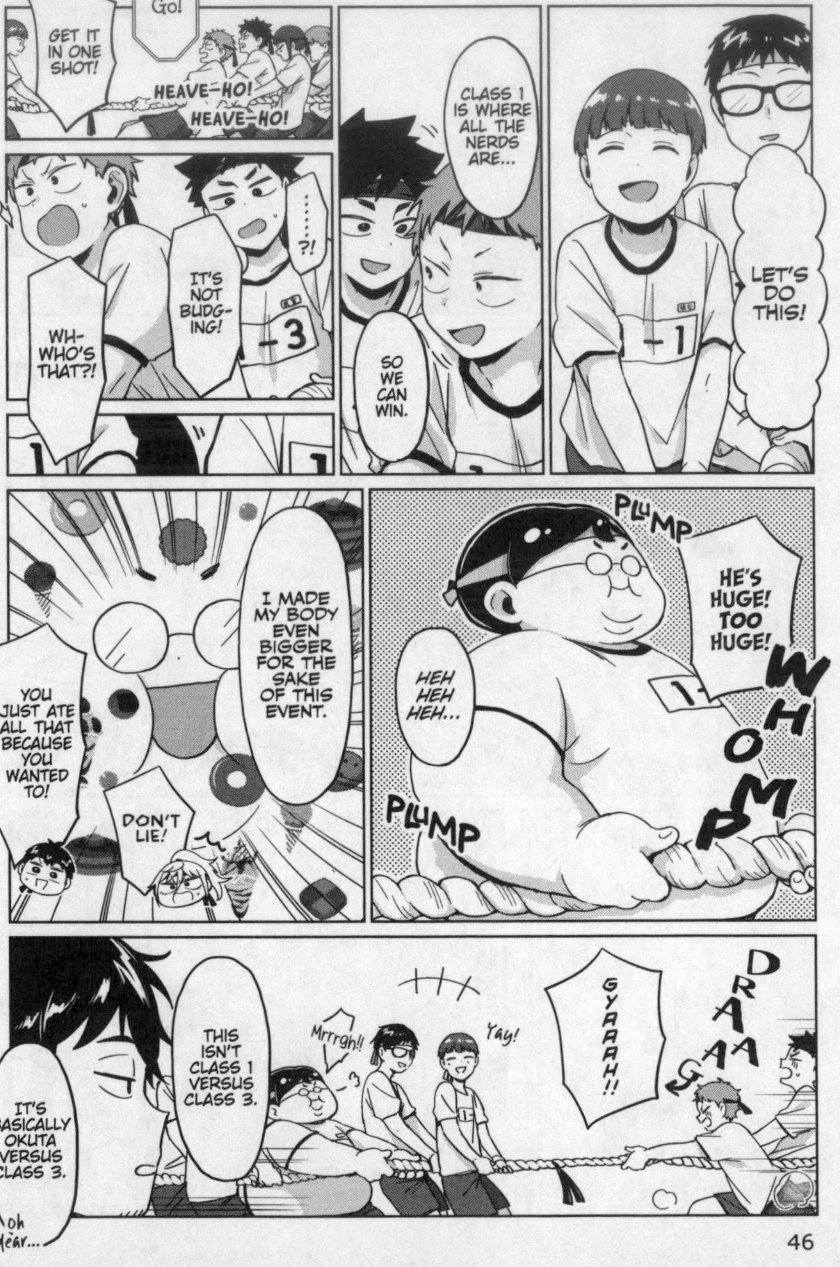
LET'S DO THIS!
CLASS 1 IS WHERE ALL THE NERDS ARE...
SO WE CAN WIN.
Go!
GET IT IN ONE SHOT!
HEAVE-HO!
HEAVE-HO!
......?!
IT'S NOT BUDGING!
WH-WHO'S THAT?!
PLUMP
HE'S HUGE! TOO HUGE!
HEH HEH HEH...
WHOMP
PLUMP
I MADE MY BODY EVEN BIGGER FOR THE SAKE OF THIS EVENT.
YOU JUST ATE ALL THAT BECAUSE YOU WANTED TO!
DON'T LIE!
DRAAAG
GYAAAH!!
Yay!
Mrrrgh!!
THIS ISN'T CLASS 1 VERSUS CLASS 3.
IT'S BASICALLY OKUTA VERSUS CLASS 3.
Oh dear...

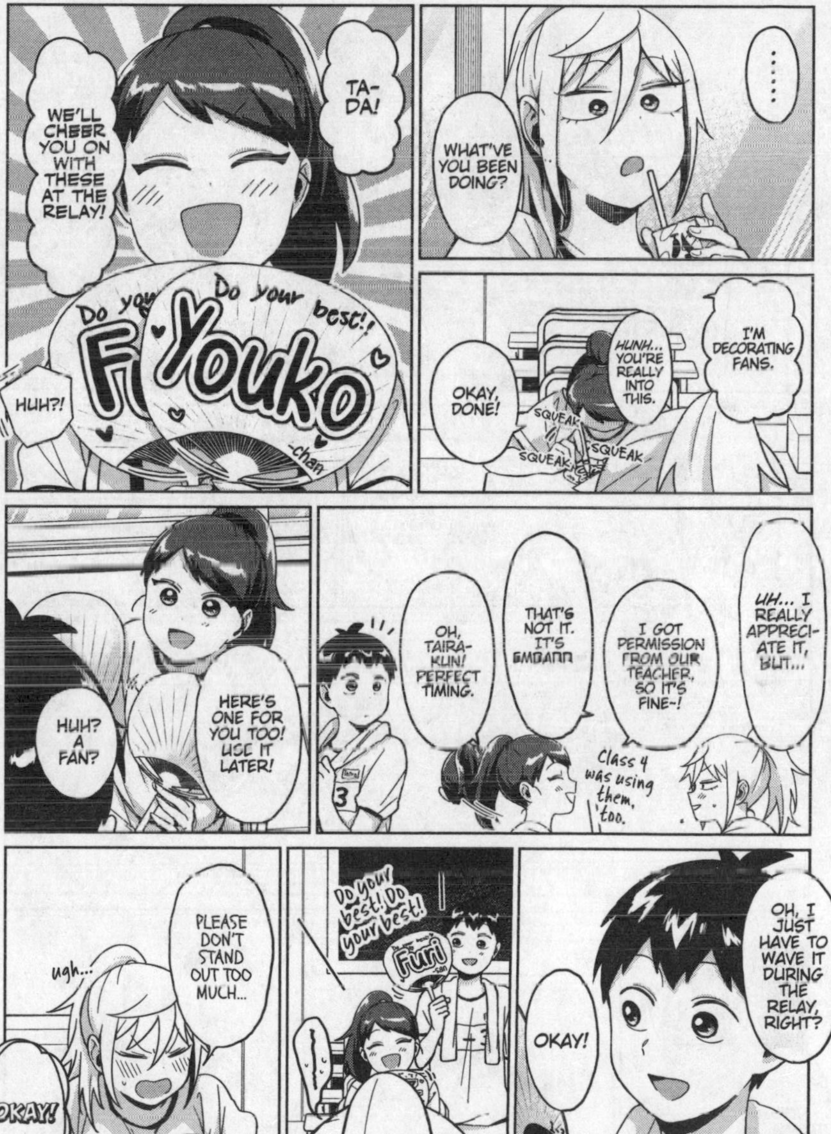
......
WHAT'VE YOU BEEN DOING?
I'M DECORATING FANS.
HUNH... YOU'RE REALLY INTO THIS.
SQUEAK
SQUEAK
SQUEAK
OKAY, DONE!
TA-DA!
WE'LL CHEER YOU ON WITH THESE AT THE RELAY!
Do your best!! Youko -chan
Do you F
HUH?!
UH... I REALLY APPRECIATE IT, BUT...
I GOT PERMISSION FROM OUR TEACHER, SO IT'S FINE~!
THAT'S NOT IT. IT'S EMBARR
OH, TAIRA-KUN! PERFECT TIMING.
Class 4 was using them, too.
HERE'S ONE FOR YOU TOO! USE IT LATER!
HUH? A FAN?
OH, I JUST HAVE TO WAVE IT DURING THE RELAY, RIGHT?
OKAY!
Do your best! Do your best!
Furi -san
PLEASE DON'T STAND OUT TOO MUCH...
ugh...
OKAY!
Furi

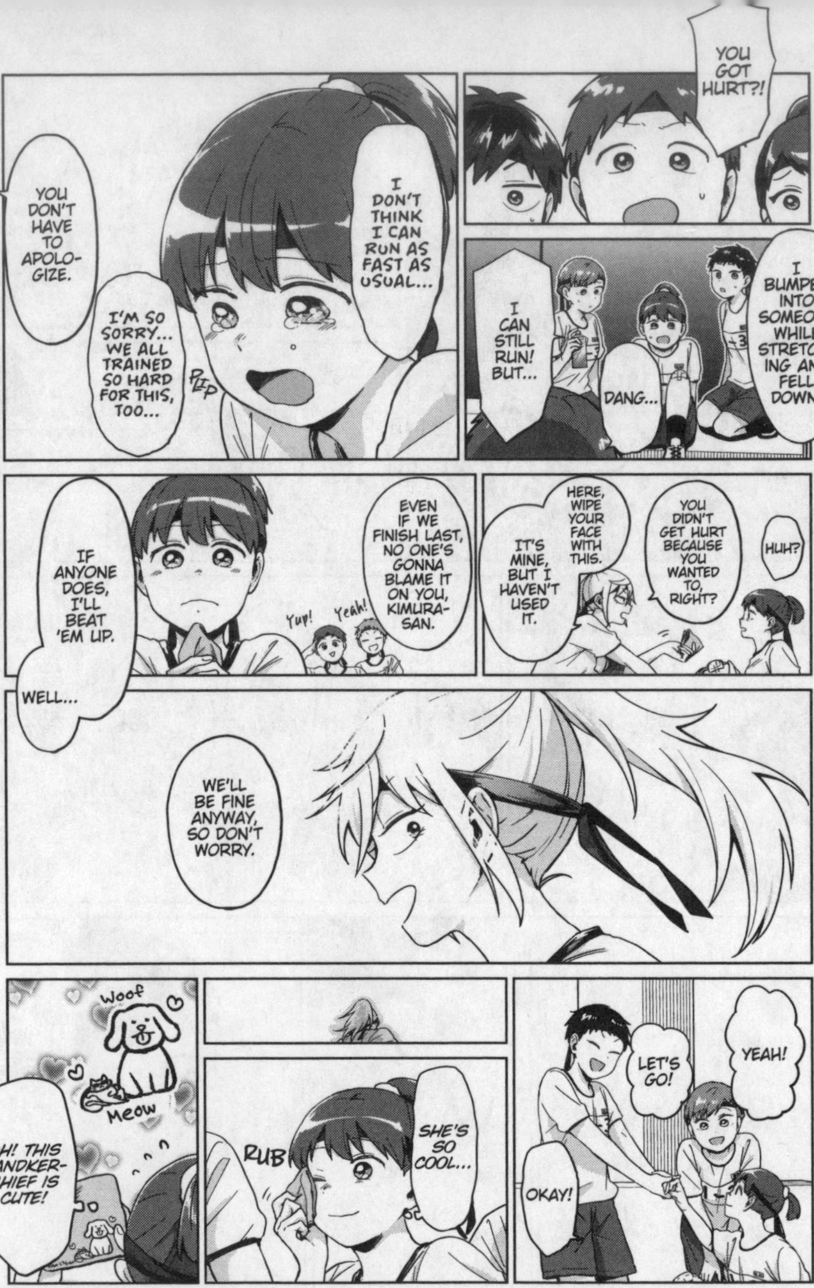
YOU GOT HURT?!
I BUMPED INTO SOMEONE WHILE STRETCHING AND FELL DOWN.
DANG...
I CAN STILL RUN! BUT...
I DON'T THINK I CAN RUN AS FAST AS USUAL...
I'M SO SORRY... WE ALL TRAINED SO HARD FOR THIS, TOO...
PLIP
YOU DON'T HAVE TO APOLOGIZE.
HUH?
YOU DIDN'T GET HURT BECAUSE YOU WANTED TO, RIGHT?
HERE, WIPE YOUR FACE WITH THIS.
IT'S MINE, BUT I HAVEN'T USED IT.
EVEN IF WE FINISH LAST, NO ONE'S GONNA BLAME IT ON YOU, KIMURA-SAN.
Yeah!
Yup!
IF ANYONE DOES, I'LL BEAT 'EM UP.
WELL...
WE'LL BE FINE ANYWAY, SO DON'T WORRY.
YEAH!
LET'S GO!
OKAY!
SHE'S SO COOL...
RUB
Woof
Meow
OH! THIS HANDKERCHIEF IS CUTE!

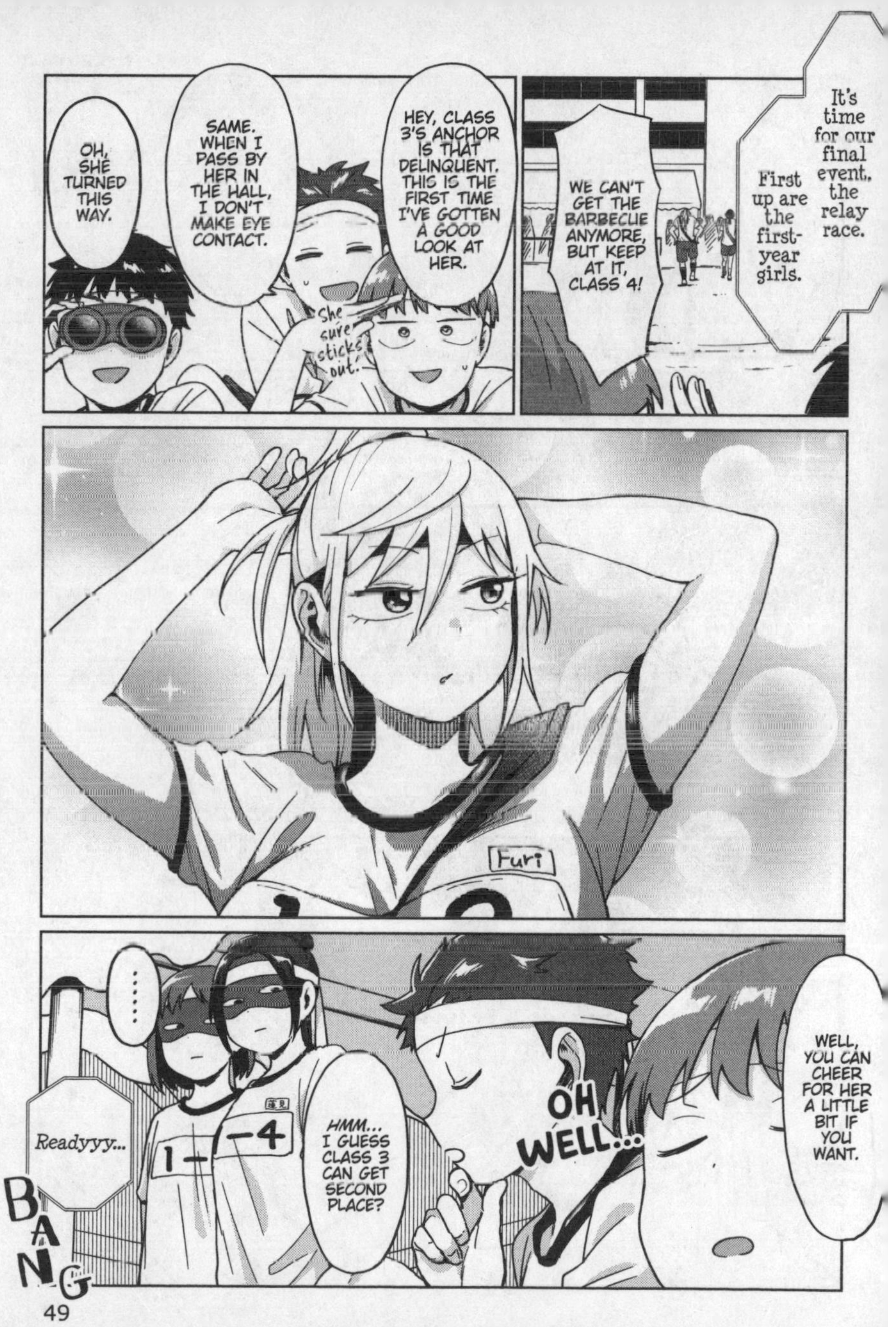
It's time for our final event, the relay race.
First up are the first-year girls.
WE CAN'T GET THE BARBECUE ANYMORE, BUT KEEP AT IT, CLASS 4!
HEY, CLASS 3'S ANCHOR IS THAT DELINQUENT. THIS IS THE FIRST TIME I'VE GOTTEN A GOOD LOOK AT HER.
SAME. WHEN I PASS BY HER IN THE HALL, I DON'T MAKE EYE CONTACT.
She sure sticks out!
OH, SHE TURNED THIS WAY.
Furi
WELL, YOU CAN CHEER FOR HER A LITTLE BIT IF YOU WANT.
OH WELL...
HMM... I GUESS CLASS 3 CAN GET SECOND PLACE?
......
1-4
Readyyy...
BANG

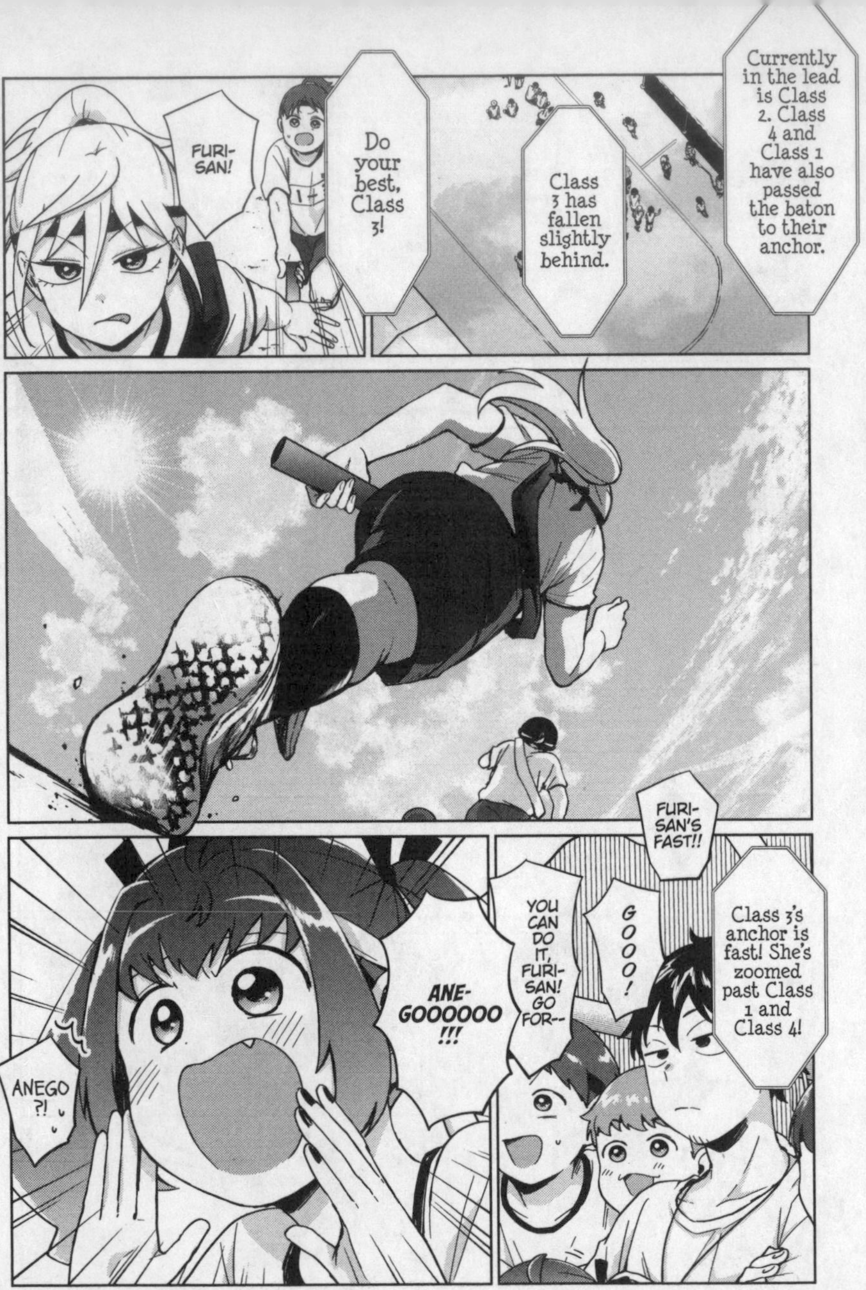
Currently in the lead is Class 2. Class 4 and Class 1 have also passed the baton to their anchor.
Class 3 has fallen slightly behind.
Do your best, Class 3!
FURI-SAN!
FURI-SAN'S FAST!!
Class 3's anchor is fast! She's zoomed past Class 1 and Class 4!
GOOOO!
YOU CAN DO IT, FURI-SAN! GO FOR--
ANE-GOOOOOO!!!
ANEGO?!

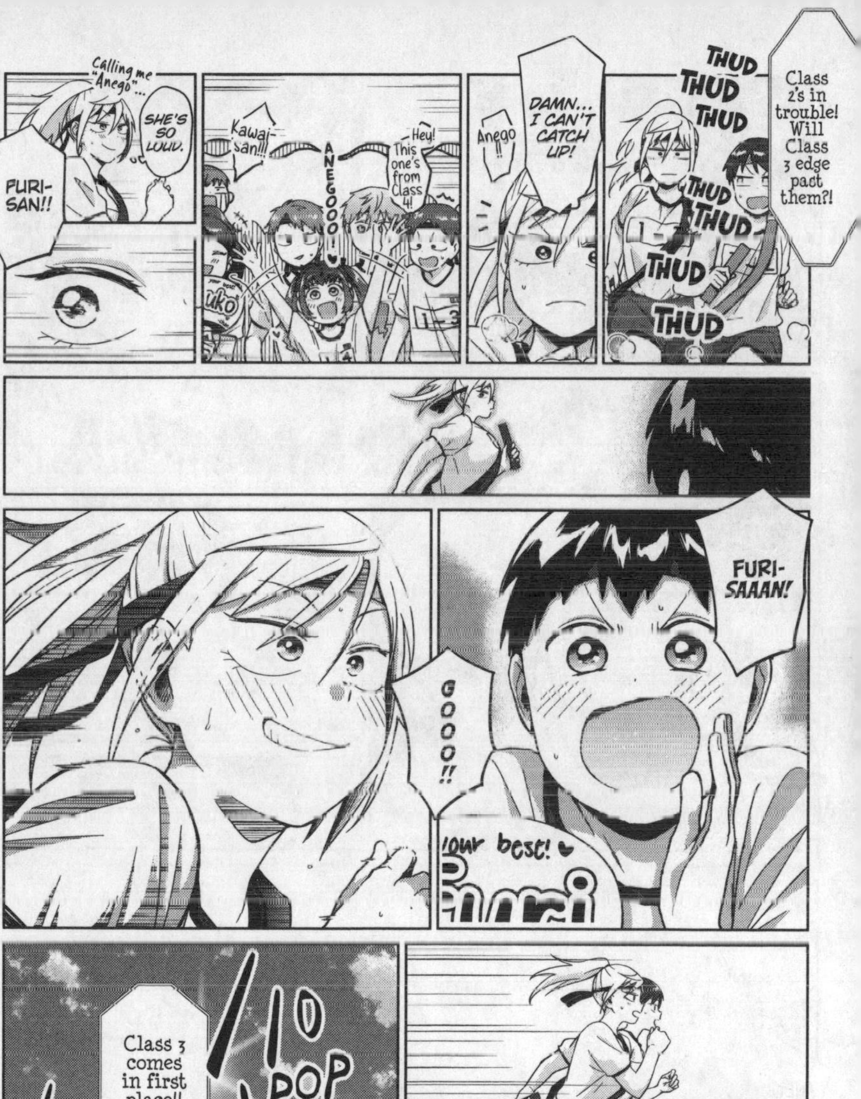
Class 2's in trouble! Will Class 3 edge past them?!
THUD THUD THUD
THUD THUD
THUD
THUD
DAMN... I CAN'T CATCH UP!
Anego!!
Hey! This one's from Class 4!
ANEGOOO!
Kawai-san!!!
Calling me "Anego"...
SHE'S SO LUUU.
FURI-SAN!!
FURI-SAAAN!
GOOOO!!
Class 3 comes in first place!!
POP
POP

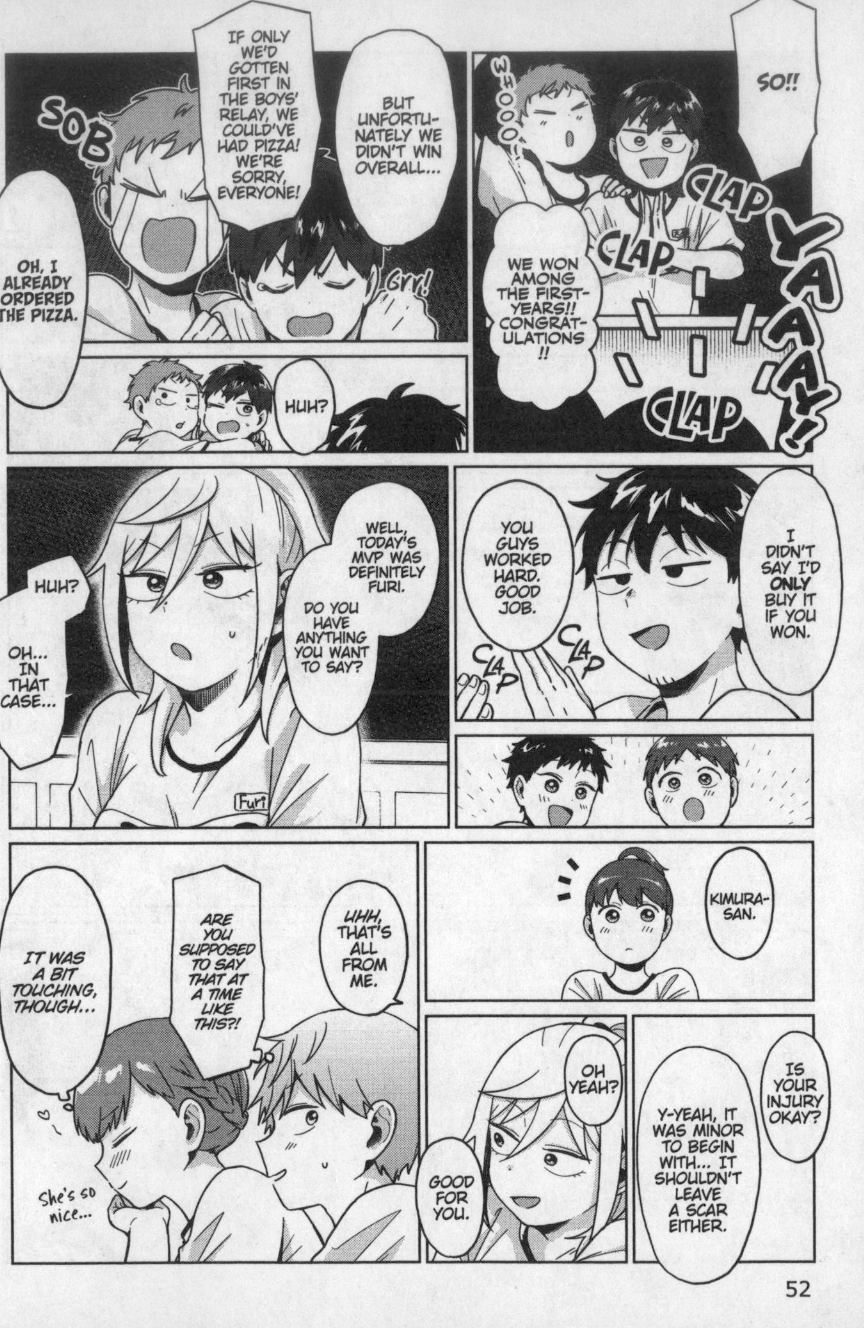
SO!!
WHOOOO
CLAP
CLAP
WE WON AMONG THE FIRST-YEARS!! CONGRATULATIONS!!
YAAAY!
CLAP
BUT UNFORTUNATELY WE DIDN'T WIN OVERALL...
IF ONLY WE'D GOTTEN FIRST IN THE BOYS' RELAY, WE COULD'VE HAD PIZZA! WE'RE SORRY, EVERYONE!
SOB
GRR!
OH, I ALREADY ORDERED THE PIZZA.
HUH?
I DIDN'T SAY I'D ONLY BUY IT IF YOU WON.
YOU GUYS WORKED HARD. GOOD JOB.
CLAP
CLAP
WELL, TODAY'S MVP WAS DEFINITELY FURI.
DO YOU HAVE ANYTHING YOU WANT TO SAY?
HUH?
OH... IN THAT CASE...
Furi
KIMURA-SAN.
IS YOUR INJURY OKAY?
Y-YEAH, IT WAS MINOR TO BEGIN WITH... IT SHOULDN'T LEAVE A SCAR EITHER.
OH YEAH?
GOOD FOR YOU.
UHH, THAT'S ALL FROM ME.
ARE YOU SUPPOSED TO SAY THAT AT A TIME LIKE THIS?!
IT WAS A BIT TOUCHING, THOUGH...
She's so nice...

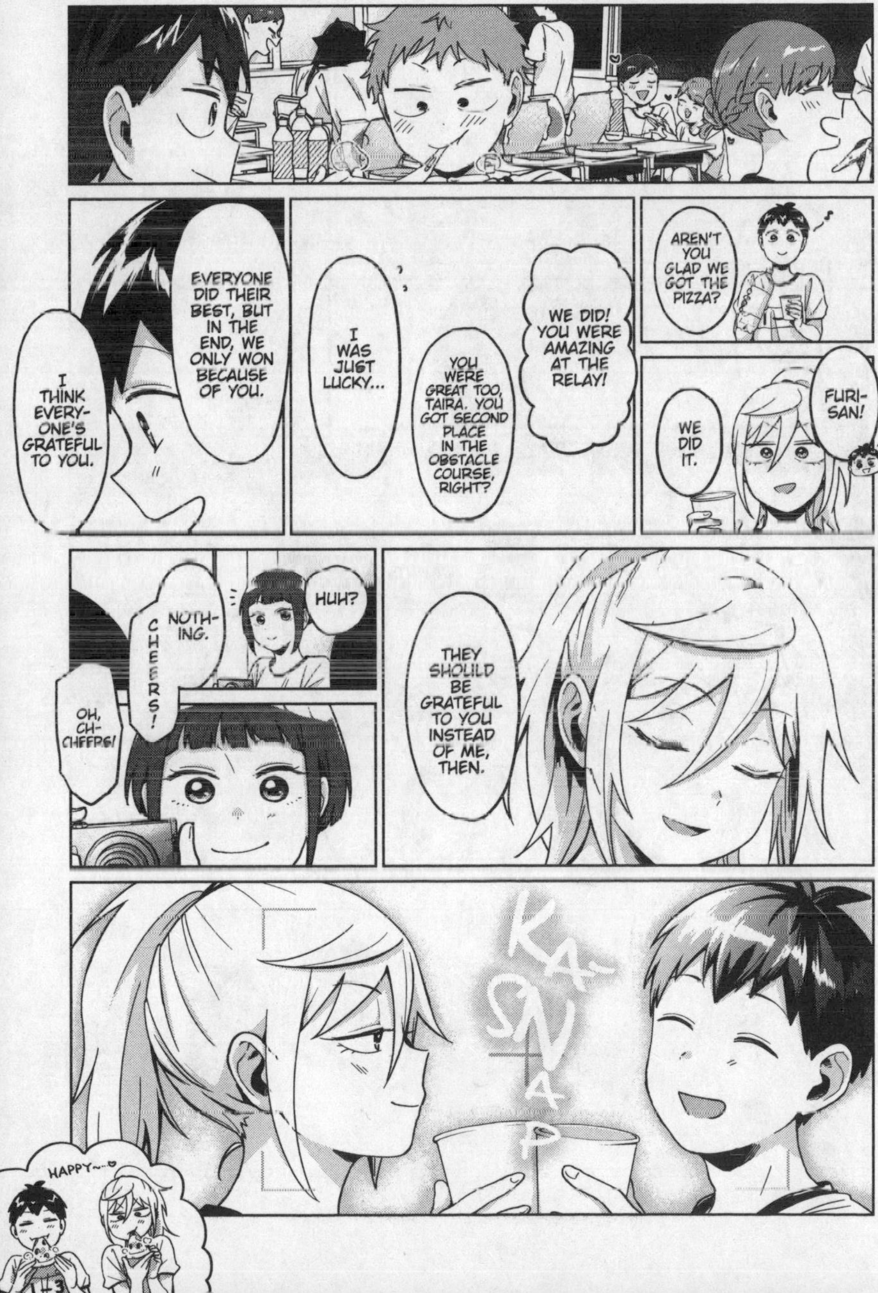
AREN'T YOU GLAD WE GOT THE PIZZA?
FURI-SAN!
WE DID IT.
WE DID! YOU WERE AMAZING AT THE RELAY!
YOU WERE GREAT TOO, TAIRA. YOU GOT SECOND PLACE IN THE OBSTACLE COURSE, RIGHT?
I WAS JUST LUCKY...
EVERYONE DID THEIR BEST, BUT IN THE END, WE ONLY WON BECAUSE OF YOU.
I THINK EVERYONE'S GRATEFUL TO YOU.
THEY SHOULD BE GRATEFUL TO YOU INSTEAD OF ME, THEN.
HUH?
NOTHING.
CHEERS!
OH, CH-CHEERS!
KA-SNAP
HAPPY~♡

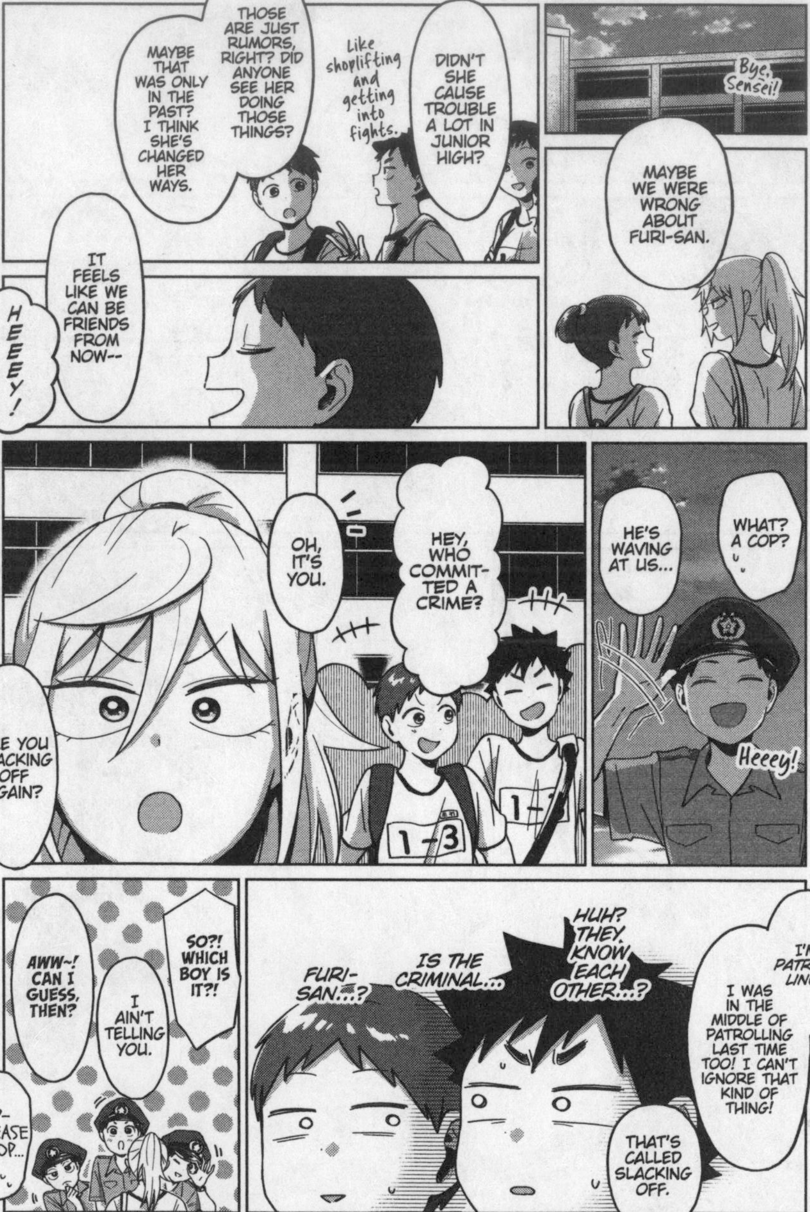
Bye, Sensei!
MAYBE WE WERE WRONG ABOUT FURI-SAN.
DIDN'T SHE CAUSE TROUBLE A LOT IN JUNIOR HIGH?
Like shoplifting and getting into fights.
THOSE ARE JUST RUMORS, RIGHT? DID ANYONE SEE HER DOING THOSE THINGS?
MAYBE THAT WAS ONLY IN THE PAST? I THINK SHE'S CHANGED HER WAYS.
IT FEELS LIKE WE CAN BE FRIENDS FROM NOW--
HEEEY!
WHAT? A COP?
HE'S WAVING AT US...
Heeey!
HEY, WHO COMMITTED A CRIME?
OH, IT'S YOU.
ARE YOU SLACKING OFF AGAIN?
I'M PATROLLING!
I WAS IN THE MIDDLE OF PATROLLING LAST TIME TOO! I CAN'T IGNORE THAT KIND OF THING!
HUH? THEY KNOW EACH OTHER...?
IS THE CRIMINAL...
FURI-SAN...?
THAT'S CALLED SLACKING OFF.
SO?! WHICH BOY IS IT?!
AWW~! CAN I GUESS, THEN?
I AIN'T TELLING YOU.
P-PLEASE STOP...

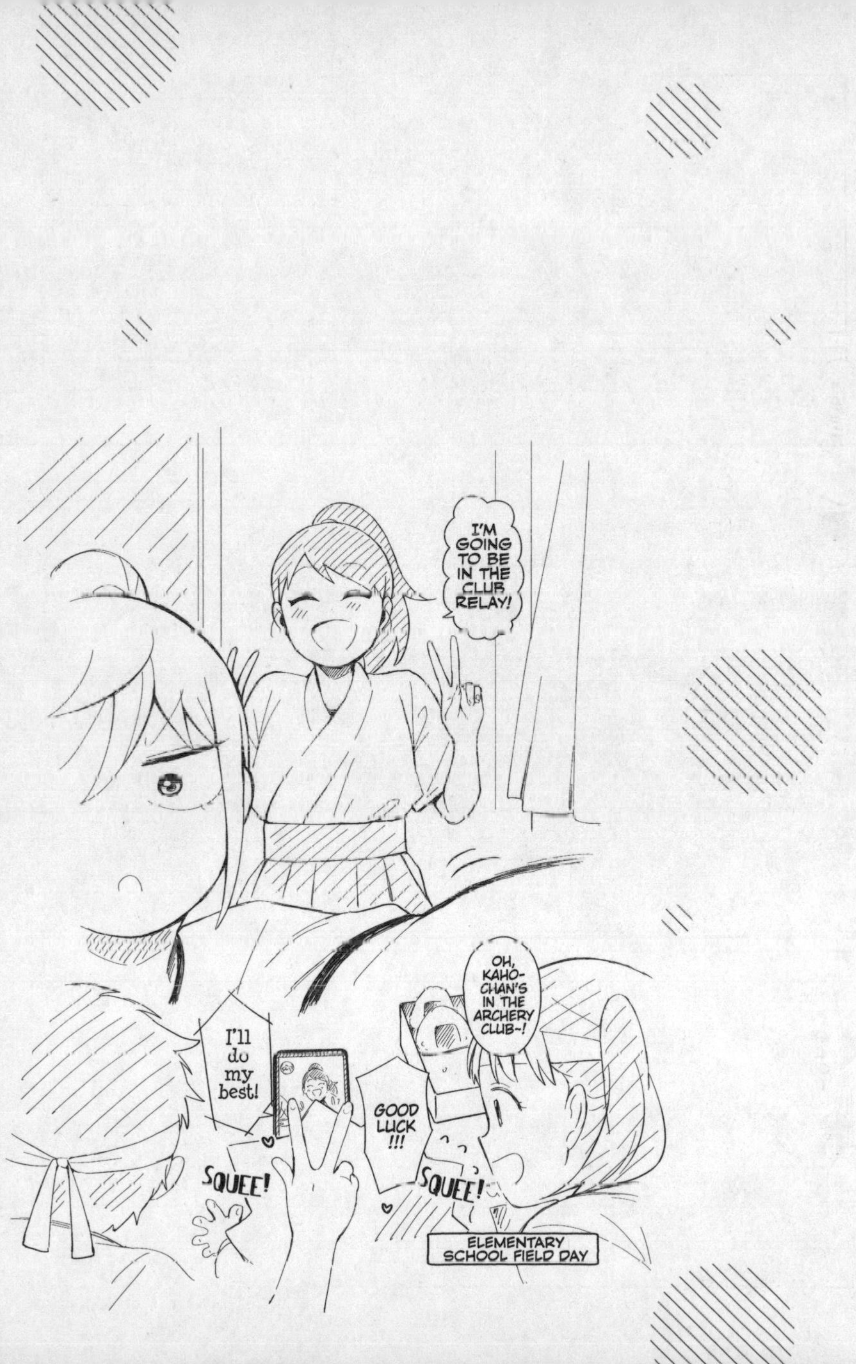
I'M GOING TO BE IN THE CLUB RELAY!
OH, KAHO-CHAN'S IN THE ARCHERY CLUB~!
GOOD LUCK!!!
SQUEE!
I'll do my best!
SQUEE!
ELEMENTARY SCHOOL FIELD DAY

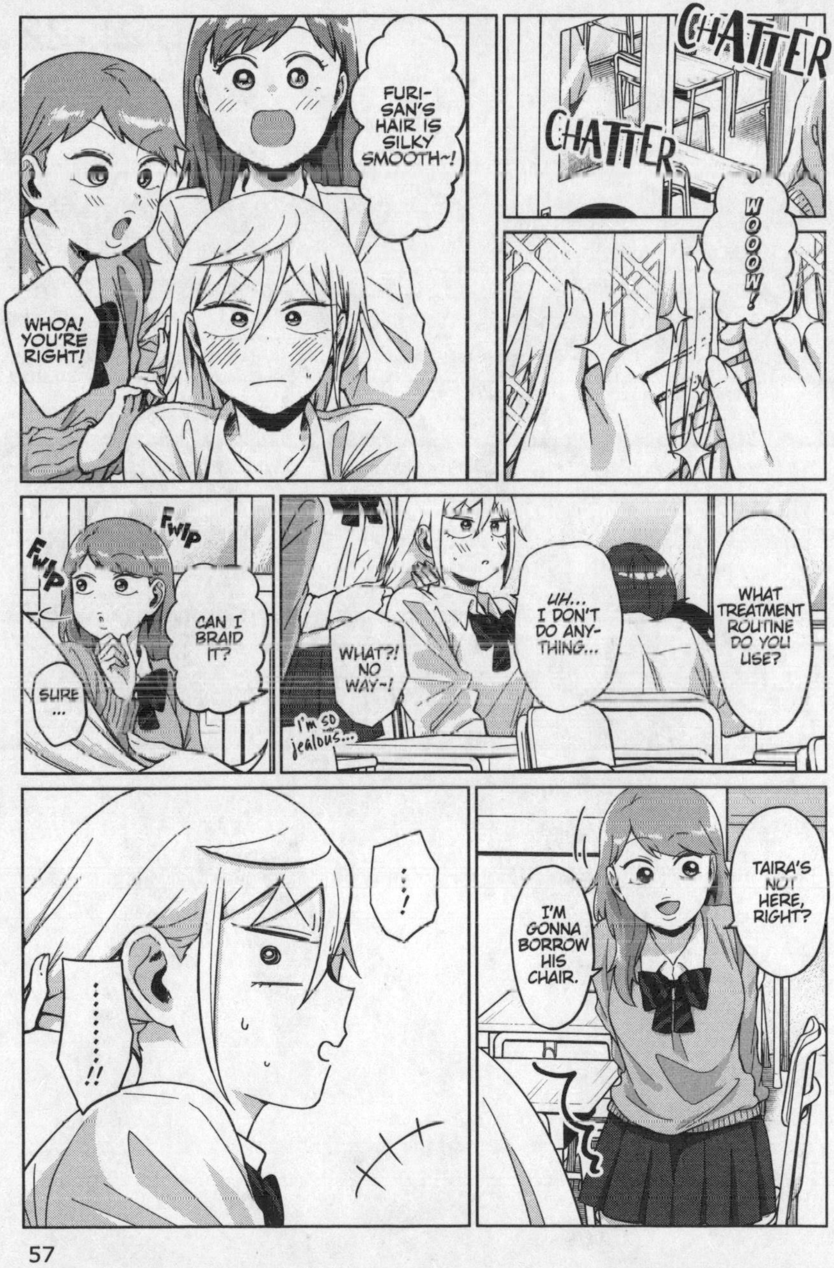
CHATTER
CHATTER
WOOOOW!
FURI-SAN'S HAIR IS SILKY SMOOTH~!
WHOA! YOU'RE RIGHT!
WHAT TREATMENT ROUTINE DO YOU USE?
UH... I DON'T DO ANY-THING...
WHAT?! NO WAY~!
I'm so jealous...
FWIP
FWIP
CAN I BRAID IT?
SURE...
TAIRA'S NOT HERE, RIGHT?
I'M GONNA BORROW HIS CHAIR.
...!
..........!!

Chapter 22

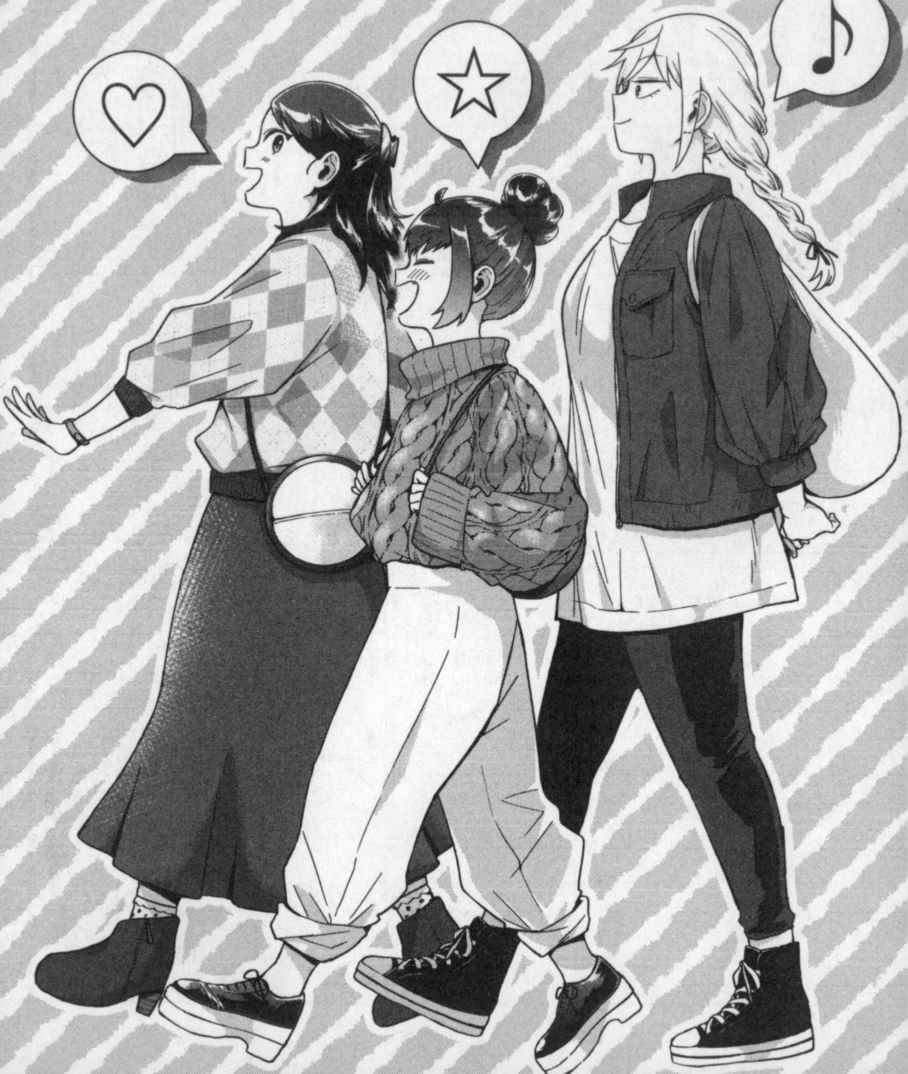

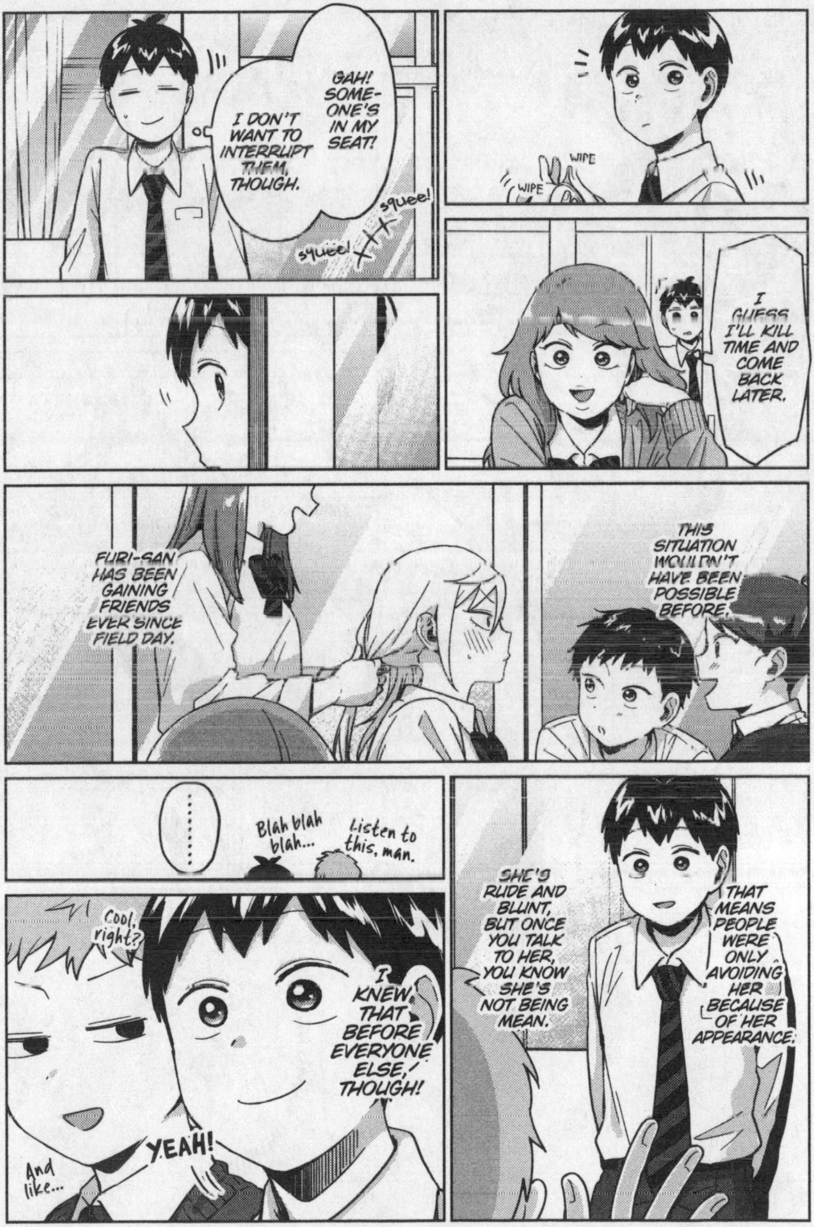
WIPE
WIPE
GAH! SOME-ONE'S IN MY SEAT!
I DON'T WANT TO INTERRUPT THEM, THOUGH.
squee!
squee!
I GUESS I'LL KILL TIME AND COME BACK LATER.
THIS SITUATION WOULDN'T HAVE BEEN POSSIBLE BEFORE.
FURI-SAN HAS BEEN GAINING FRIENDS EVER SINCE FIELD DAY.
THAT MEANS PEOPLE WERE ONLY AVOIDING HER BECAUSE OF HER APPEARANCE.
SHE'S RUDE AND BLUNT, BUT ONCE YOU TALK TO HER, YOU KNOW SHE'S NOT BEING MEAN.
Listen to this, man.
Blah blah blah...
......
Cool, right?
I KNEW THAT BEFORE EVERYONE ELSE, THOUGH!
YEAH!
And like...

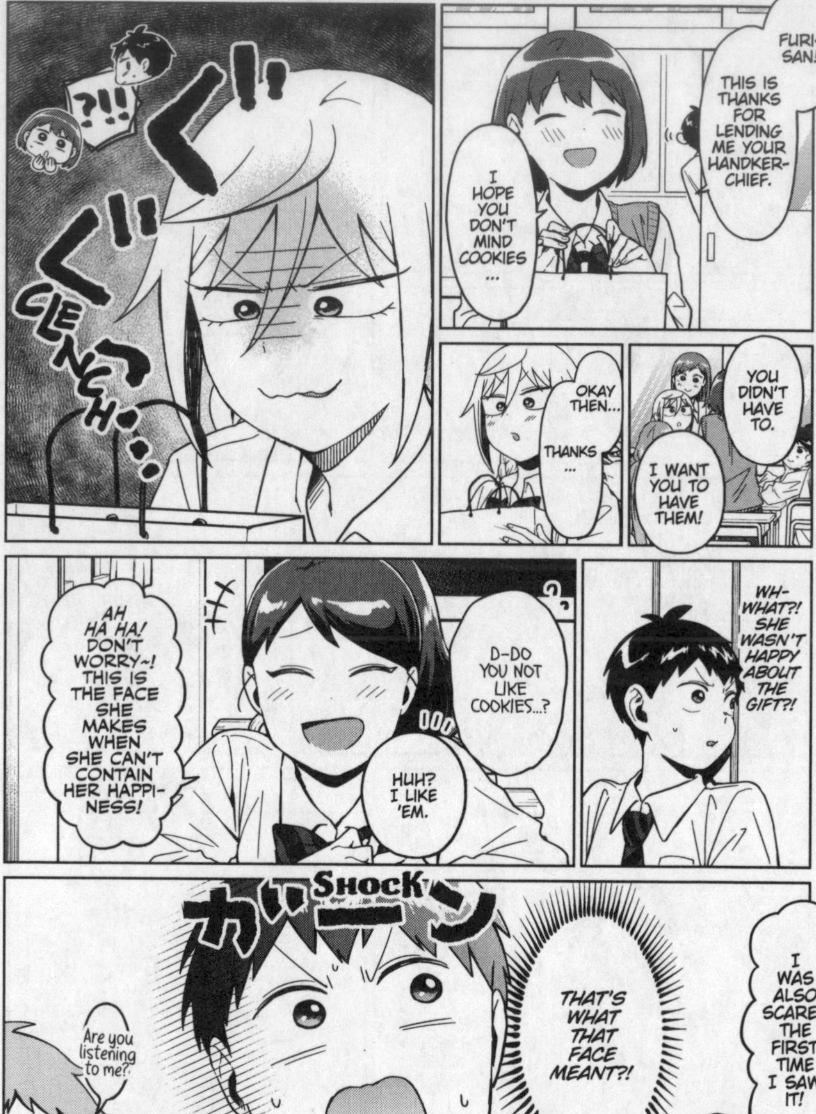
FURI-SAN!
THIS IS THANKS FOR LENDING ME YOUR HANDKER-CHIEF.
I HOPE YOU DON'T MIND COOKIES ...
YOU DIDN'T HAVE TO.
I WANT YOU TO HAVE THEM!
OKAY THEN...
THANKS ...
?!!
CLENCH
WH-WHAT?! SHE WASN'T HAPPY ABOUT THE GIFT?!
D-DO YOU NOT LIKE COOKIES...?
HUH? I LIKE 'EM.
AH HA HA! DON'T WORRY~! THIS IS THE FACE SHE MAKES WHEN SHE CAN'T CONTAIN HER HAPPI-NESS!
SHOCK
I WAS ALSO SCARED THE FIRST TIME I SAW IT!
GAH... MY FACE MOVES ON ITS OWN.
THAT'S WHAT THAT FACE MEANT?!
Are you listening to me?

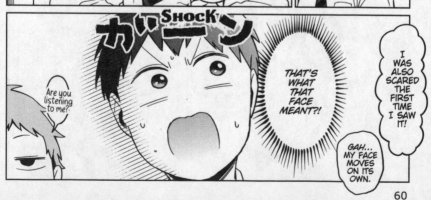

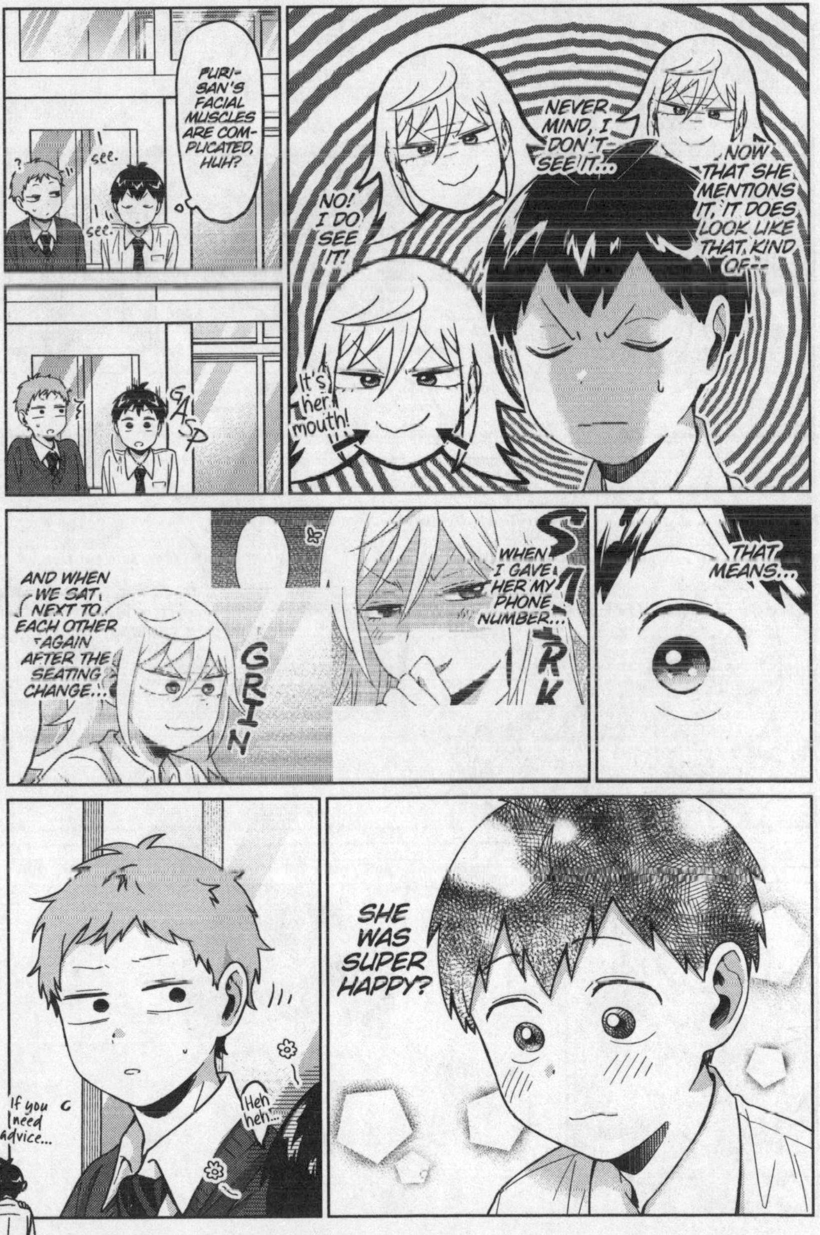
NOW THAT SHE MENTIONS IT, IT DOES LOOK LIKE THAT, KIND OF--
NEVER MIND, I DON'T SEE IT...
NO! I DO SEE IT!
It's her mouth!
FURI-SAN'S FACIAL MUSCLES ARE COMPLICATED, HUH?
I see.
I see.
GASP
THAT MEANS...
WHEN I GAVE HER MY PHONE NUMBER...
SMIRK
AND WHEN WE SAT NEXT TO EACH OTHER AGAIN AFTER THE SEATING CHANGE...
GRIN
SHE WAS SUPER HAPPY?
Heh heh...
If you need advice...
just ask me.

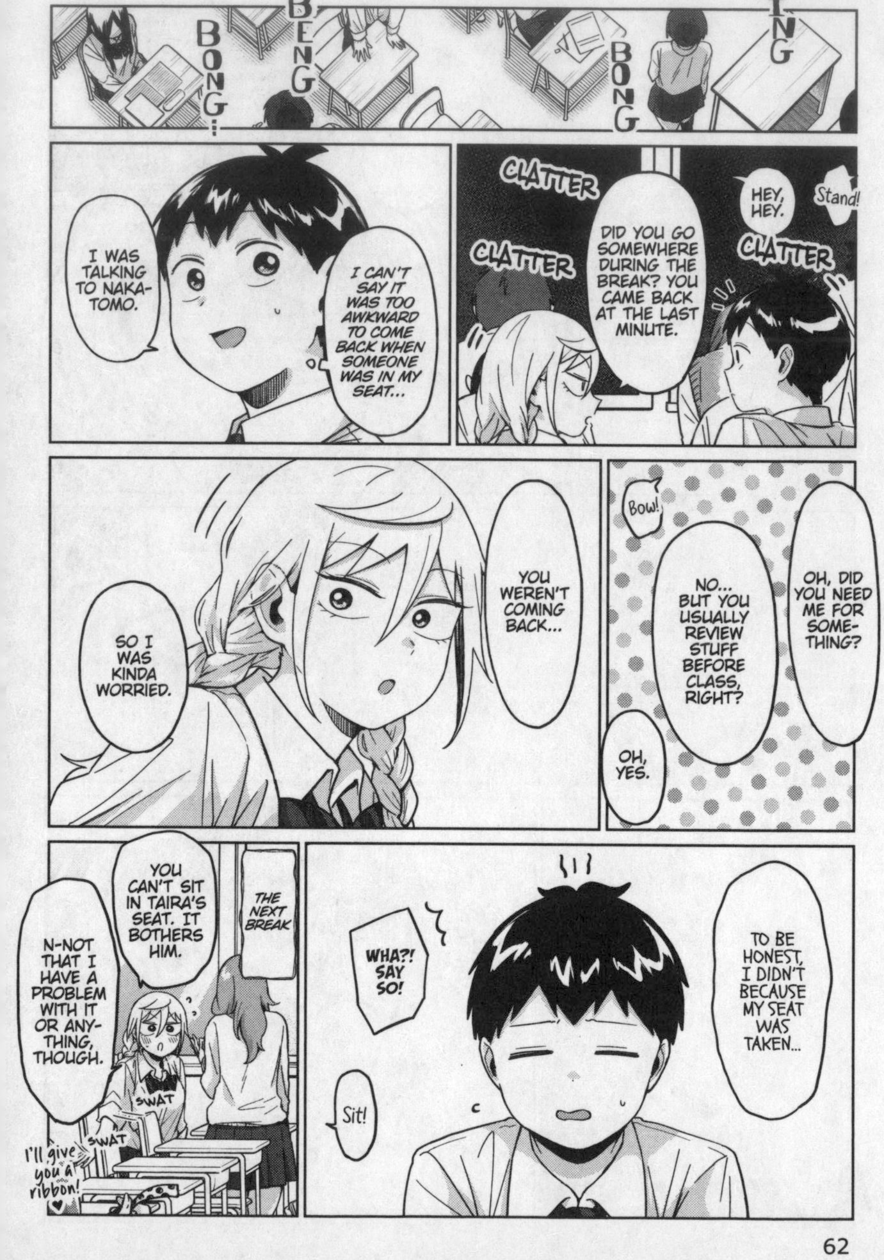
BING
BONG
BENG
BONG...
Stand!
HEY, HEY.
CLATTER
DID YOU GO SOMEWHERE DURING THE BREAK? YOU CAME BACK AT THE LAST MINUTE.
CLATTER
CLATTER
I CAN'T SAY IT WAS TOO AWKWARD TO COME BACK WHEN SOMEONE WAS IN MY SEAT...
I WAS TALKING TO NAKA-TOMO.
Bow!
OH, DID YOU NEED ME FOR SOME-THING?
NO... BUT YOU USUALLY REVIEW STUFF BEFORE CLASS, RIGHT?
OH, YES.
YOU WEREN'T COMING BACK...
SO I WAS KINDA WORRIED.
TO BE HONEST, I DIDN'T BECAUSE MY SEAT WAS TAKEN...
WHA?! SAY SO!
Sit!
THE NEXT BREAK
YOU CAN'T SIT IN TAIRA'S SEAT. IT BOTHERS HIM.
N-NOT THAT I HAVE A PROBLEM WITH IT OR ANY-THING, THOUGH.
SWAT
SWAT
I'll give you a ribbon! ♥

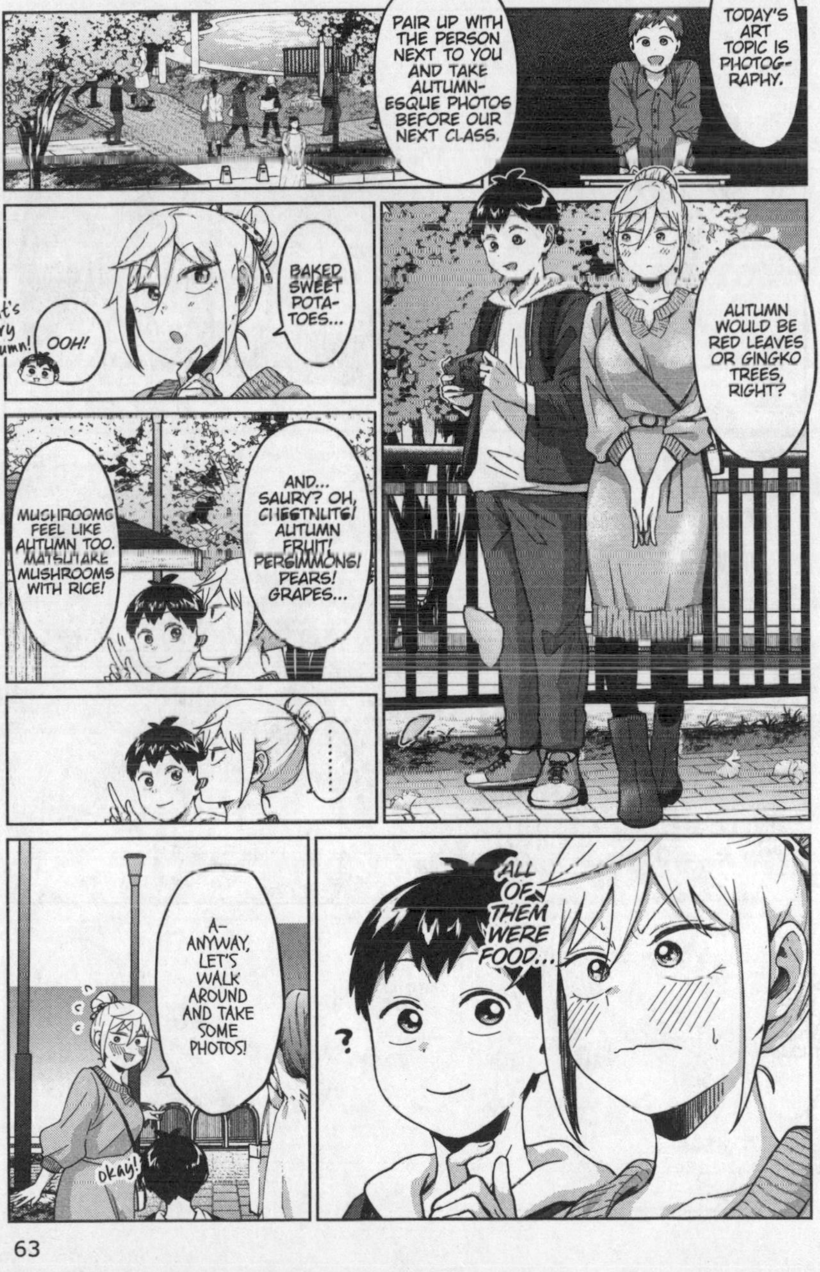
TODAY'S ART TOPIC IS PHOTOGRAPHY.
PAIR UP WITH THE PERSON NEXT TO YOU AND TAKE AUTUMN-ESQUE PHOTOS BEFORE OUR NEXT CLASS.
AUTUMN WOULD BE RED LEAVES OR GINGKO TREES, RIGHT?
BAKED SWEET POTATOES...
OOH!
That's very autumn!
AND... SAURY? OH, CHESTNUTS! AUTUMN FRUIT! PERSIMMONS! PEARS! GRAPES...
MUSHROOMS FEEL LIKE AUTUMN TOO. MATSUTAKE MUSHROOMS WITH RICE!
......
ALL OF THEM WERE FOOD...
?
A-ANYWAY, LET'S WALK AROUND AND TAKE SOME PHOTOS!
Okay!

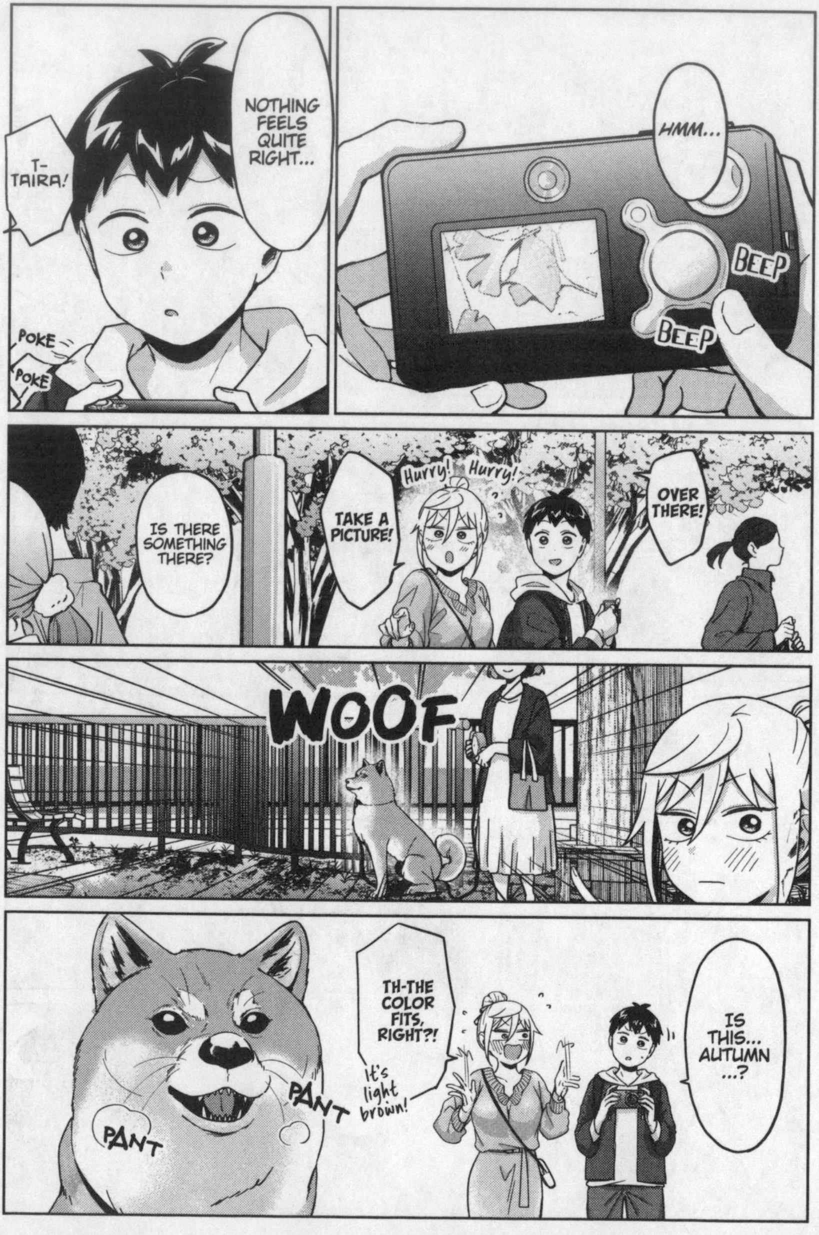
HMM...
BEEP
BEEP
NOTHING FEELS QUITE RIGHT...
T-TAIRA!
POKE
POKE
OVER THERE!
Hurry! Hurry!
TAKE A PICTURE!
IS THERE SOMETHING THERE?
WOOF
IS THIS... AUTUMN ...?
TH-THE COLOR FITS, RIGHT?!
It's light brown!
PANT
PANT

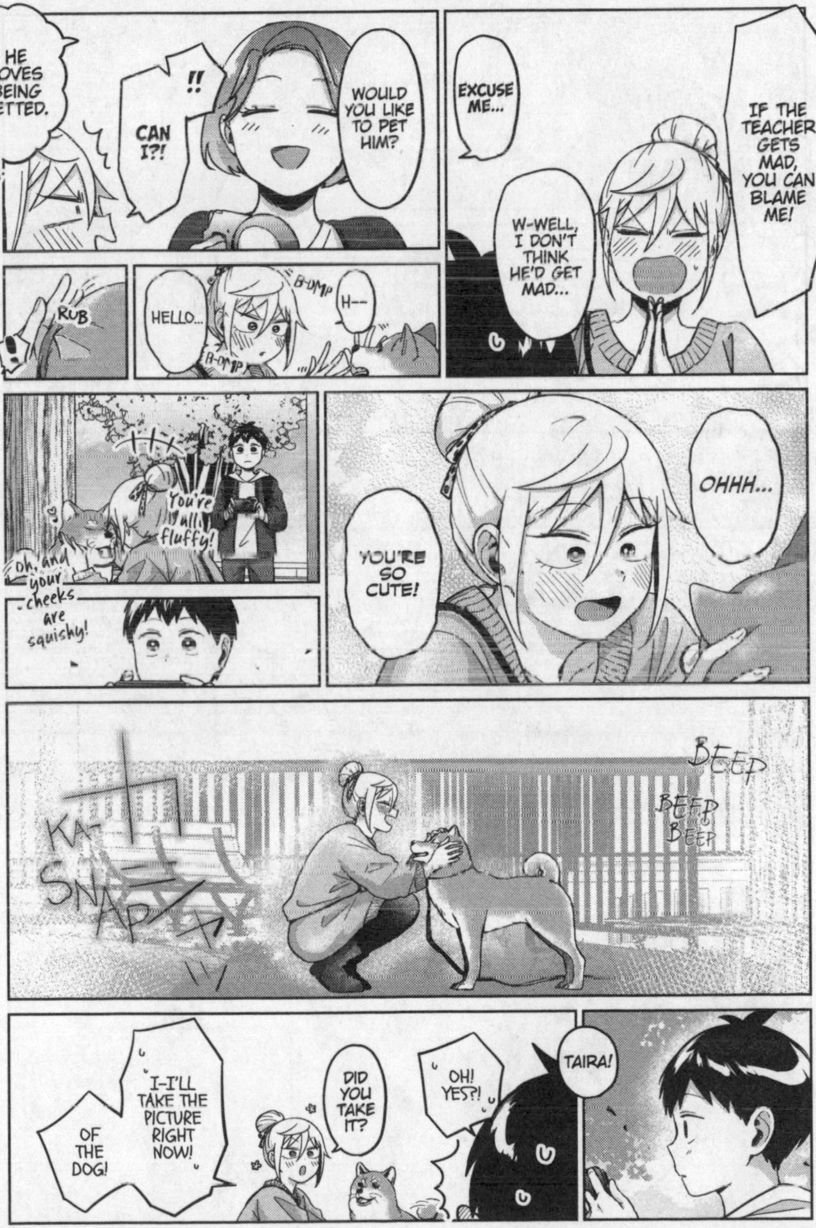
EXCUSE ME...
IF THE TEACHER GETS MAD, YOU CAN BLAME ME!
W-WELL, I DON'T THINK HE'D GET MAD...
WOULD YOU LIKE TO PET HIM?
!!
CAN I?!
HE LOVES BEING PETTED.
Go ahead!
B-DMP
H--
HELLO...
B-DMP
RUB
OHHH...
YOU'RE SO CUTE!
You're all fluffy!
Oh, and your cheeks are squishy!
BEEP
BEEP
BEEP
KA-SNAP
TAIRA!
OH! YES?!
DID YOU TAKE IT?
I-I'LL TAKE THE PICTURE RIGHT NOW!
OF THE DOG!

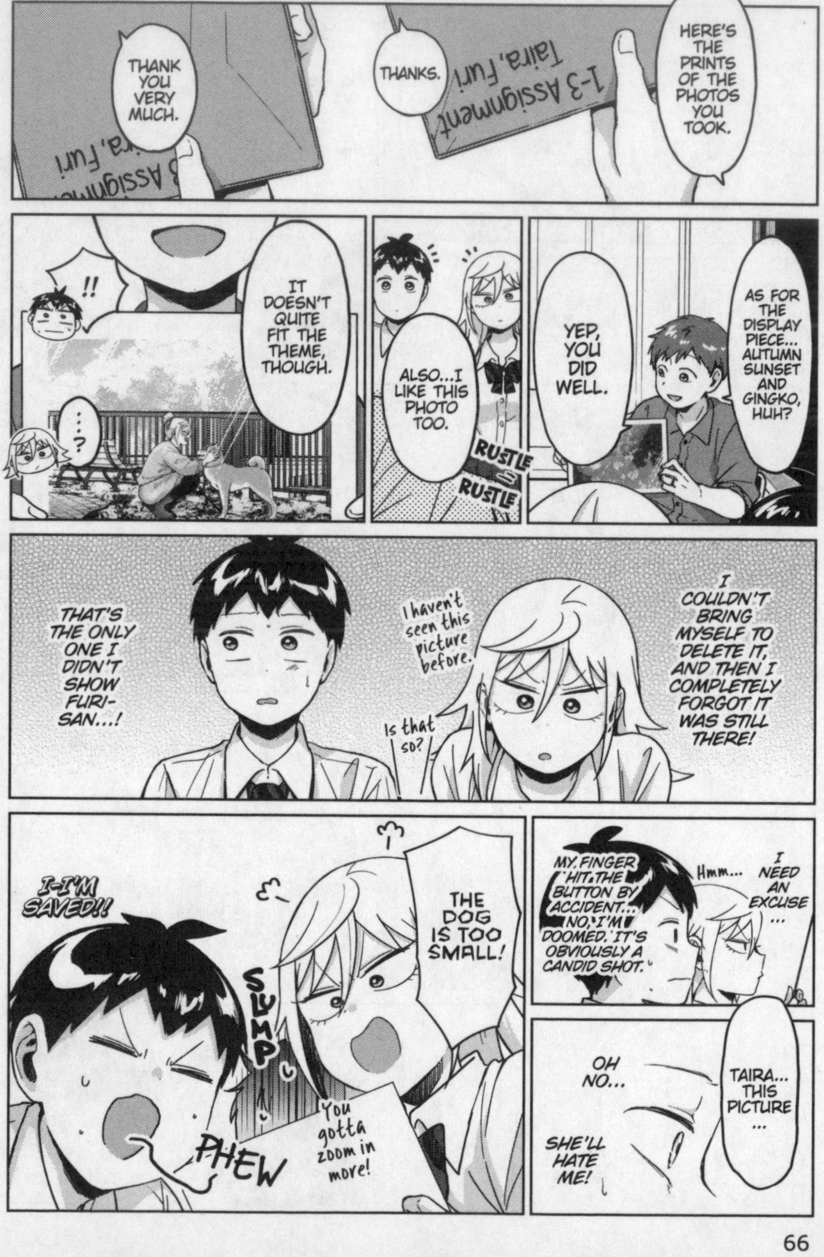
HERE'S THE PRINTS OF THE PHOTOS YOU TOOK.
1-3 Assignment Taira, Furi
THANKS.
THANK YOU VERY MUCH.
AS FOR THE DISPLAY PIECE... AUTUMN SUNSET AND GINGKO, HUH?
YEP, YOU DID WELL.
RUSTLE RUSTLE
ALSO...I LIKE THIS PHOTO TOO.
IT DOESN'T QUITE FIT THE THEME, THOUGH.
!!
...?
I COULDN'T BRING MYSELF TO DELETE IT, AND THEN I COMPLETELY FORGOT IT WAS STILL THERE!
I haven't seen this picture before.
Is that so?
THAT'S THE ONLY ONE I DIDN'T SHOW FURI-SAN...!
I NEED AN EXCUSE...
Hmm...
MY FINGER HIT THE BUTTON BY ACCIDENT... NO, I'M DOOMED. IT'S OBVIOUSLY A CANDID SHOT.
TAIRA... THIS PICTURE...
OH NO...
SHE'LL HATE ME!
THE DOG IS TOO SMALL!
You gotta zoom in more!
SLUMP
I-I'M SAVED!!
PHEW

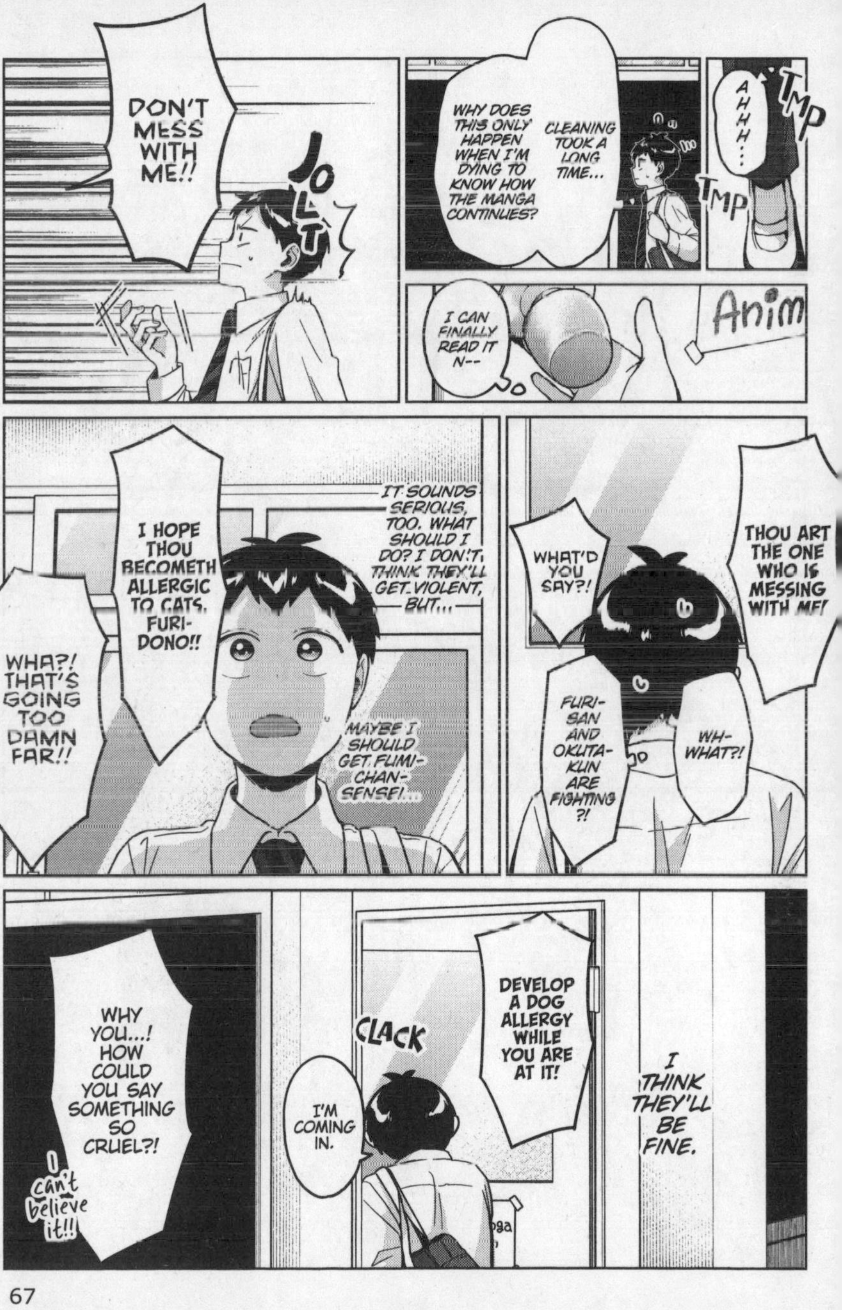
TMP
AHHH...
TMP
CLEANING TOOK A LONG TIME...
WHY DOES THIS ONLY HAPPEN WHEN I'M DYING TO KNOW HOW THE MANGA CONTINUES?
Anim
I CAN FINALLY READ IT N--
DON'T MESS WITH ME!!
JOLT
THOU ART THE ONE WHO IS MESSING WITH ME!
WHAT'D YOU SAY?!
FURI-SAN AND OKUTA-KUN ARE FIGHTING?!
WH-WHAT?!
I HOPE THOU BECOMETH ALLERGIC TO CATS, FURI-DONO!!
IT SOUNDS SERIOUS, TOO. WHAT SHOULD I DO? I DON'T THINK THEY'LL GET VIOLENT, BUT...
WHA?! THAT'S GOING TOO DAMN FAR!!
MAYBE I SHOULD GET FUMI-CHAN-SENSEI...
DEVELOP A DOG ALLERGY WHILE YOU ARE AT IT!
I THINK THEY'LL BE FINE.
CLACK
I'M COMING IN.
WHY YOU...! HOW COULD YOU SAY SOMETHING SO CRUEL?!
I can't believe it!!

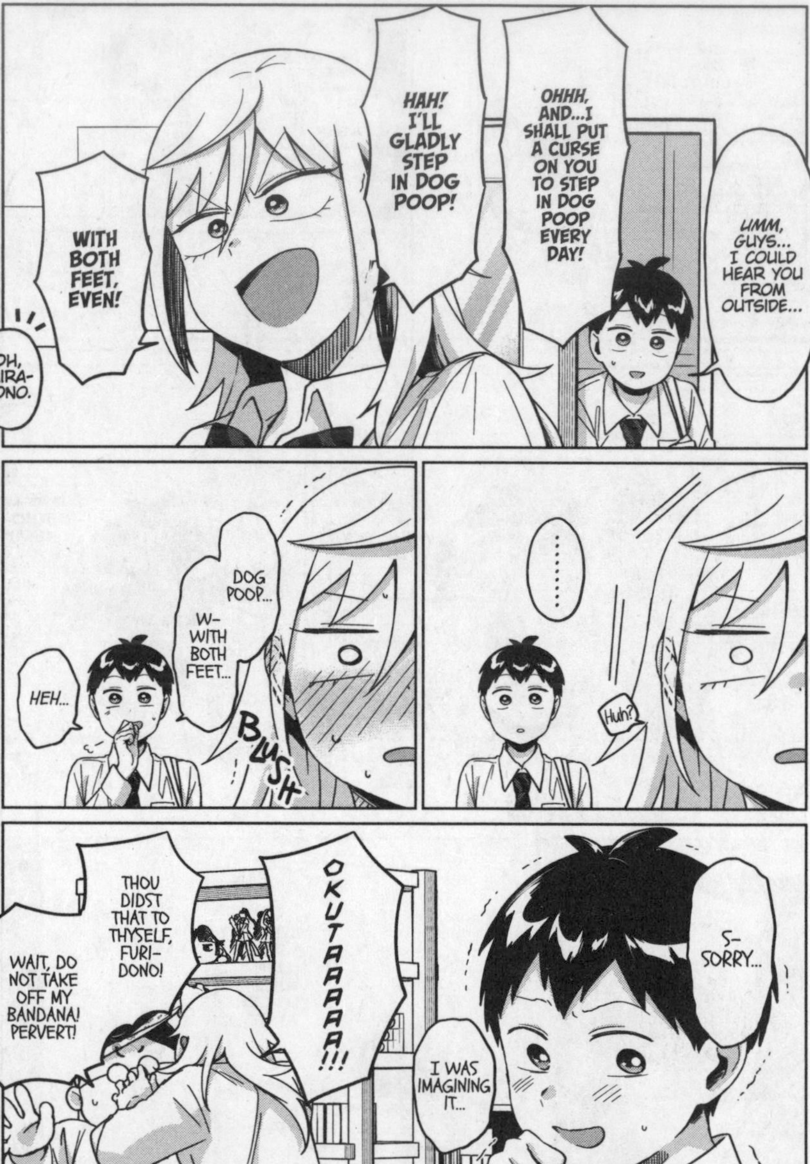
OHHH, AND...I SHALL PUT A CURSE ON YOU TO STEP IN DOG POOP EVERY DAY!
HAH! I'LL GLADLY STEP IN DOG POOP!
WITH BOTH FEET, EVEN!
UMM, GUYS... I COULD HEAR YOU FROM OUTSIDE...
OH, TAIRA-DONO.
......
Huh?
DOG POOP...
W-WITH BOTH FEET...
BLUSH
HEH...
S-SORRY...
I WAS IMAGINING IT...
OKUTAAAAA!!!
THOU DIDST THAT TO THYSELF, FURI-DONO!
WAIT, DO NOT TAKE OFF MY BANDANA! PERVERT!

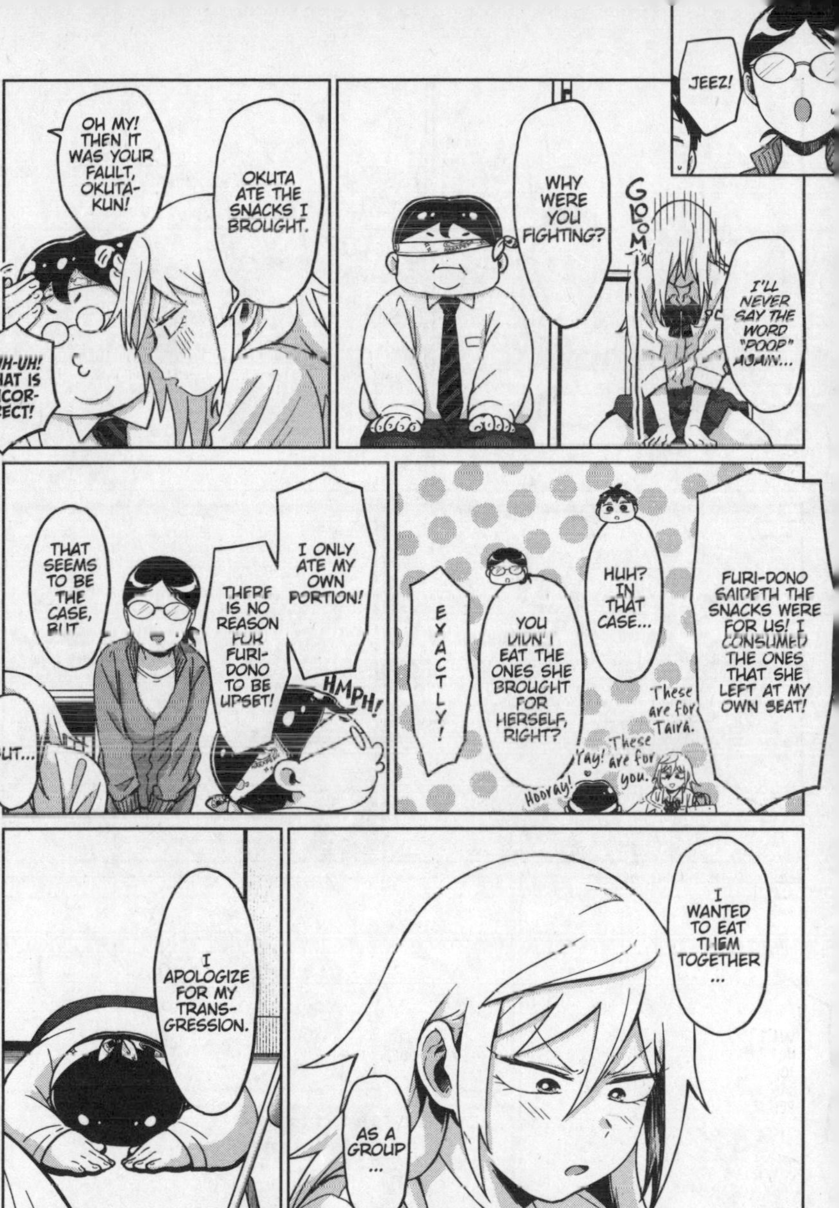
JEEZ!
GLOOM
I'LL NEVER SAY THE WORD "POOP" AGAIN...
WHY WERE YOU FIGHTING?
OKUTA ATE THE SNACKS I BROUGHT.
OH MY! THEN IT WAS YOUR FAULT, OKUTA-KUN!
NUH-UH! THAT IS INCORRECT!
FURI-DONO SAIDETH THE SNACKS WERE FOR US! I CONSUMED THE ONES THAT SHE LEFT AT MY OWN SEAT!
These are for Taira.
These are for you.
Yay!
Hooray!
HUH? IN THAT CASE...
YOU DIDN'T EAT THE ONES SHE BROUGHT FOR HERSELF, RIGHT?
EXACTLY!
I ONLY ATE MY OWN PORTION!
THERE IS NO REASON FOR FURI-DONO TO BE UPSET!
HMPH!
THAT SEEMS TO BE THE CASE, BUT
BUT...
I WANTED TO EAT THEM TOGETHER...
AS A GROUP...
I APOLOGIZE FOR MY TRANS-GRESSION.

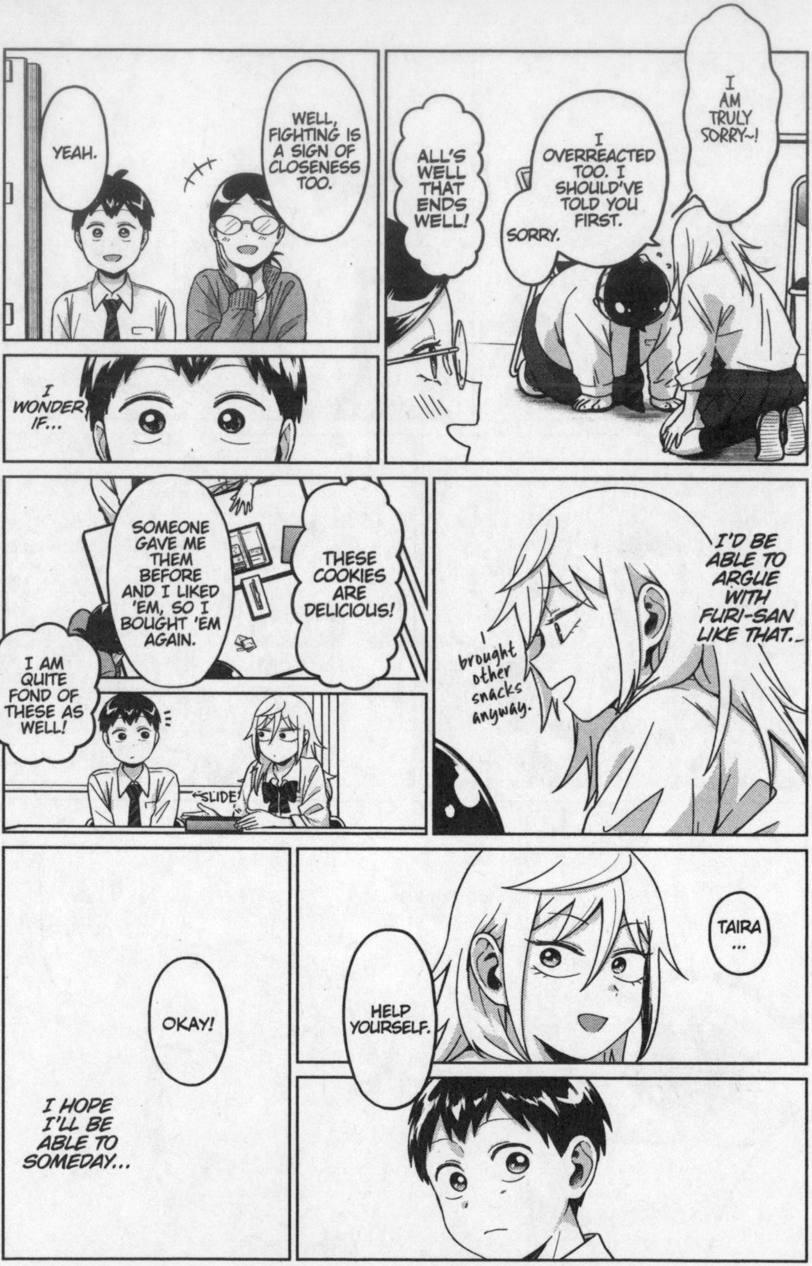
I AM TRULY SORRY~!
I OVERREACTED TOO. I SHOULD'VE TOLD YOU FIRST.
SORRY.
ALL'S WELL THAT ENDS WELL!
WELL, FIGHTING IS A SIGN OF CLOSENESS TOO.
YEAH.
I WONDER IF...
I'D BE ABLE TO ARGUE WITH FURI-SAN LIKE THAT...
I brought other snacks anyway.
THESE COOKIES ARE DELICIOUS!
SOMEONE GAVE ME THEM BEFORE AND I LIKED 'EM, SO I BOUGHT 'EM AGAIN.
I AM QUITE FOND OF THESE AS WELL!
SLIDE
TAIRA...
HELP YOURSELF.
OKAY!
I HOPE I'LL BE ABLE TO SOMEDAY...

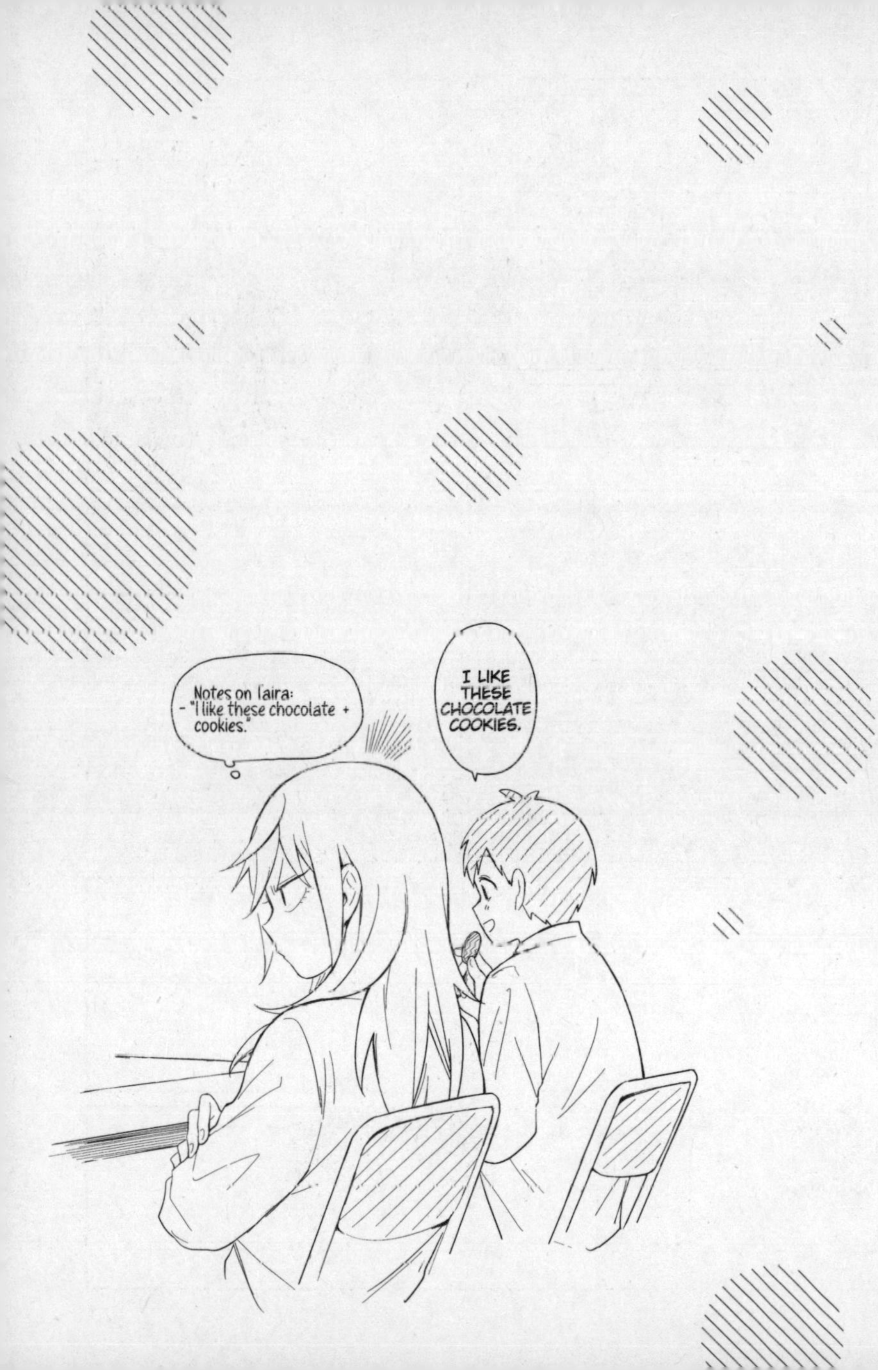

I LIKE THESE CHOCOLATE COOKIES.
Notes on Taira: - "I like these chocolate + cookies."

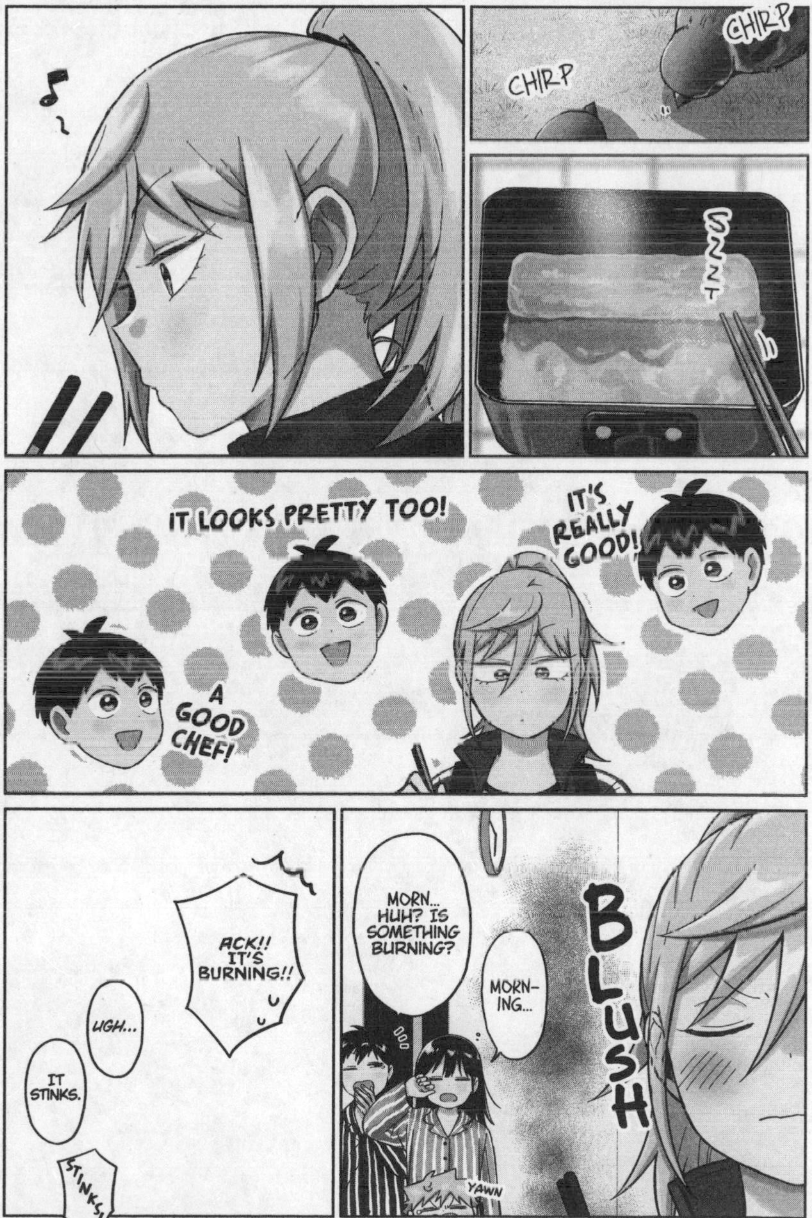
CHIRP
CHIRP
SZZT
IT'S REALLY GOOD!
IT LOOKS PRETTY TOO!
A GOOD CHEF!
BLUSH
MORN-ING...
MORN... HUH? IS SOMETHING BURNING?
YAWN
ACK!! IT'S BURNING!!
UGH...
IT STINKS.
STINKS!

Chapter 23

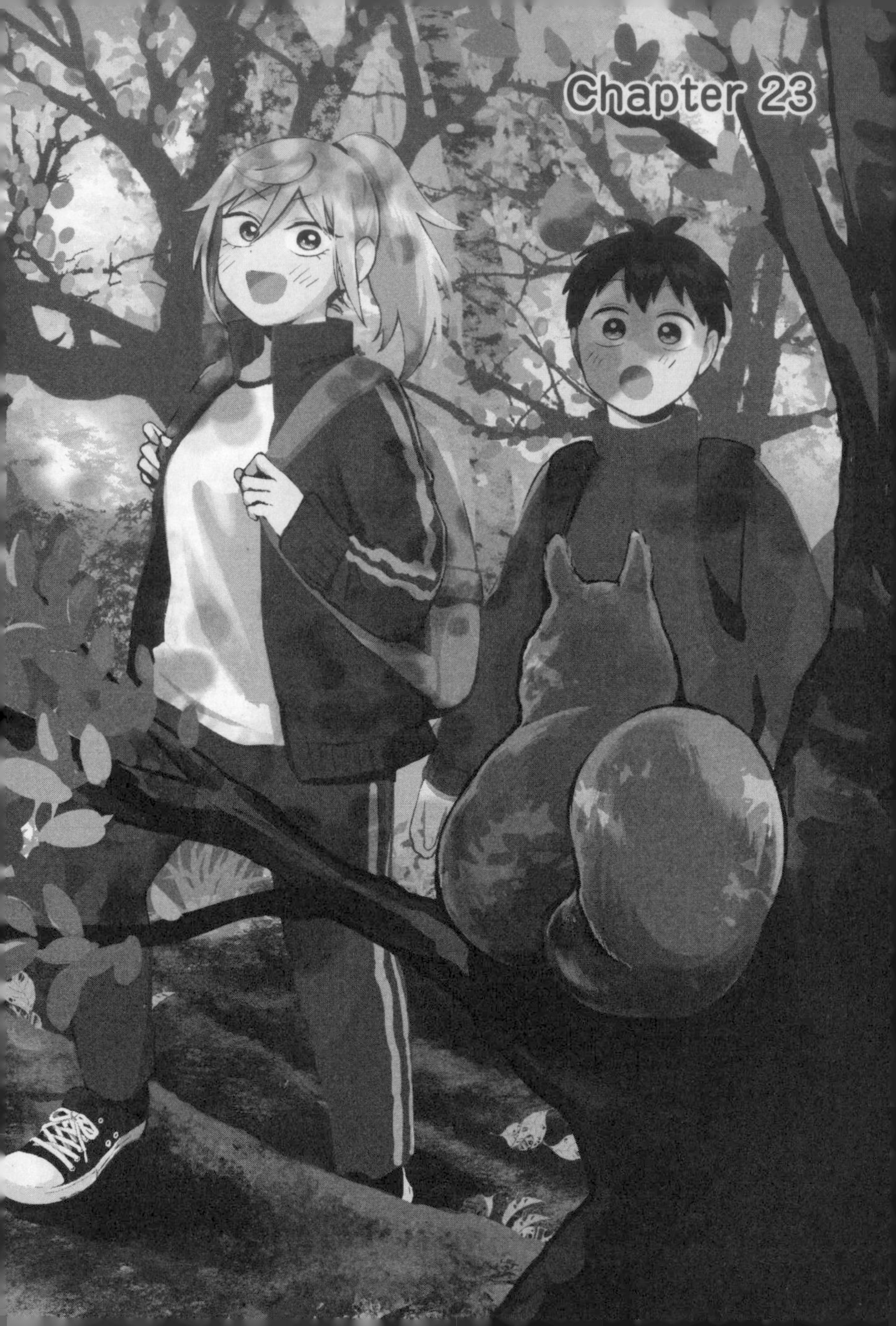

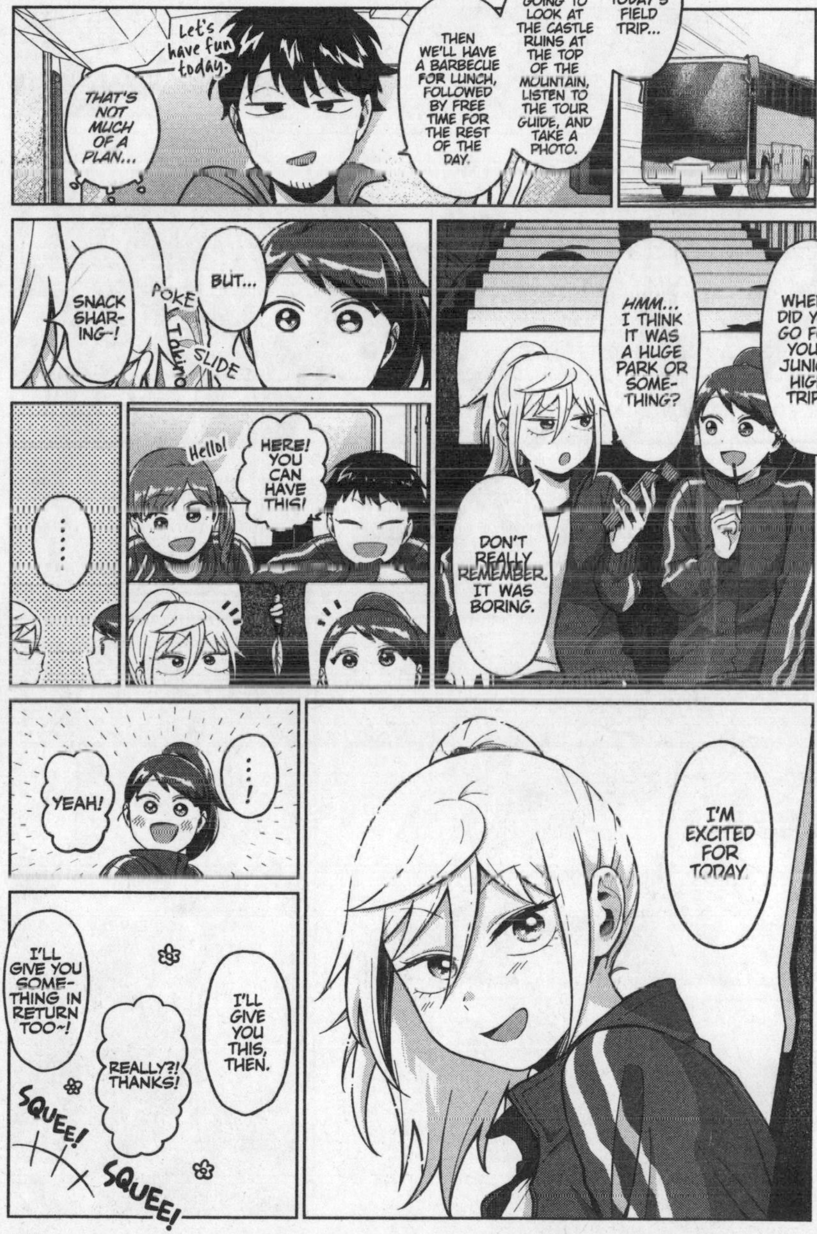
FOR TODAY'S FIELD TRIP...
WE'RE GOING TO LOOK AT THE CASTLE RUINS AT THE TOP OF THE MOUNTAIN, LISTEN TO THE TOUR GUIDE, AND TAKE A PHOTO.
THEN WE'LL HAVE A BARBECUE FOR LUNCH, FOLLOWED BY FREE TIME FOR THE REST OF THE DAY.
Let's have fun today.
THAT'S NOT MUCH OF A PLAN...
WHERE DID YOU GO FOR YOUR JUNIOR HIGH TRIP?
HMM... I THINK IT WAS A HUGE PARK OR SOME-THING?
DON'T REALLY REMEMBER. IT WAS BORING.
BUT...
POKE
SLIDE
SNACK SHAR-ING~!
HERE! YOU CAN HAVE THIS!
Hello!
......
...!
YEAH!
I'M EXCITED FOR TODAY.
I'LL GIVE YOU THIS, THEN.
REALLY?! THANKS!
I'LL GIVE YOU SOME-THING IN RETURN TOO~!
SQUEE!
SQUEE!

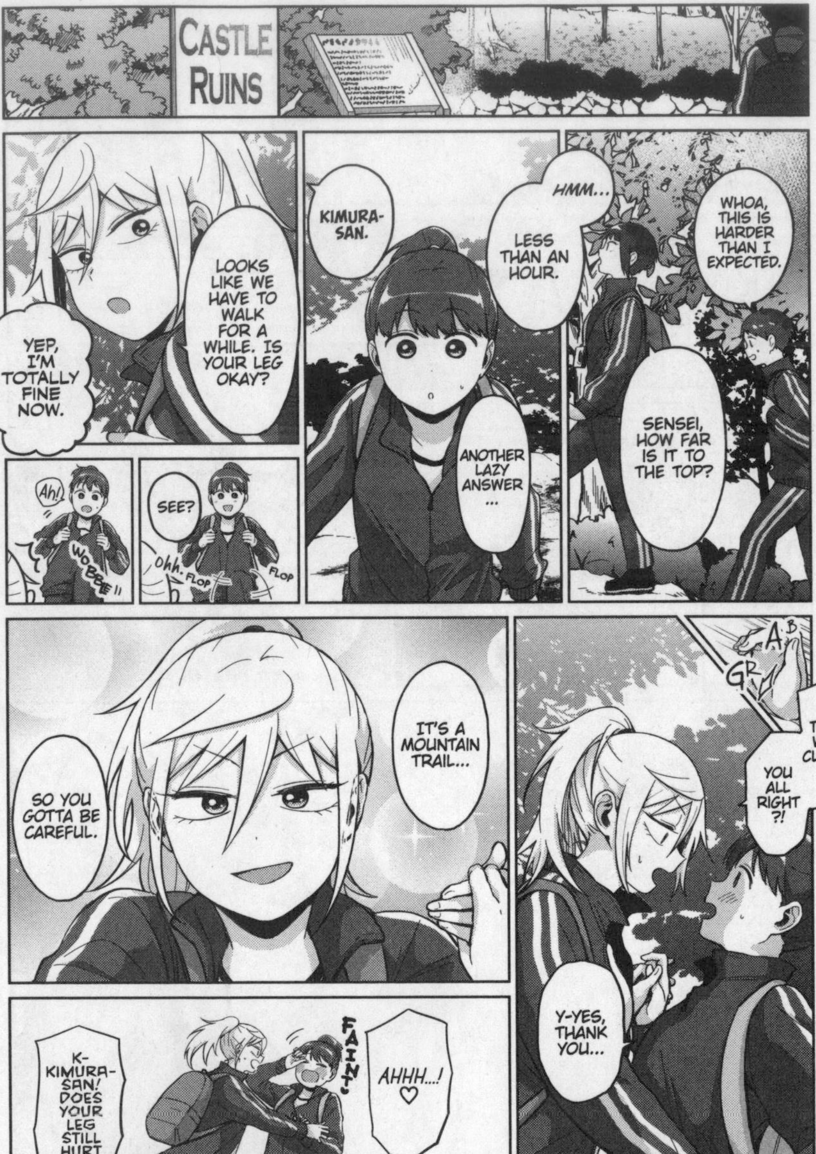
CASTLE RUINS
WHOA, THIS IS HARDER THAN I EXPECTED.
SENSEI, HOW FAR IS IT TO THE TOP?
HMM...
LESS THAN AN HOUR.
KIMURA-SAN.
ANOTHER LAZY ANSWER ...
LOOKS LIKE WE HAVE TO WALK FOR A WHILE. IS YOUR LEG OKAY?
YEP, I'M TOTALLY FINE NOW.
SEE?
Ohh.
FLOP
FLOP
Ah!
WOBBLE
GRAB
THAT WAS CLOSE!
YOU ALL RIGHT?!
Y-YES, THANK YOU...
IT'S A MOUNTAIN TRAIL...
SO YOU GOTTA BE CAREFUL.
AHHH...! ♡
FAINT
K-KIMURA-SAN! DOES YOUR LEG STILL HURT AFTER ALL?!

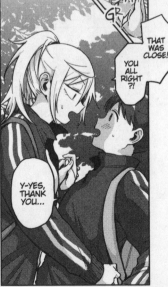

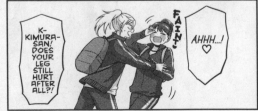

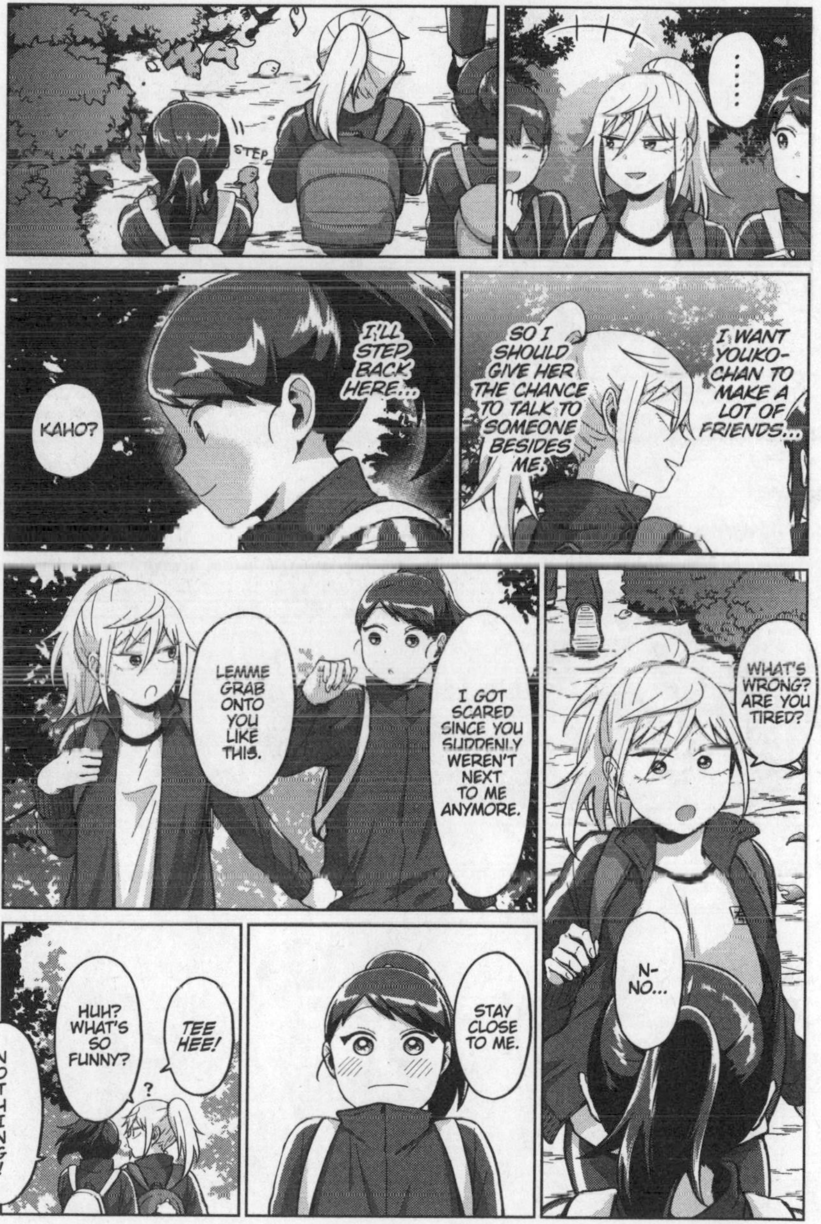
......
STEP
I WANT YOUKO-CHAN TO MAKE A LOT OF FRIENDS...
SO I SHOULD GIVE HER THE CHANCE TO TALK TO SOMEONE BESIDES ME.
I'LL STEP BACK HERE...
KAHO?
WHAT'S WRONG? ARE YOU TIRED?
N-NO...
I GOT SCARED SINCE YOU SUDDENLY WEREN'T NEXT TO ME ANYMORE.
LEMME GRAB ONTO YOU LIKE THIS.
STAY CLOSE TO ME.
TEE HEE!
HUH? WHAT'S SO FUNNY?
?
NOTHING!

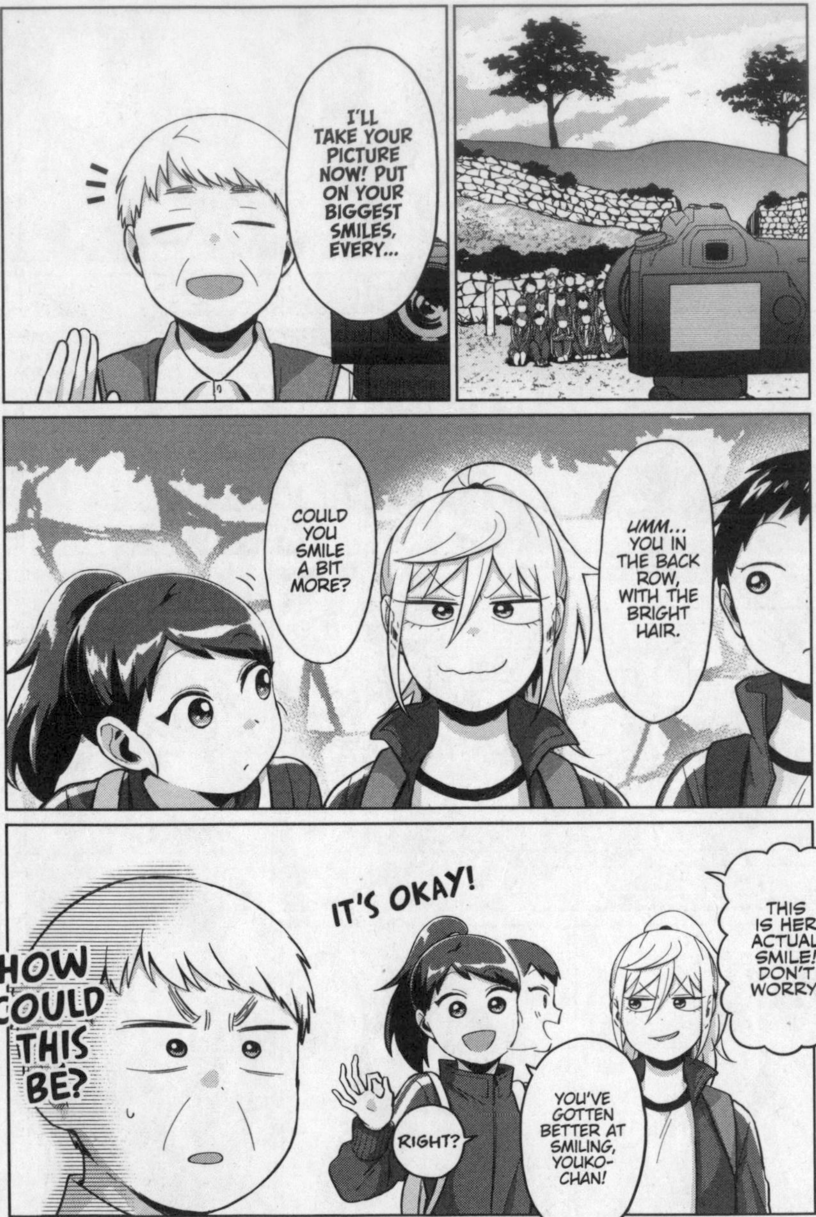
I'LL TAKE YOUR PICTURE NOW! PUT ON YOUR BIGGEST SMILES, EVERY...
UMM... YOU IN THE BACK ROW, WITH THE BRIGHT HAIR.
COULD YOU SMILE A BIT MORE?
THIS IS HER ACTUAL SMILE! DON'T WORRY!
IT'S OKAY!
YOU'VE GOTTEN BETTER AT SMILING, YOUKO-CHAN!
RIGHT?
HOW COULD THIS BE?

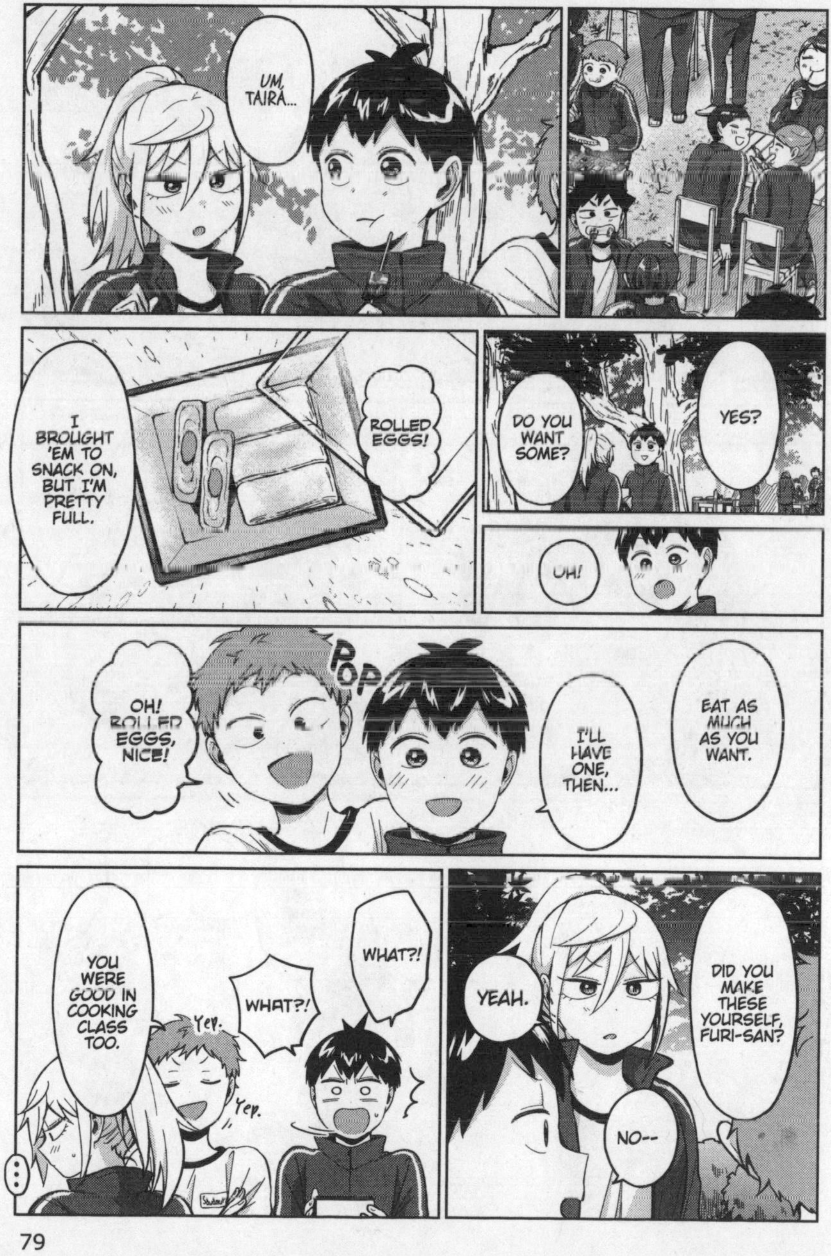
UM, TAIRA...
YES?
DO YOU WANT SOME?
UH!
ROLLED EGGS!
I BROUGHT 'EM TO SNACK ON, BUT I'M PRETTY FULL.
EAT AS MUCH AS YOU WANT.
I'LL HAVE ONE, THEN...
POP
OH! ROLLED EGGS, NICE!
DID YOU MAKE THESE YOURSELF, FURI-SAN?
YEAH.
NO--
WHAT?!
WHAT?!
YOU WERE GOOD IN COOKING CLASS TOO.
Yep.
Yep.
...

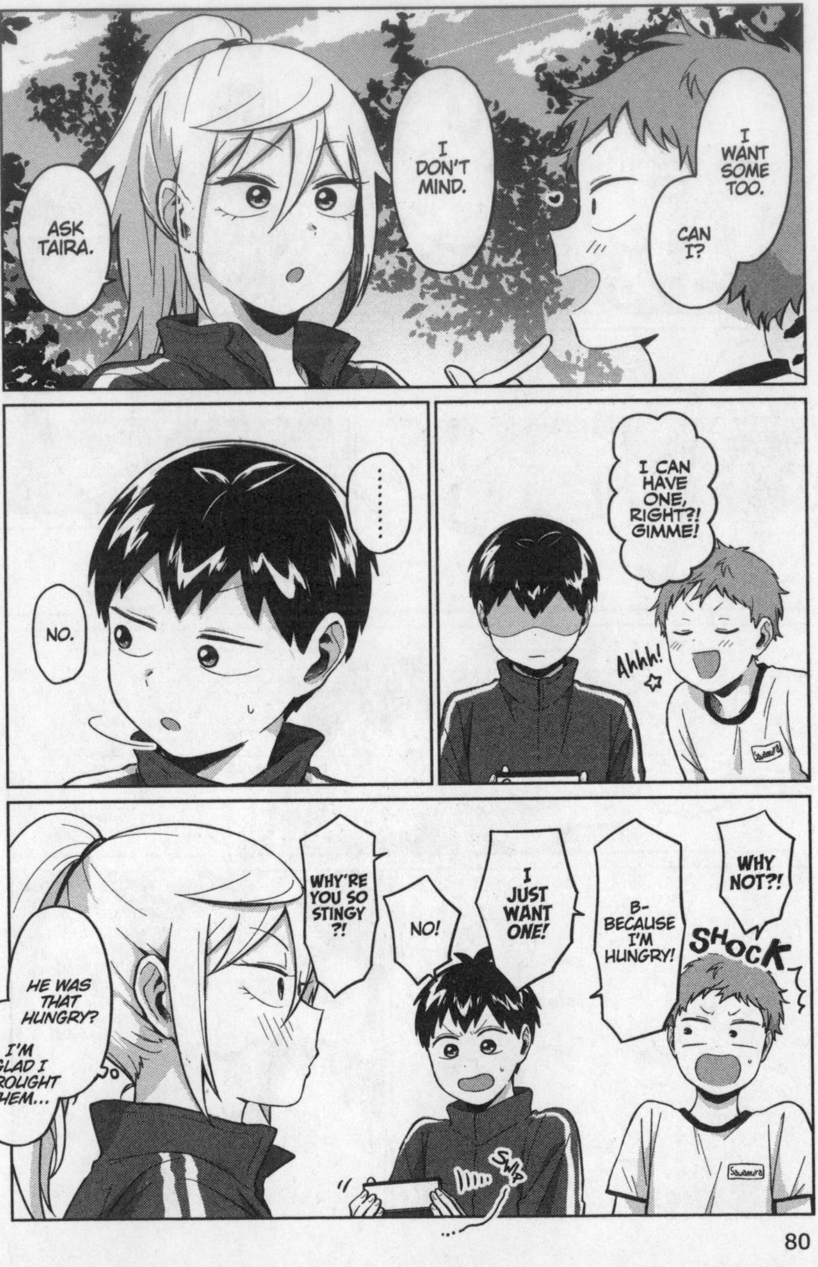
I WANT SOME TOO.
CAN I?
I DON'T MIND.
ASK TAIRA.
I CAN HAVE ONE, RIGHT?! GIMME!
Ahhh!
......
NO.
WHY NOT?!
SHOCK
B-BECAUSE I'M HUNGRY!
I JUST WANT ONE!
NO!
WHY'RE YOU SO STINGY?!
HE WAS THAT HUNGRY?
I'M GLAD I BROUGHT THEM...
...

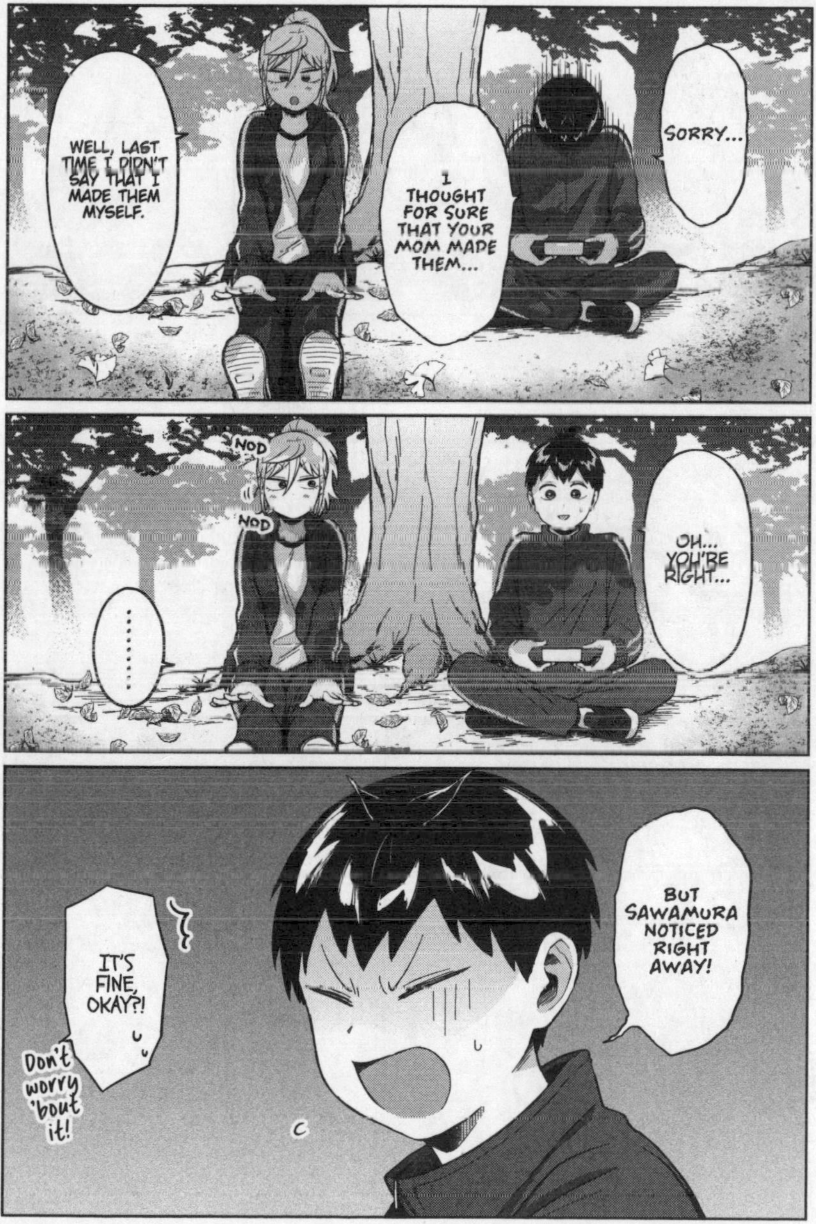
SORRY...
I THOUGHT FOR SURE THAT YOUR MOM MADE THEM...
WELL, LAST TIME I DIDN'T SAY THAT I MADE THEM MYSELF.
OH... YOU'RE RIGHT...
NOD
NOD
......
BUT SAWAMURA NOTICED RIGHT AWAY!
IT'S FINE, OKAY?!
Don't worry 'bout it!

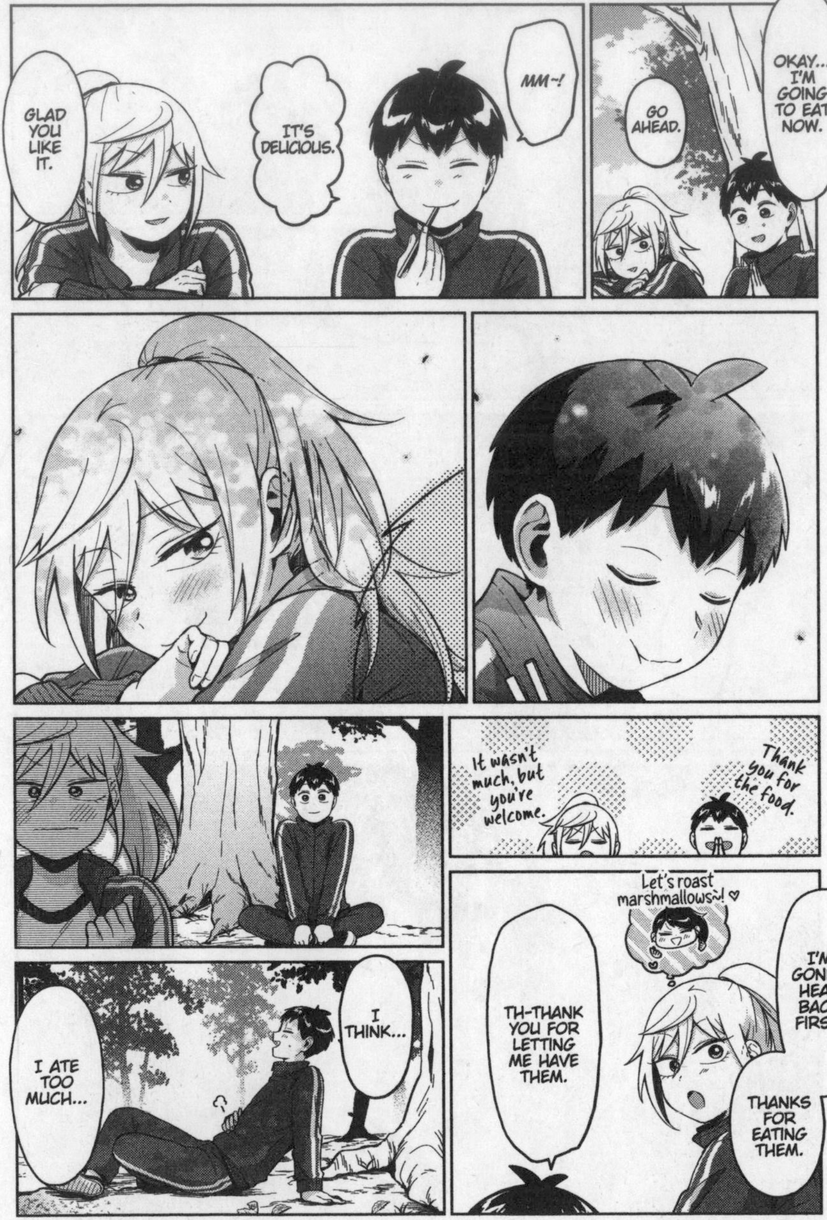
OKAY... I'M GOING TO EAT NOW.
GO AHEAD.
MM~!
IT'S DELICIOUS.
GLAD YOU LIKE IT.
Thank you for the food.
It wasn't much, but you're welcome.
I'M GONNA HEAD BACK FIRST.
Let's roast marshmallows~! ♡
TH-THANK YOU FOR LETTING ME HAVE THEM.
THANKS FOR EATING THEM.
I THINK...
I ATE TOO MUCH...

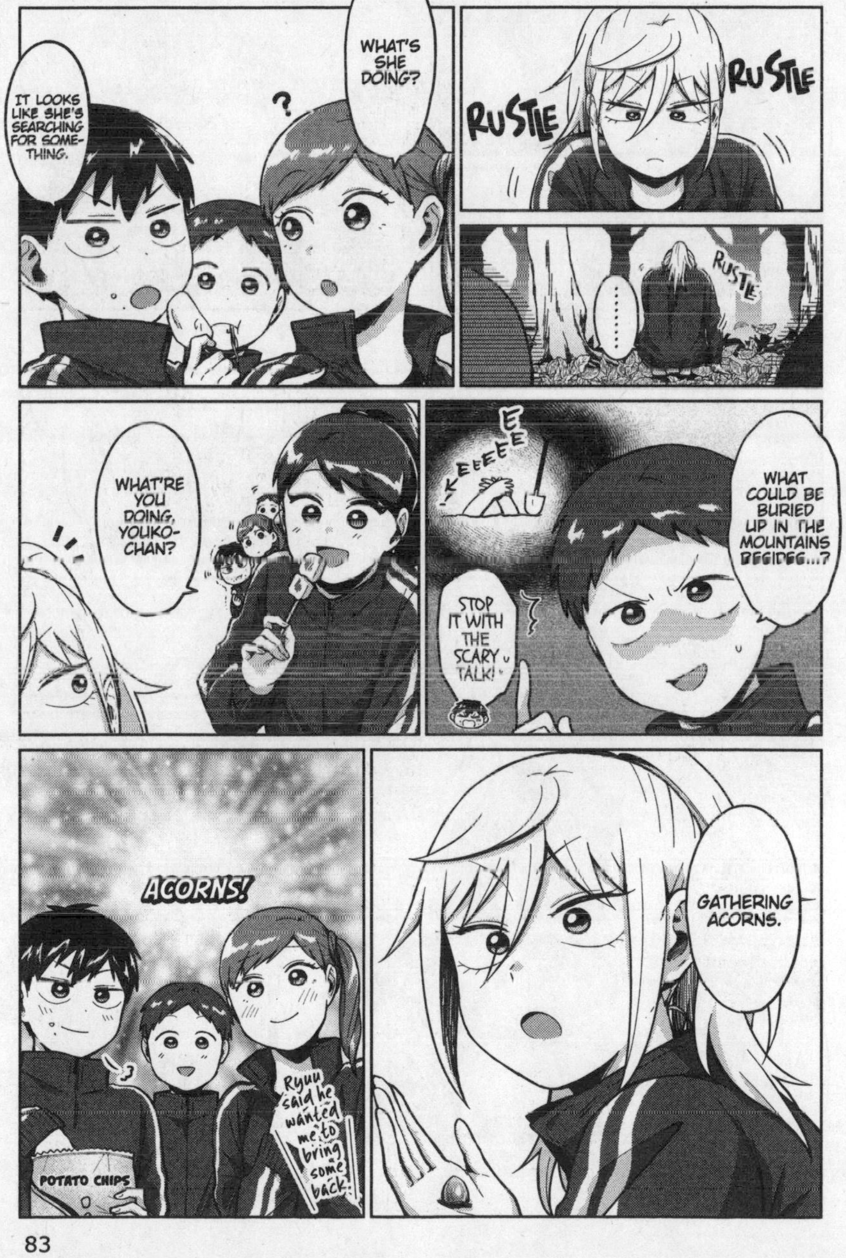
RUSTLE
RUSTLE
RUSTLE
......
WHAT'S SHE DOING?
?
IT LOOKS LIKE SHE'S SEARCHING FOR SOMETHING.
WHAT COULD BE BURIED UP IN THE MOUNTAINS BESIDES...?
STOP IT WITH THE SCARY TALK!
WHAT'RE YOU DOING, YOUKO-CHAN?
GATHERING ACORNS.
ACORNS!
Ryuu said he wanted me to bring some back!
POTATO CHIPS

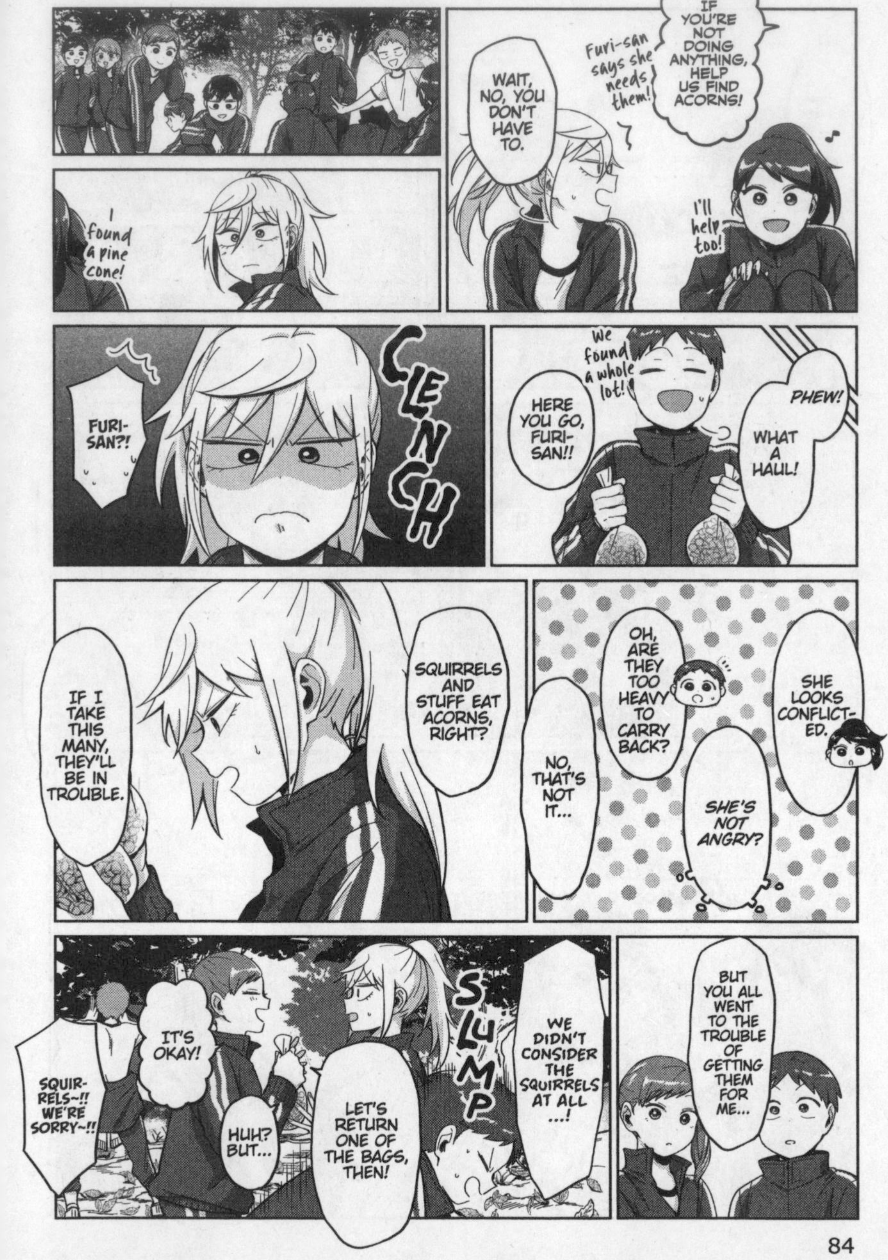
IF YOU'RE NOT DOING ANYTHING, HELP US FIND ACORNS!
Furi-san says she needs them!
WAIT, NO, YOU DON'T HAVE TO.
I'll help too!
I found a pine cone!
PHEW!
WHAT A HAUL!
We found a whole lot!
HERE YOU GO, FURI-SAN!!
CLENCH
FURI-SAN?!
SHE LOOKS CONFLICT-ED.
SHE'S NOT ANGRY?
OH, ARE THEY TOO HEAVY TO CARRY BACK?
NO, THAT'S NOT IT...
SQUIRRELS AND STUFF EAT ACORNS, RIGHT?
IF I TAKE THIS MANY, THEY'LL BE IN TROUBLE.
BUT YOU ALL WENT TO THE TROUBLE OF GETTING THEM FOR ME...
WE DIDN'T CONSIDER THE SQUIRRELS AT ALL ...!
SLUMP
LET'S RETURN ONE OF THE BAGS, THEN!
HUH? BUT...
IT'S OKAY!
SQUIRRELS~!! WE'RE SORRY~!!

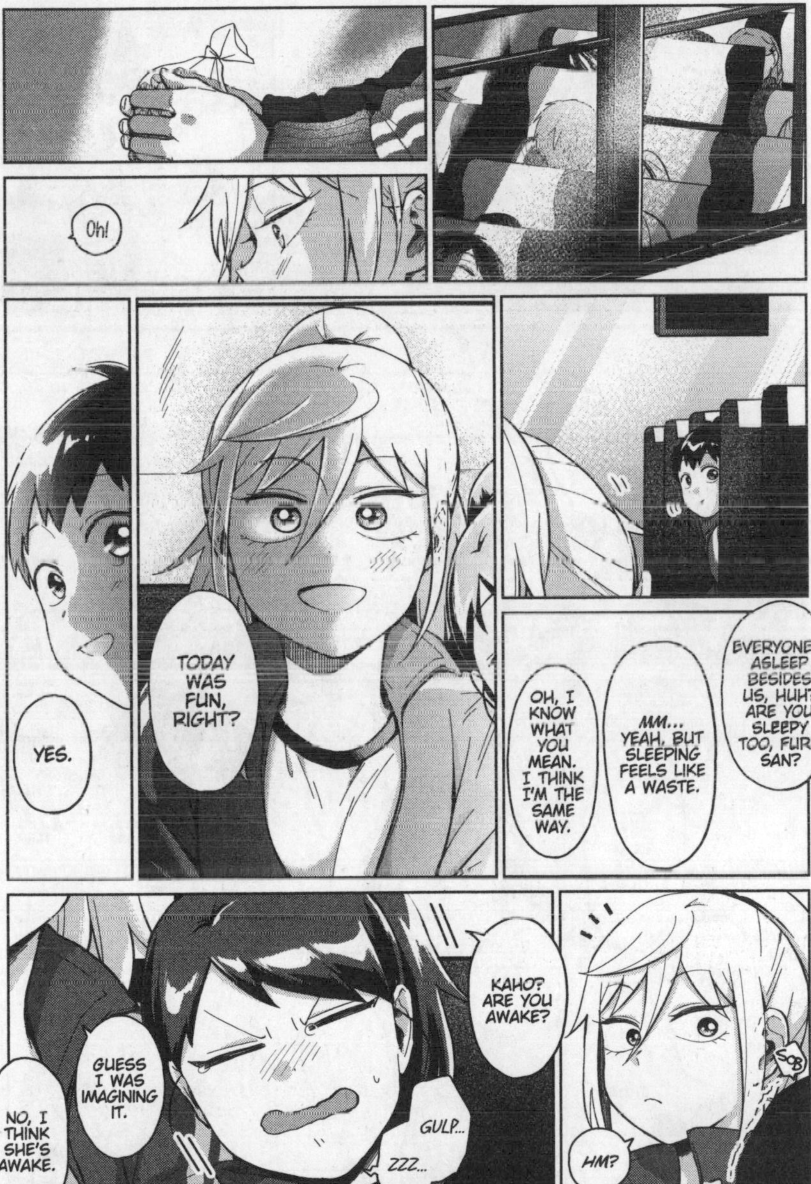
Oh!
EVERYONE'S ASLEEP BESIDES US, HUH? ARE YOU SLEEPY TOO, FURI-SAN?
MM... YEAH, BUT SLEEPING FEELS LIKE A WASTE.
OH, I KNOW WHAT YOU MEAN. I THINK I'M THE SAME WAY.
TODAY WAS FUN, RIGHT?
YES.
SOB
HM?
SOB
KAHO? ARE YOU AWAKE?
GULP...
ZZZ...
GUESS I WAS IMAGINING IT.
NO, I THINK SHE'S AWAKE.

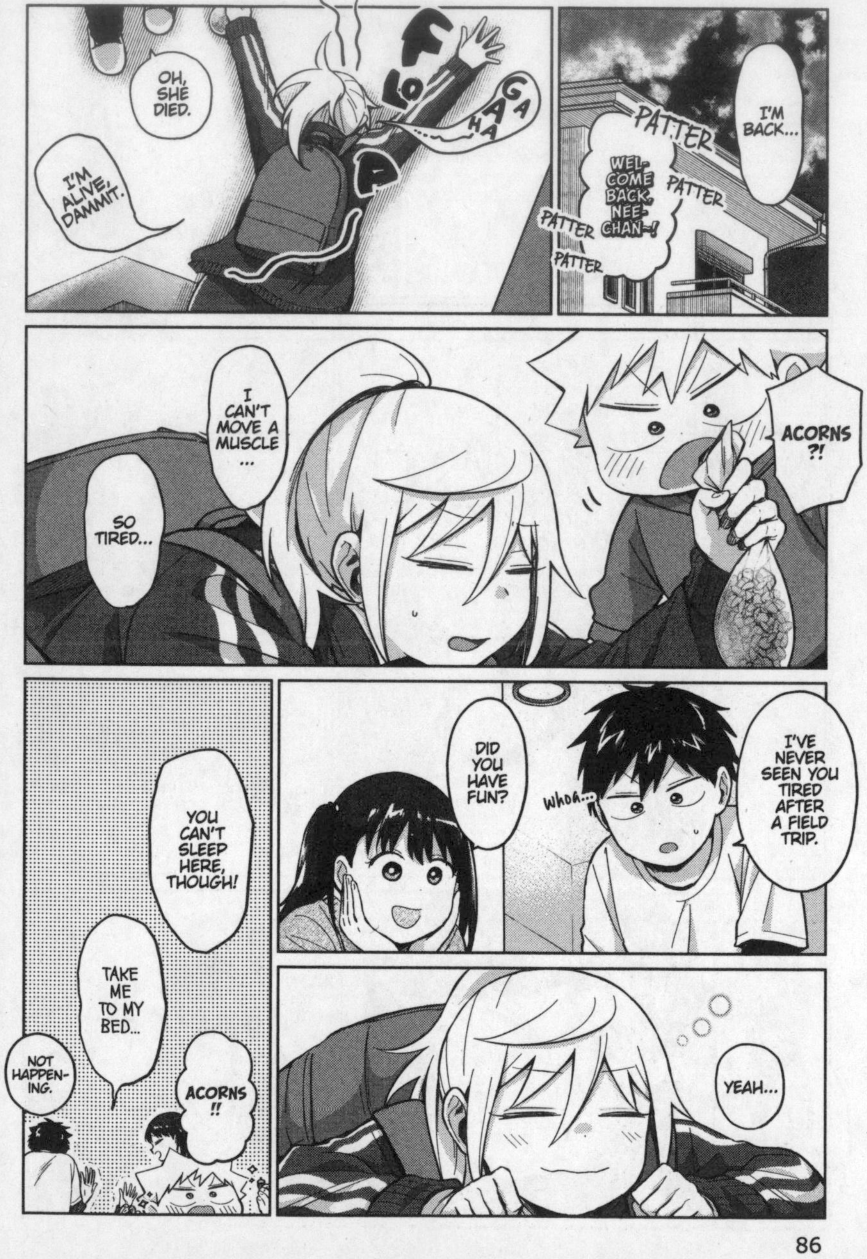
I'M BACK...
PATTER
WEL-COME BACK, NEE-CHAN~!
PATTER
PATTER
PATTER
FLOP
GAHAHA
OH, SHE DIED.
I'M ALIVE, DAMMIT.
ACORNS?!
I CAN'T MOVE A MUSCLE...
SO TIRED...
I'VE NEVER SEEN YOU TIRED AFTER A FIELD TRIP.
WHOA...
DID YOU HAVE FUN?
YEAH...
YOU CAN'T SLEEP HERE, THOUGH!
TAKE ME TO MY BED...
ACORNS!!
NOT HAPPEN-ING.

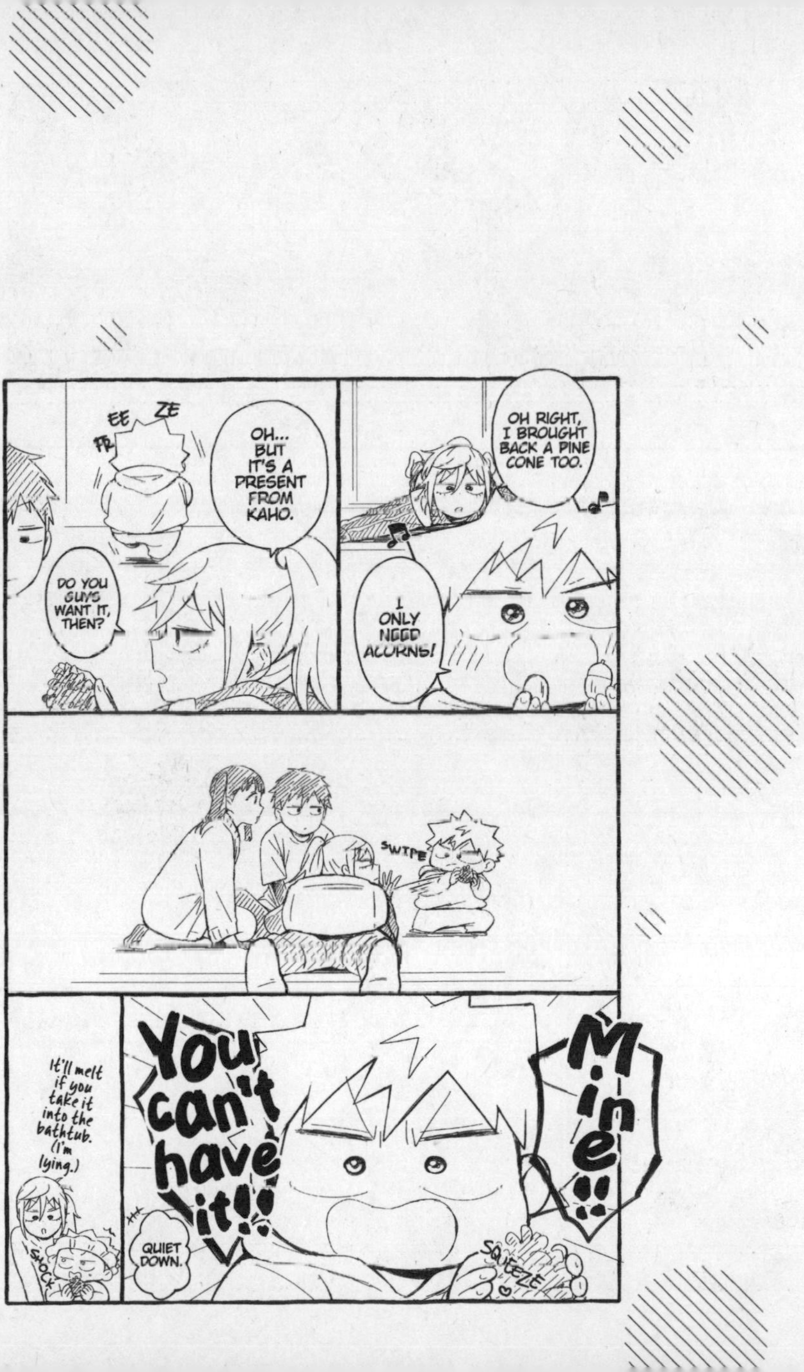
OH RIGHT, I BROUGHT BACK A PINE CONE TOO.
I ONLY NEED ACORNS!
FR EE ZE
OH... BUT IT'S A PRESENT FROM KAHO.
DO YOU GUYS WANT IT, THEN?
SWIPE
Mine!!
You can't have it!!
SQUEEZE
It'll melt if you take it into the bathtub. (I'm lying.)
SHOCK
QUIET DOWN.

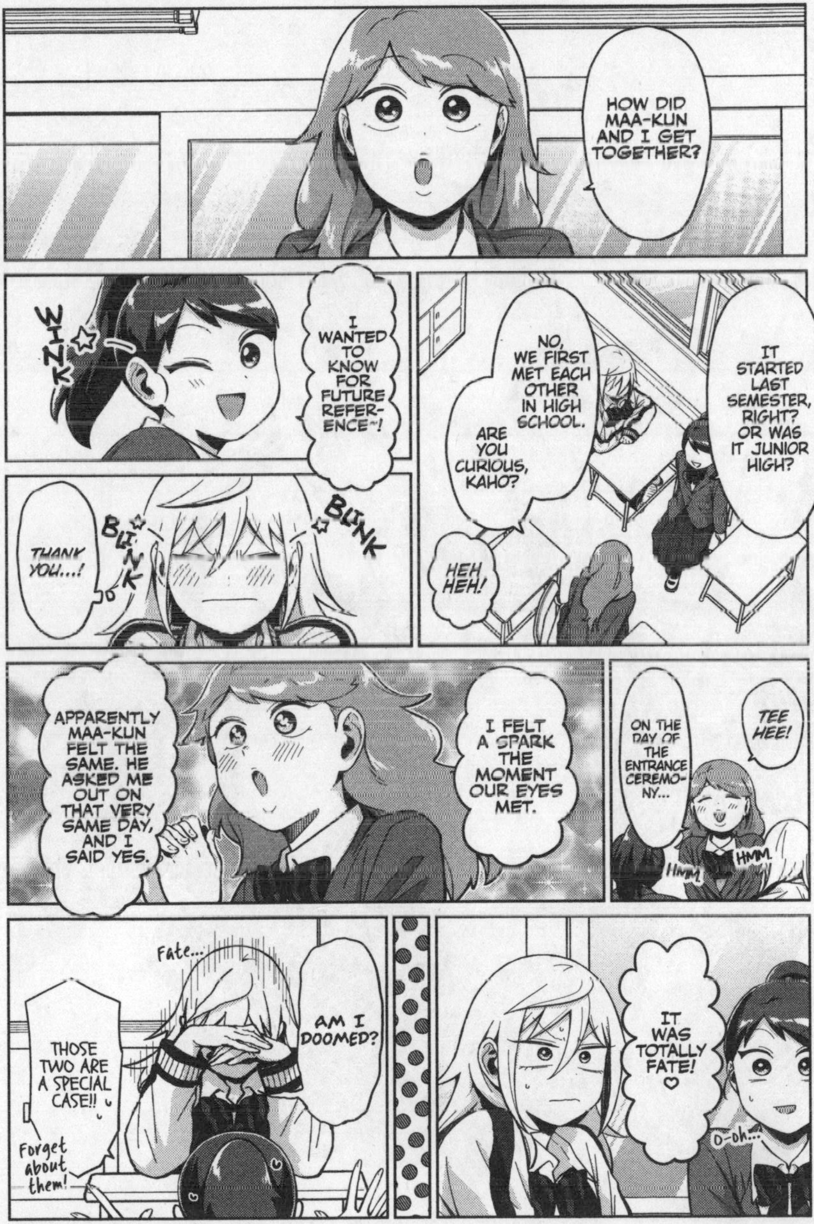
HOW DID MAA-KUN AND I GET TOGETHER?
IT STARTED LAST SEMESTER, RIGHT? OR WAS IT JUNIOR HIGH?
NO, WE FIRST MET EACH OTHER IN HIGH SCHOOL.
ARE YOU CURIOUS, KAHO?
HEH HEH!
WINK
I WANTED TO KNOW FOR FUTURE REFERENCE~!
BLINK
BLINK
THANK YOU...!
TEE HEE!
ON THE DAY OF THE ENTRANCE CEREMONY...
HMM.
HMM.
I FELT A SPARK THE MOMENT OUR EYES MET.
APPARENTLY MAA-KUN FELT THE SAME. HE ASKED ME OUT ON THAT VERY SAME DAY, AND I SAID YES.
IT WAS TOTALLY FATE! ♥
O-oh...
AM I DOOMED?
Fate...
THOSE TWO ARE A SPECIAL CASE!!
Forget about them!

Chapter 24

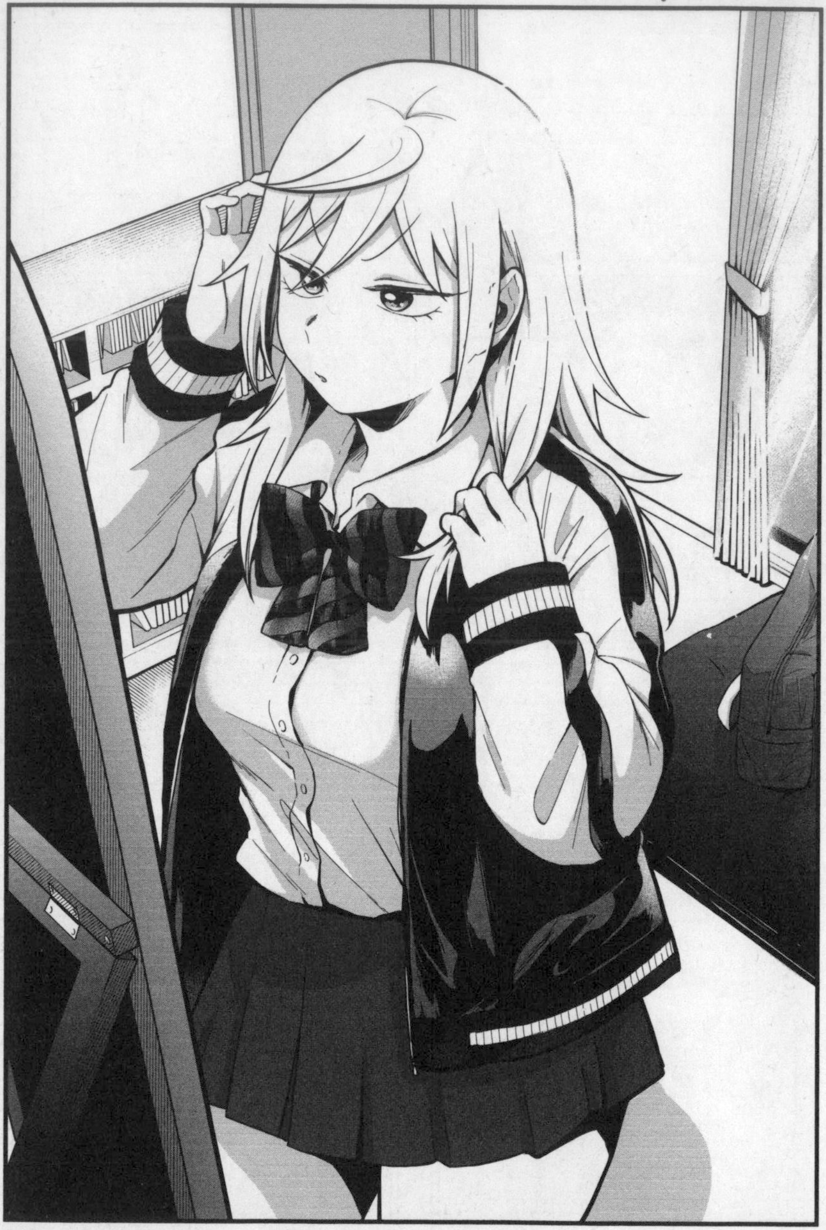

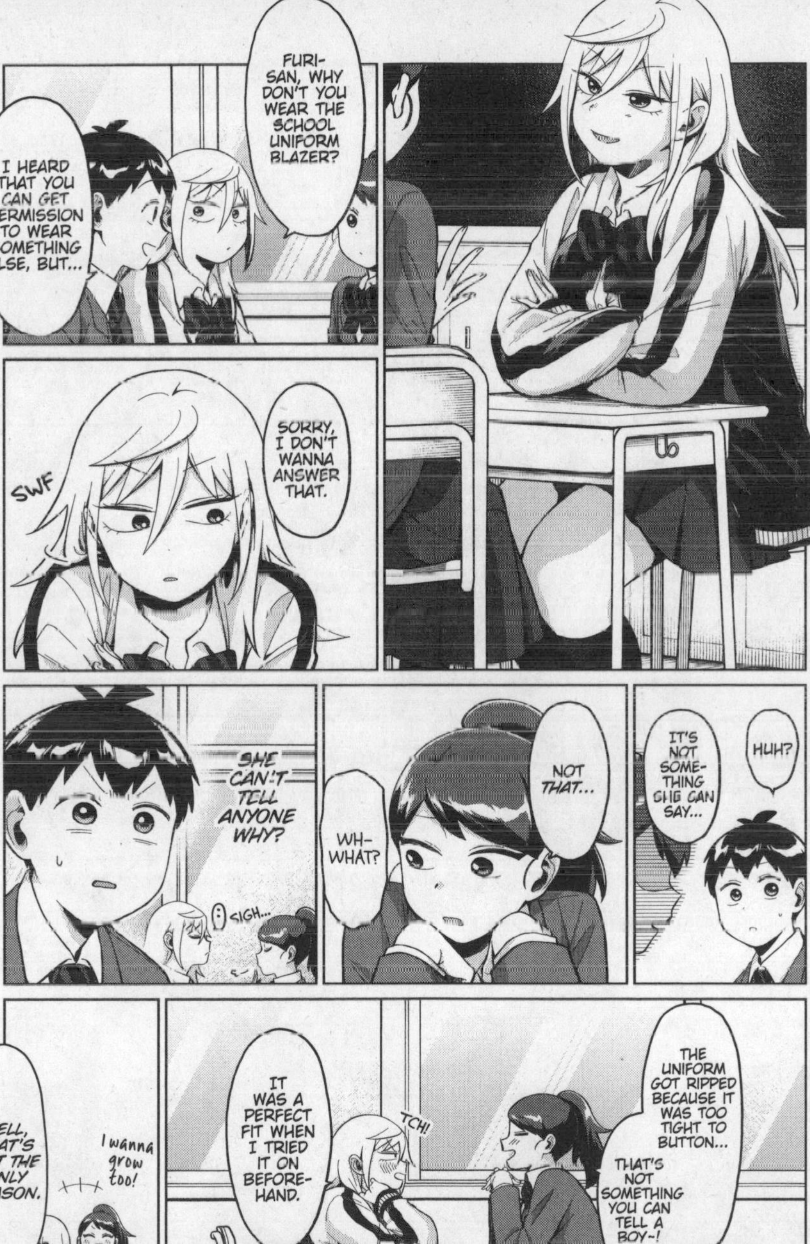
FURI-SAN, WHY DON'T YOU WEAR THE SCHOOL UNIFORM BLAZER?
I HEARD THAT YOU CAN GET PERMISSION TO WEAR SOMETHING ELSE, BUT...
SORRY, I DON'T WANNA ANSWER THAT.
SWF
HUH?
IT'S NOT SOMETHING SHE CAN SAY...
NOT THAT...
WH-WHAT?
SHE CAN'T TELL ANYONE WHY?
SIGH...
THE UNIFORM GOT RIPPED BECAUSE IT WAS TOO TIGHT TO BUTTON...
THAT'S NOT SOMETHING YOU CAN TELL A BOY~!
TCH!
IT WAS A PERFECT FIT WHEN I TRIED IT ON BEFOREHAND.
WELL, THAT'S NOT THE ONLY REASON.
I wanna grow too!

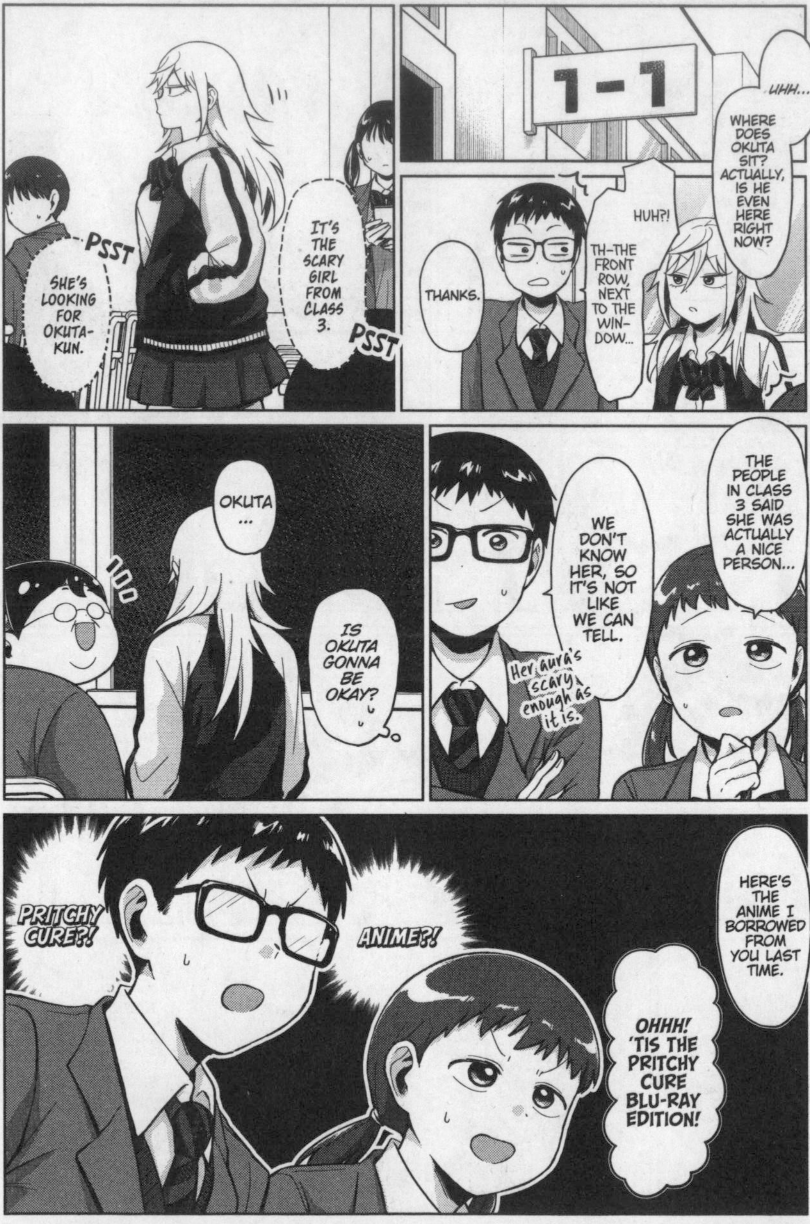
1-1
UHH...
WHERE DOES OKUTA SIT? ACTUALLY, IS HE EVEN HERE RIGHT NOW?
HUH?!
TH-THE FRONT ROW, NEXT TO THE WIN-DOW...
THANKS.
IT'S THE SCARY GIRL FROM CLASS 3.
PSST
SHE'S LOOKING FOR OKUTA-KUN.
PSST
THE PEOPLE IN CLASS 3 SAID SHE WAS ACTUALLY A NICE PERSON...
WE DON'T KNOW HER, SO IT'S NOT LIKE WE CAN TELL.
Her aura's scary enough as it is.
OKUTA ...
IS OKUTA GONNA BE OKAY?
HERE'S THE ANIME I BORROWED FROM YOU LAST TIME.
OHHH! 'TIS THE PRITCHY CURE BLU-RAY EDITION!
ANIME?!
PRITCHY CURE?!

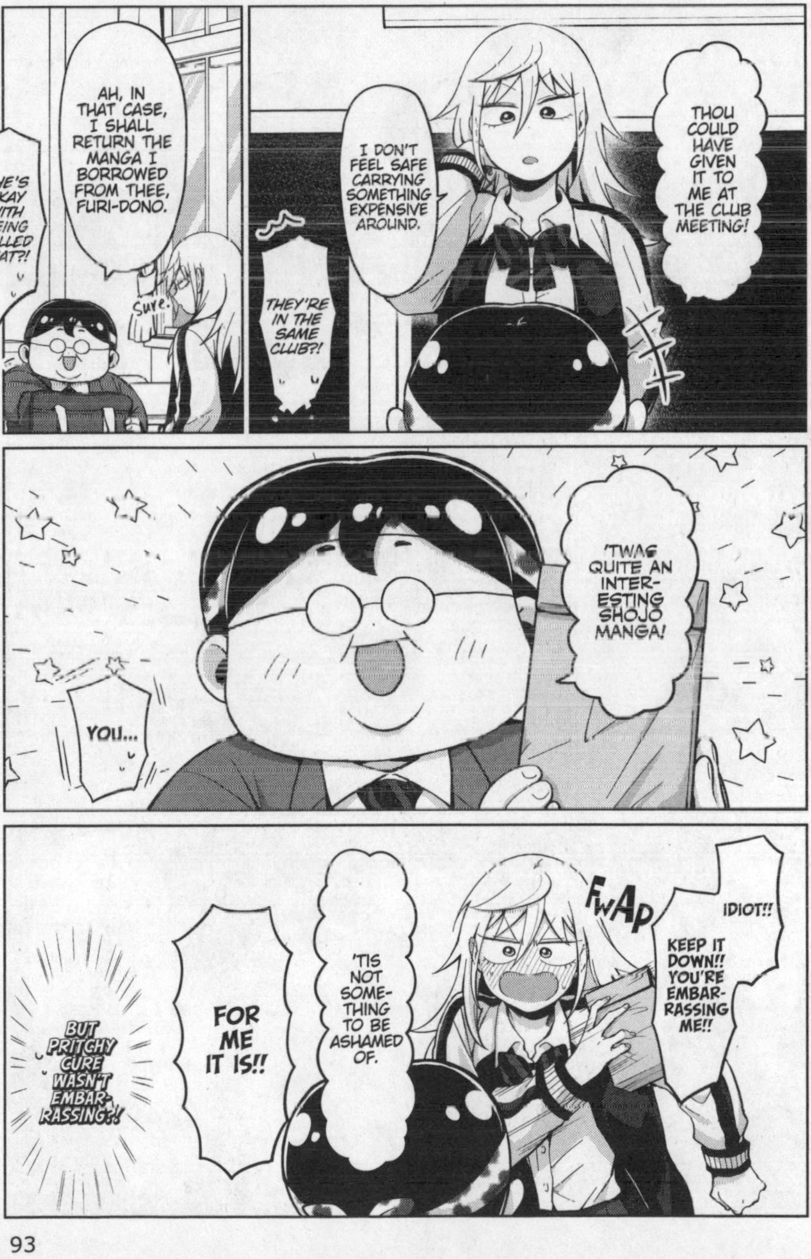
THOU COULD HAVE GIVEN IT TO ME AT THE CLUB MEETING!
I DON'T FEEL SAFE CARRYING SOMETHING EXPENSIVE AROUND.
THEY'RE IN THE SAME CLUB?!
AH, IN THAT CASE, I SHALL RETURN THE MANGA I BORROWED FROM THEE, FURI-DONO.
Sure.
SHE'S OKAY WITH BEING CALLED THAT?!
'TWAS QUITE AN INTERESTING SHOJO MANGA!
YOU...
IDIOT!!
KEEP IT DOWN!! YOU'RE EMBARRASSING ME!!
FWAP
'TIS NOT SOMETHING TO BE ASHAMED OF.
FOR ME IT IS!!
BUT PRITCHY CURE WASN'T EMBARRASSING?!

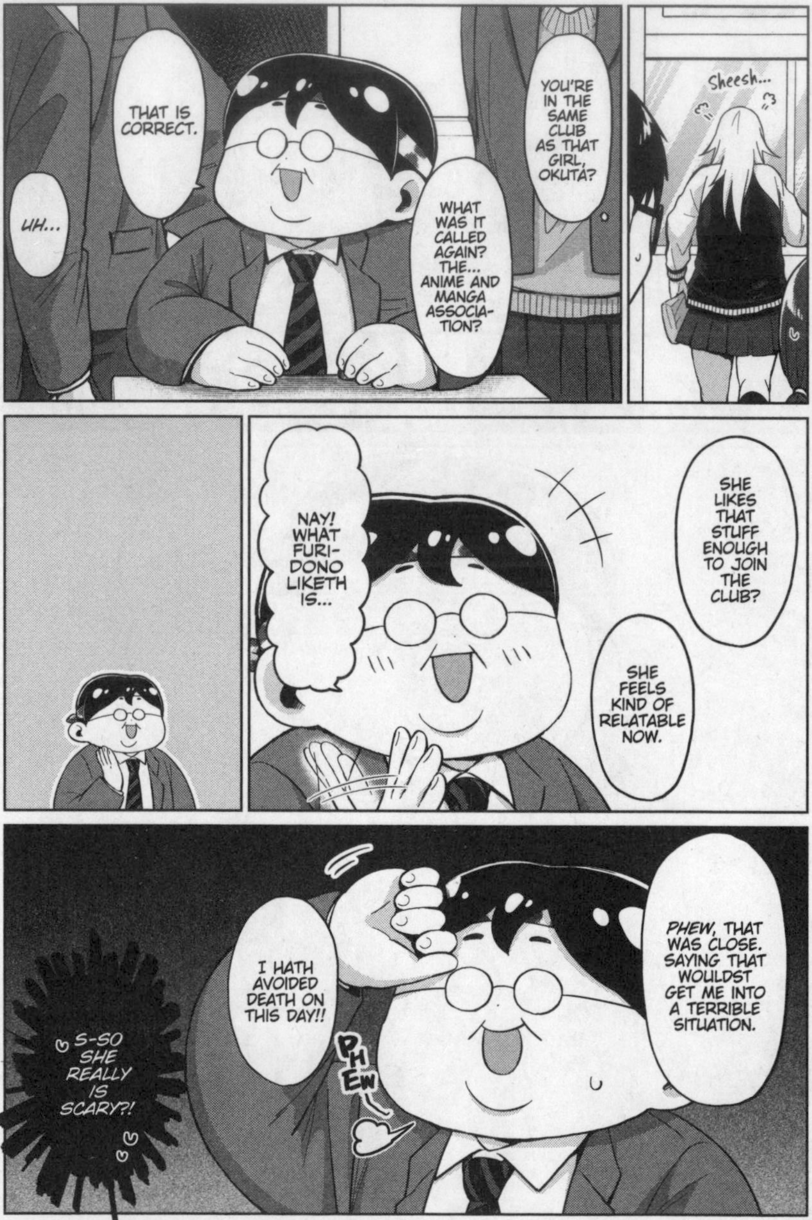
Sheesh...
YOU'RE IN THE SAME CLUB AS THAT GIRL, OKUTA?
WHAT WAS IT CALLED AGAIN? THE... ANIME AND MANGA ASSOCIATION?
THAT IS CORRECT.
UH...
SHE LIKES THAT STUFF ENOUGH TO JOIN THE CLUB?
SHE FEELS KIND OF RELATABLE NOW.
NAY! WHAT FURI-DONO LIKETH IS...
PHEW, THAT WAS CLOSE. SAYING THAT WOULDST GET ME INTO A TERRIBLE SITUATION.
I HATH AVOIDED DEATH ON THIS DAY!!
PHEW
S-SO SHE REALLY IS SCARY?!

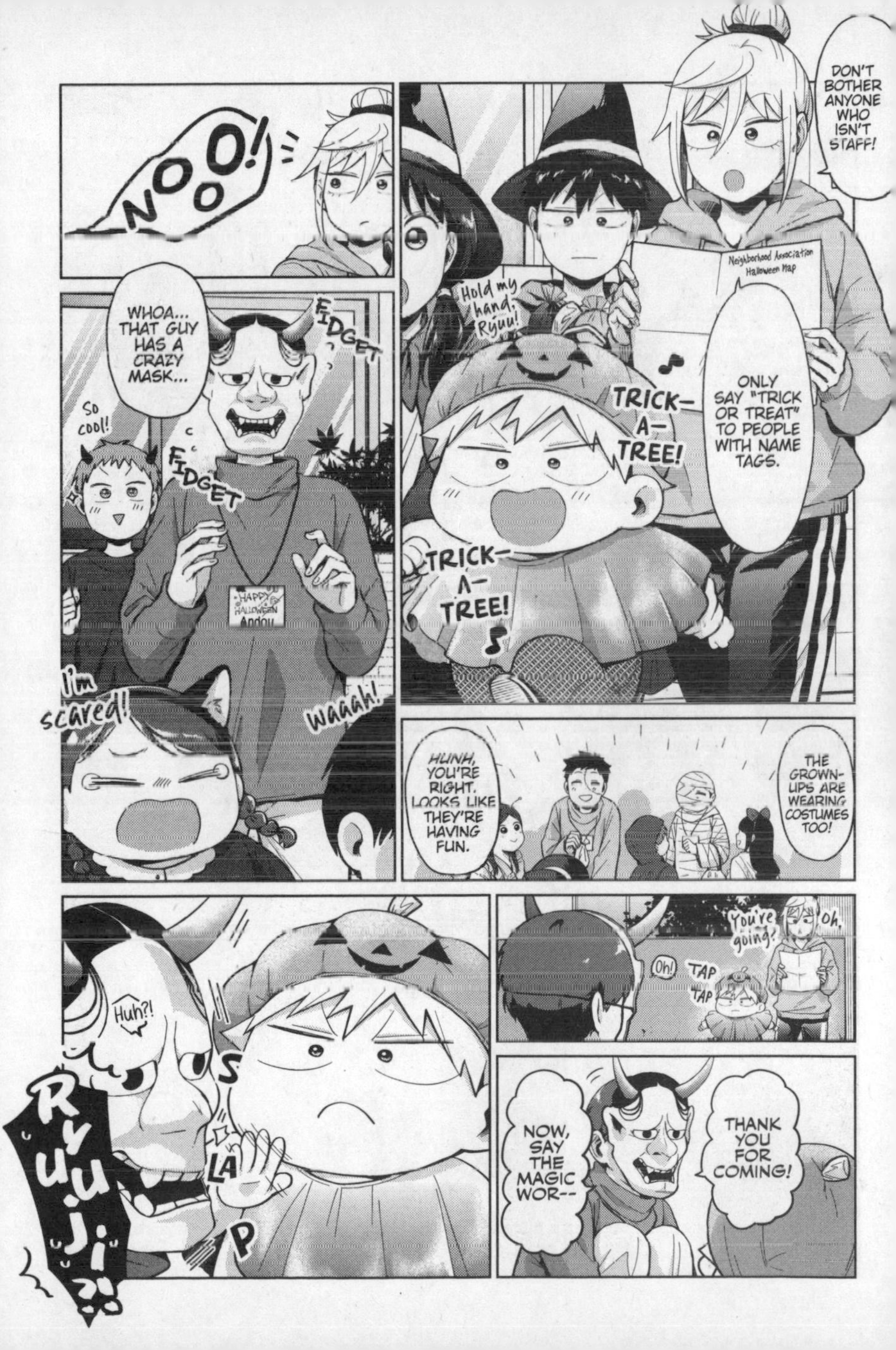
DON'T BOTHER ANYONE WHO ISN'T STAFF!
Neighborhood Association Halloween Map
ONLY SAY "TRICK OR TREAT" TO PEOPLE WITH NAME TAGS.
Hold my hand, Ryuu!
TRICK-A-TREE!
TRICK-A-TREE!
NOOO!
THE GROWN-UPS ARE WEARING COSTUMES TOO!
HUNH, YOU'RE RIGHT. LOOKS LIKE THEY'RE HAVING FUN.
FIDGET
WHOA... THAT GUY HAS A CRAZY MASK...
So cool!
FIDGET
HAPPY HALLOWEEN
Andou
Waaah!
I'm scared!
Oh,
You're going?
Oh!
TAP TAP
THANK YOU FOR COMING!
NOW, SAY THE MAGIC WOR--
Huh?!
SLAP
Ryuuji?!

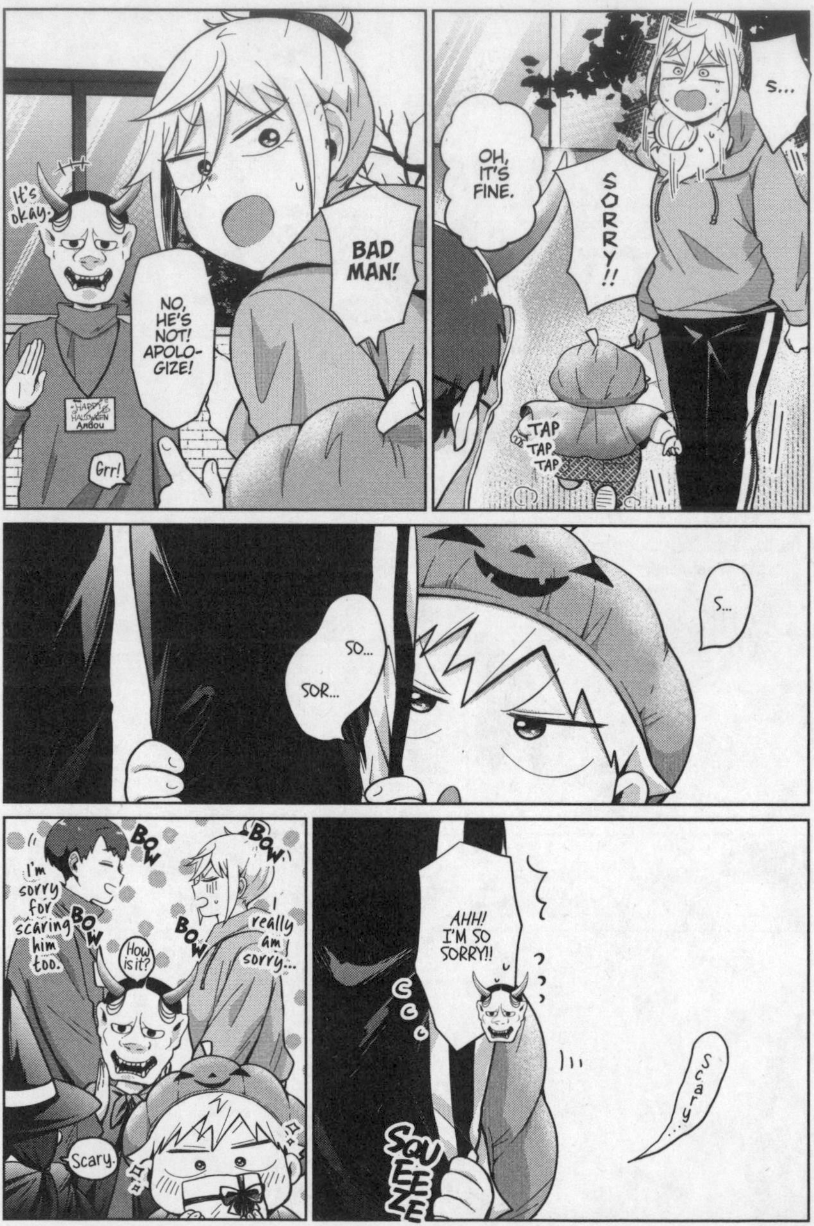
S...
SORRY!!
OH, IT'S FINE.
TAP TAP TAP
BAD MAN!
NO, HE'S NOT! APOLOGIZE!
It's okay.
HAPPY HALLOWEEN Andou
Grr!
S...
SO...
SOR...
AHH! I'M SO SORRY!!
Scary...
SQUEEZE
BOW
BOW
I really am sorry...
BOW
BOW
I'm sorry for scaring him too.
How is it?
Scary.

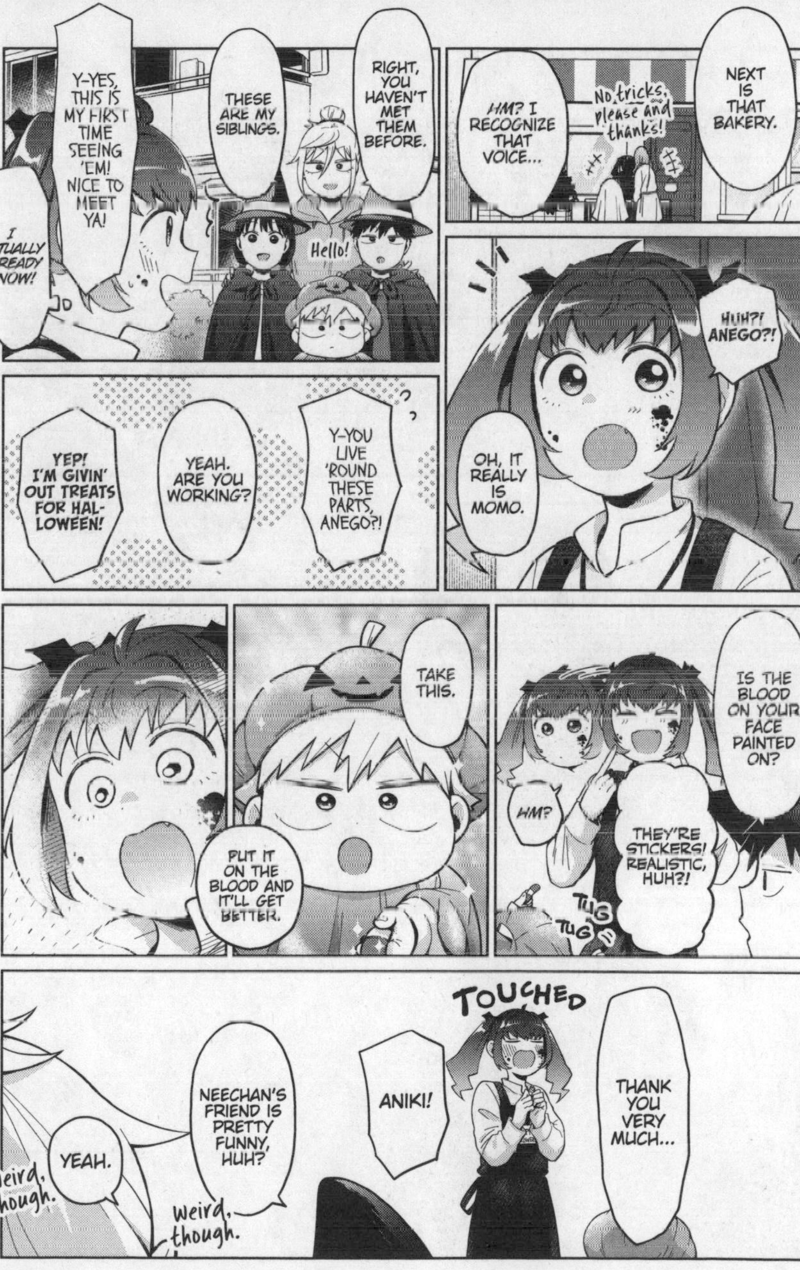
NEXT IS THAT BAKERY.
No tricks, please and thanks!
HM? I RECOGNIZE THAT VOICE...
RIGHT, YOU HAVEN'T MET THEM BEFORE.
THESE ARE MY SIBLINGS.
Hello!
Y-YES, THIS IS MY FIRST TIME SEEING 'EM! NICE TO MEET YA!
I ACTUALLY ALREADY KNOW!
HUH?! ANEGO?!
OH, IT REALLY IS MOMO.
Y-YOU LIVE 'ROUND THESE PARTS, ANEGO?!
YEAH. ARE YOU WORKING?
YEP! I'M GIVIN' OUT TREATS FOR HAL-LOWEEN!
IS THE BLOOD ON YOUR FACE PAINTED ON?
HM?
THEY'RE STICKERS! REALISTIC, HUH?!
TUG TUG
TAKE THIS.
PUT IT ON THE BLOOD AND IT'LL GET BETTER.
TOUCHED
THANK YOU VERY MUCH...
ANIKI!
NEECHAN'S FRIEND IS PRETTY FUNNY, HUH?
YEAH.
Weird, though.
weird, though.

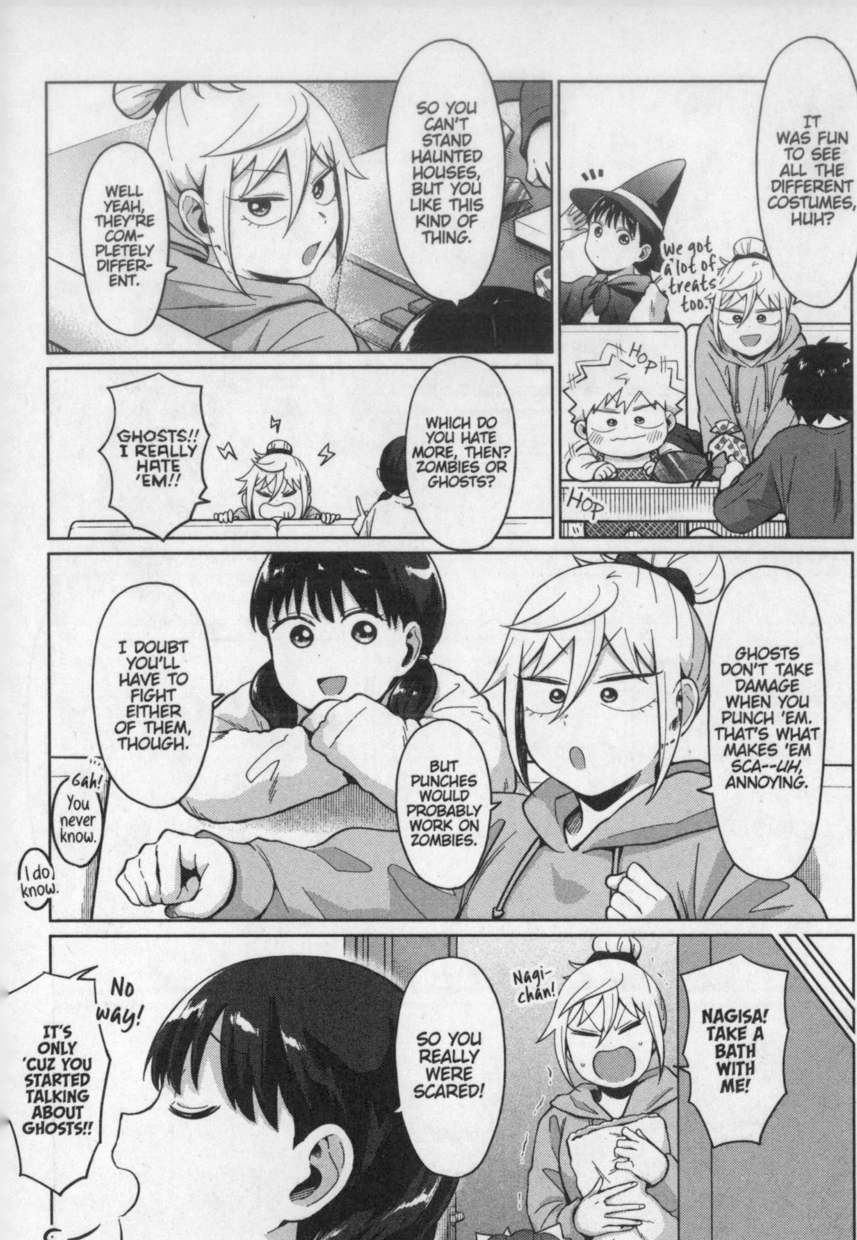
IT WAS FUN TO SEE ALL THE DIFFERENT COSTUMES, HUH?
We got a lot of treats too.
HOP
HOP
SO YOU CAN'T STAND HAUNTED HOUSES, BUT YOU LIKE THIS KIND OF THING.
WELL YEAH, THEY'RE COM- PLETELY DIFFER- ENT.
WHICH DO YOU HATE MORE, THEN? ZOMBIES OR GHOSTS?
GHOSTS!! I REALLY HATE 'EM!!
GHOSTS DON'T TAKE DAMAGE WHEN YOU PUNCH 'EM. THAT'S WHAT MAKES 'EM SCA--UH, ANNOYING.
BUT PUNCHES WOULD PROBABLY WORK ON ZOMBIES.
I DOUBT YOU'LL HAVE TO FIGHT EITHER OF THEM, THOUGH.
Gah! You never know.
I do know.
NAGISA! TAKE A BATH WITH ME!
Nagi-chan!
SO YOU REALLY WERE SCARED!
No way!
IT'S ONLY 'CUZ YOU STARTED TALKING ABOUT GHOSTS!!

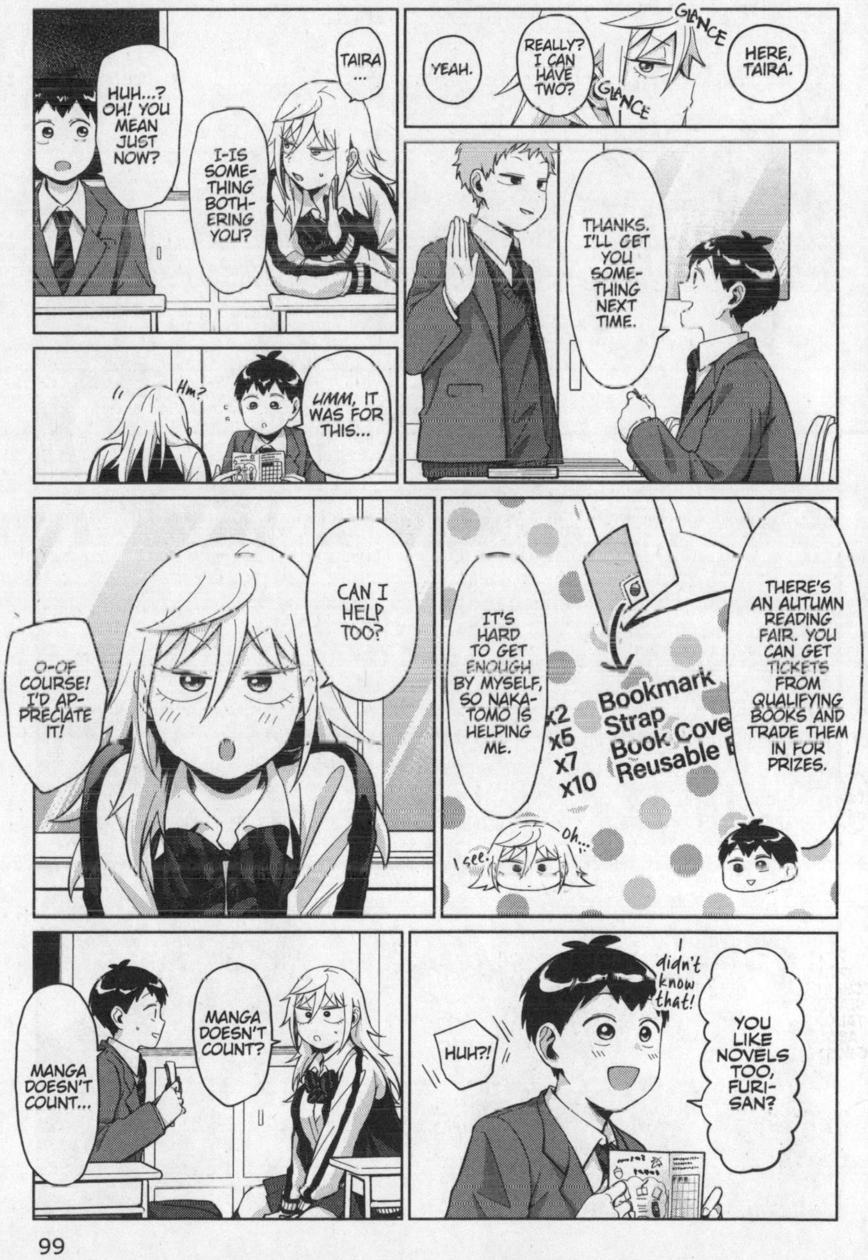
HERE, TAIRA.
GLANCE
GLANCE
REALLY? I CAN HAVE TWO?
YEAH.
THANKS. I'LL GET YOU SOME-THING NEXT TIME.
TAIRA...
I-IS SOME-THING BOTH-ERING YOU?
HUH...? OH! YOU MEAN JUST NOW?
Hm?
UMM, IT WAS FOR THIS...
THERE'S AN AUTUMN READING FAIR. YOU CAN GET TICKETS FROM QUALIFYING BOOKS AND TRADE THEM IN FOR PRIZES.
IT'S HARD TO GET ENOUGH BY MYSELF, SO NAKA-TOMO IS HELPING ME.
x2 Bookmark
x5 Strap
x7 Book Cove
x10 Reusable B
Oh...
I see.
CAN I HELP TOO?
O-OF COURSE! I'D AP-PRECIATE IT!
YOU LIKE NOVELS TOO, FURI-SAN?
I didn't know that!
HUH?!
MANGA DOESN'T COUNT?
MANGA DOESN'T COUNT...

UM, DON'T FORCE YOURSELF TO BUY THEM...
I-I AIN'T FORCING MYSELF! I CAN READ NOVELS TOO!
DO YOU HAVE ANY RECOMMENDATIONS?
WHAT'RE YOU READING NOW? IS IT GOOD?
THIS IS...
I CAN'T REALLY RECOMMEND IT.
OH...
IT HAS SOME PERVERTED SCENES...

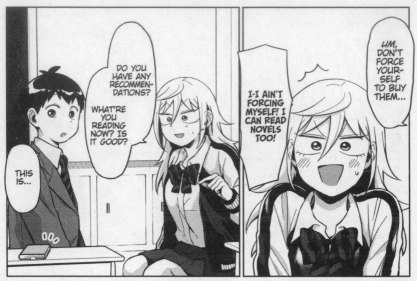

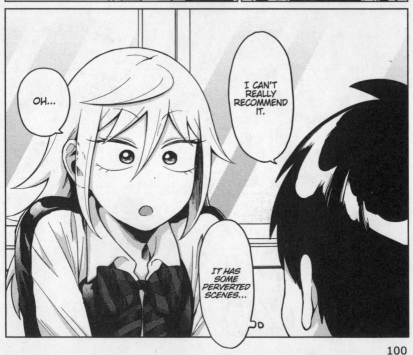

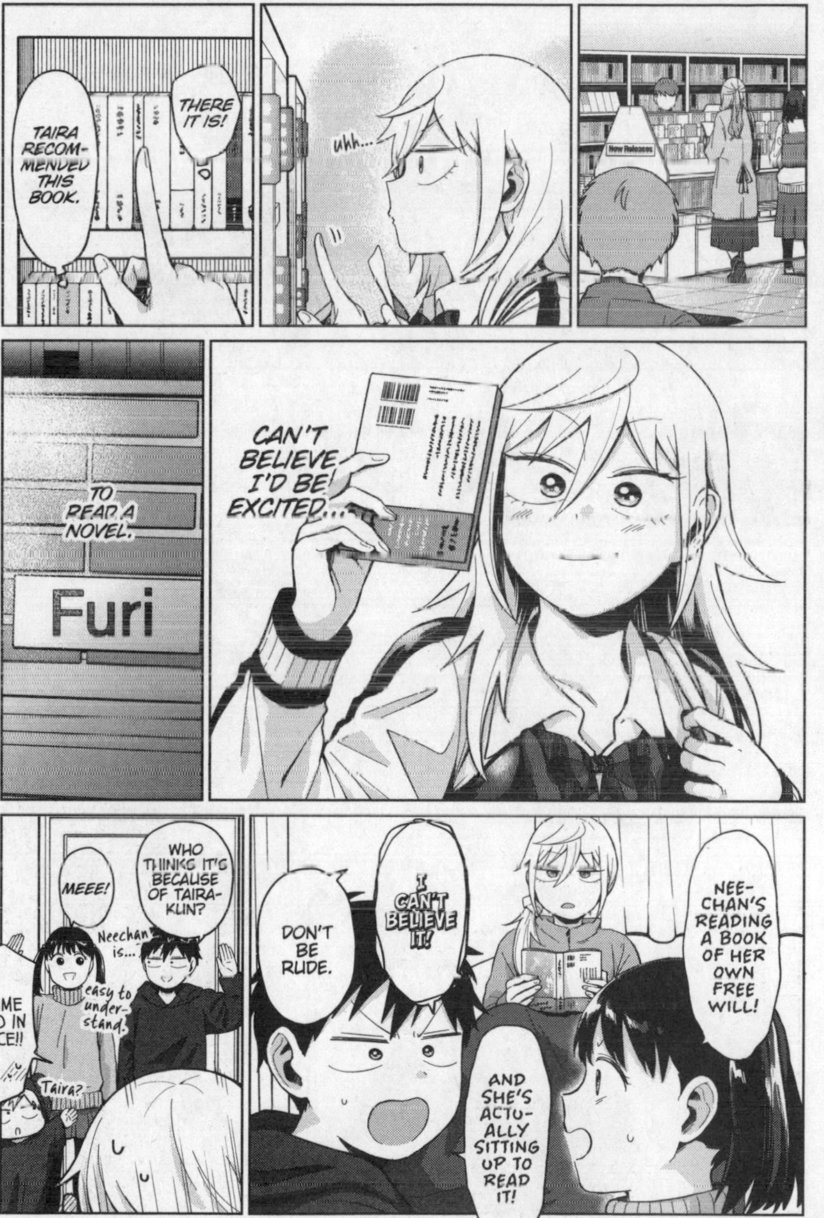
New Releases
uhh...
THERE IT IS!
TAIRA RECOMMENDED THIS BOOK.
CAN'T BELIEVE I'D BE EXCITED...
TO READ A NOVEL.
Furi
NEE-CHAN'S READING A BOOK OF HER OWN FREE WILL!
I CAN'T BELIEVE IT!
DON'T BE RUDE.
AND SHE'S ACTUALLY SITTING UP TO READ IT!
WHO THINKS IT'S BECAUSE OF TAIRA-KUN?
MEEE!
Neechan is...
easy to understand.
LEMME READ IN PEACE!!
Taira?

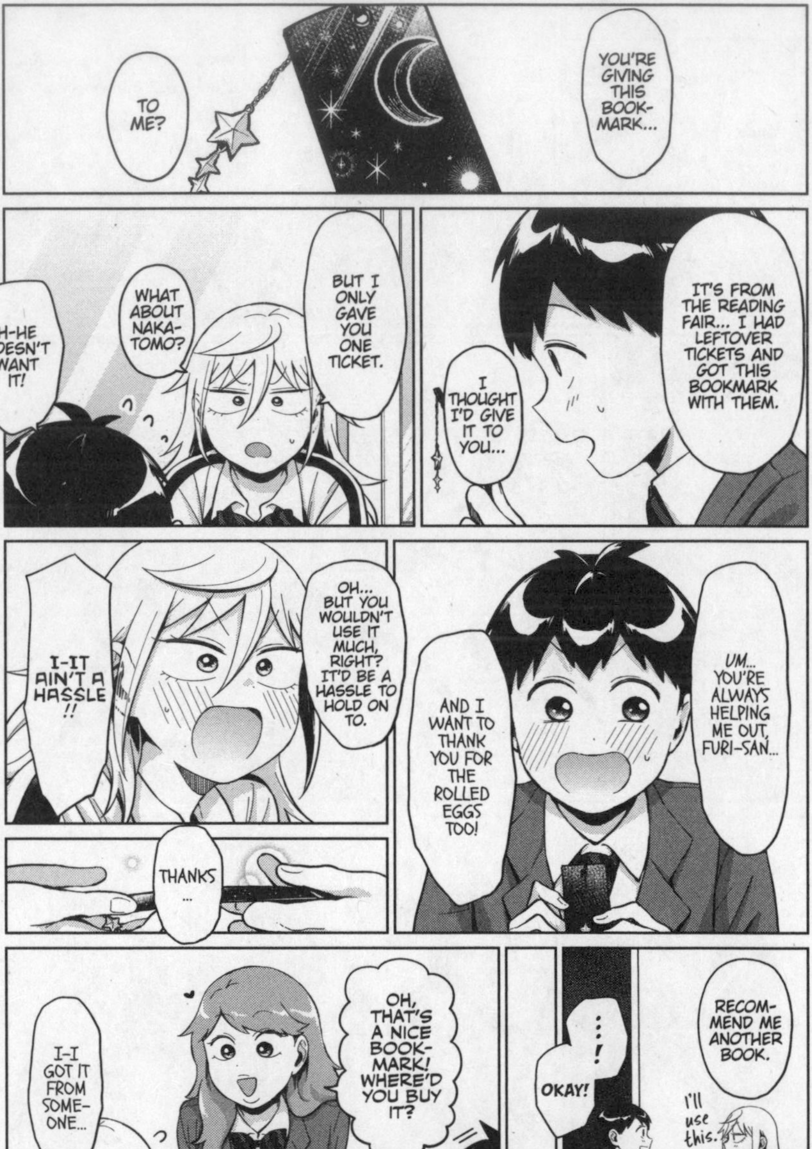
YOU'RE GIVING THIS BOOK-MARK...
TO ME?
IT'S FROM THE READING FAIR... I HAD LEFTOVER TICKETS AND GOT THIS BOOKMARK WITH THEM.
I THOUGHT I'D GIVE IT TO YOU...
BUT I ONLY GAVE YOU ONE TICKET.
WHAT ABOUT NAKA-TOMO?
H-HE DOESN'T WANT IT!
UM... YOU'RE ALWAYS HELPING ME OUT, FURI-SAN...
AND I WANT TO THANK YOU FOR THE ROLLED EGGS TOO!
OH... BUT YOU WOULDN'T USE IT MUCH, RIGHT? IT'D BE A HASSLE TO HOLD ON TO.
I-IT AIN'T A HASSLE!!
THANKS...
RECOM-MEND ME ANOTHER BOOK.
...!
OKAY!
I'll use this.
OH, THAT'S A NICE BOOK-MARK! WHERE'D YOU BUY IT?
FLINCH
I-I GOT IT FROM SOME-ONE...

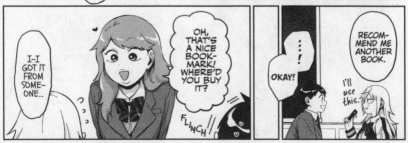

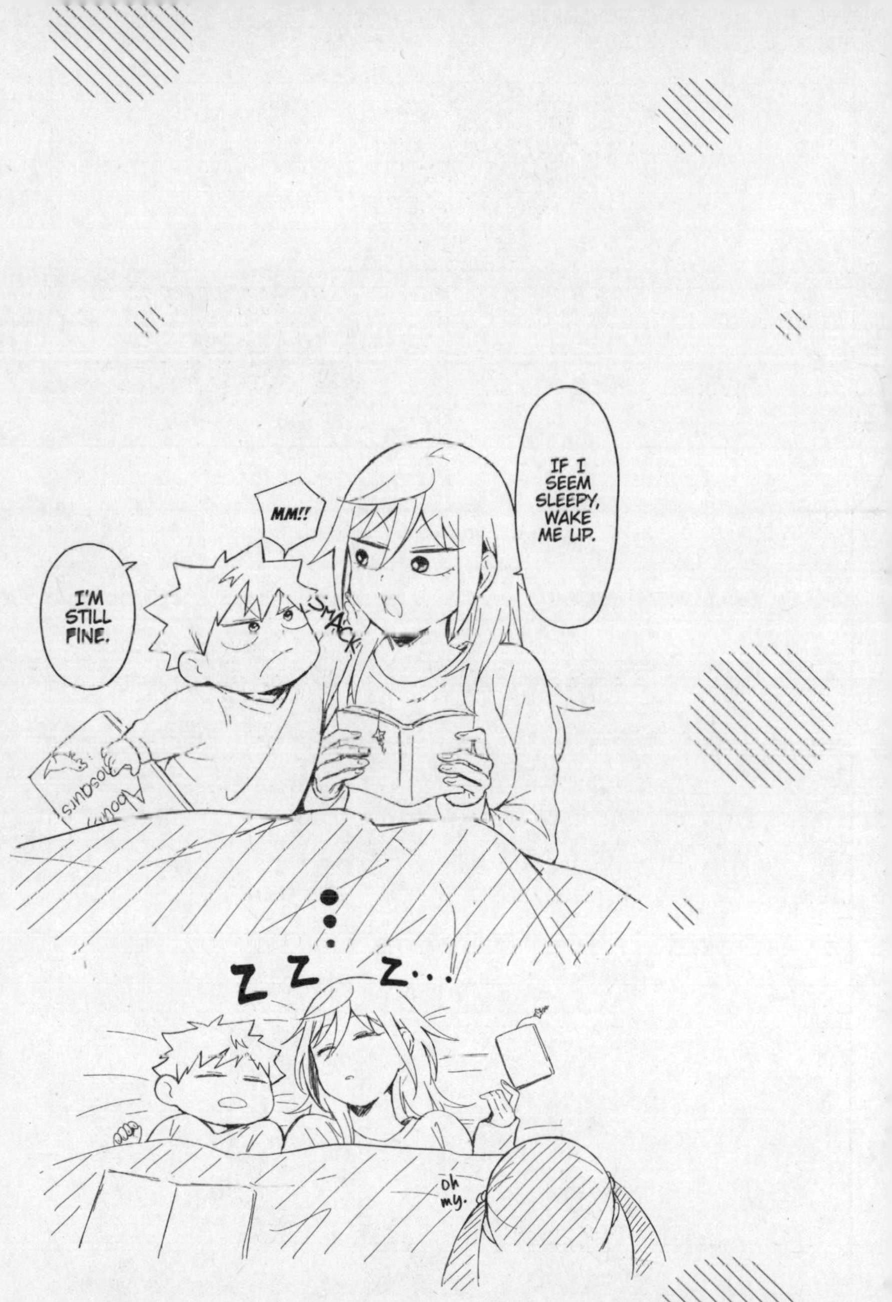
IF I SEEM SLEEPY, WAKE ME UP.
MM!!
SMACK
I'M STILL FINE.
...
Z Z Z...
oh my.

Chapter 25

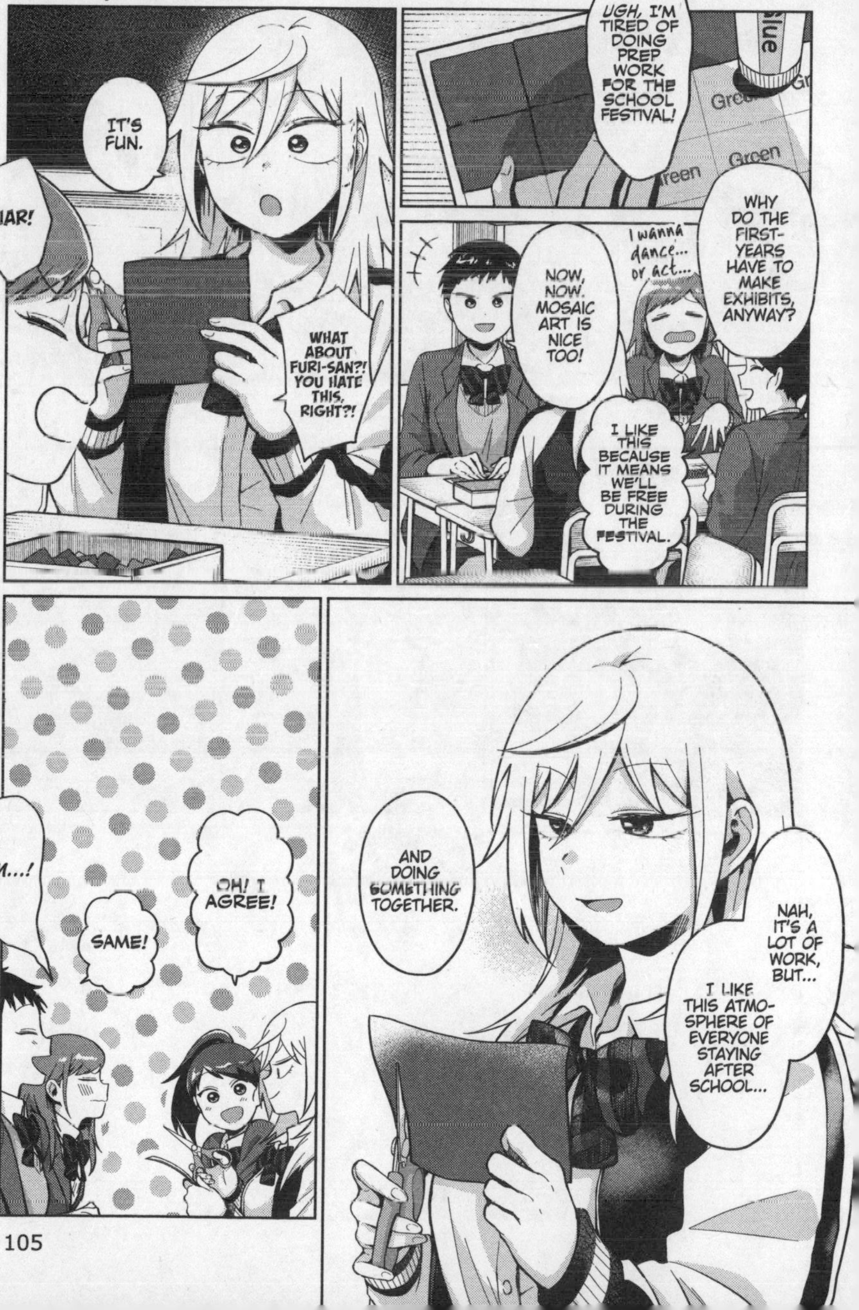

UGH, I'M TIRED OF DOING PREP WORK FOR THE SCHOOL FESTIVAL!
Glue
Green
Green
Green
Green
WHY DO THE FIRST-YEARS HAVE TO MAKE EXHIBITS, ANYWAY?
I wanna dance... or act...
NOW, NOW. MOSAIC ART IS NICE TOO!
I LIKE THIS BECAUSE IT MEANS WE'LL BE FREE DURING THE FESTIVAL.
WHAT ABOUT FURI-SAN?! YOU HATE THIS, RIGHT?!
IT'S FUN.
LIAR!
NAH, IT'S A LOT OF WORK, BUT...
I LIKE THIS ATMOSPHERE OF EVERYONE STAYING AFTER SCHOOL...
AND DOING SOMETHING TOGETHER.
OH! I AGREE!
SAME!
MM...!

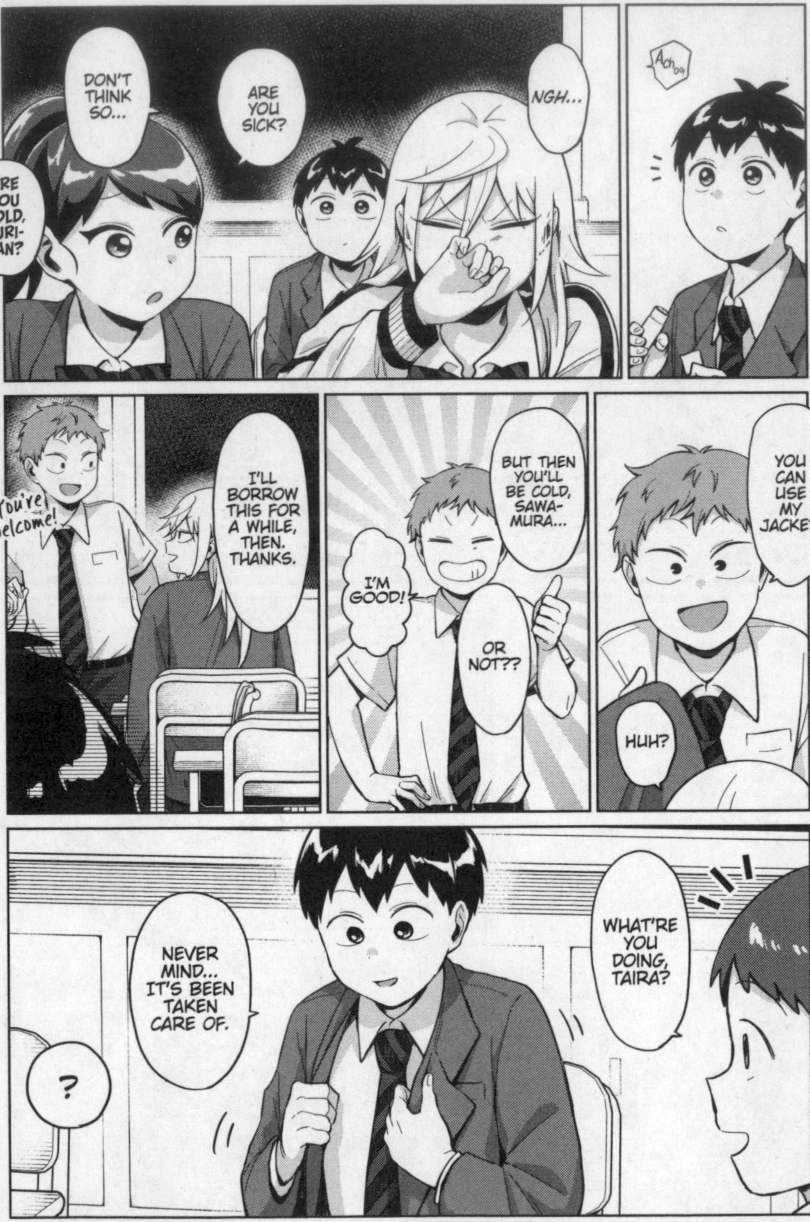
Achoo
NGH...
ARE YOU SICK?
DON'T THINK SO...
ARE YOU COLD, FURI-SAN?
YOU CAN USE MY JACKET!
HUH?
BUT THEN YOU'LL BE COLD, SAWAMURA...
I'M GOOD!
OR NOT??
I'LL BORROW THIS FOR A WHILE, THEN. THANKS.
You're welcome!
WHAT'RE YOU DOING, TAIRA?
NEVER MIND... IT'S BEEN TAKEN CARE OF.
?

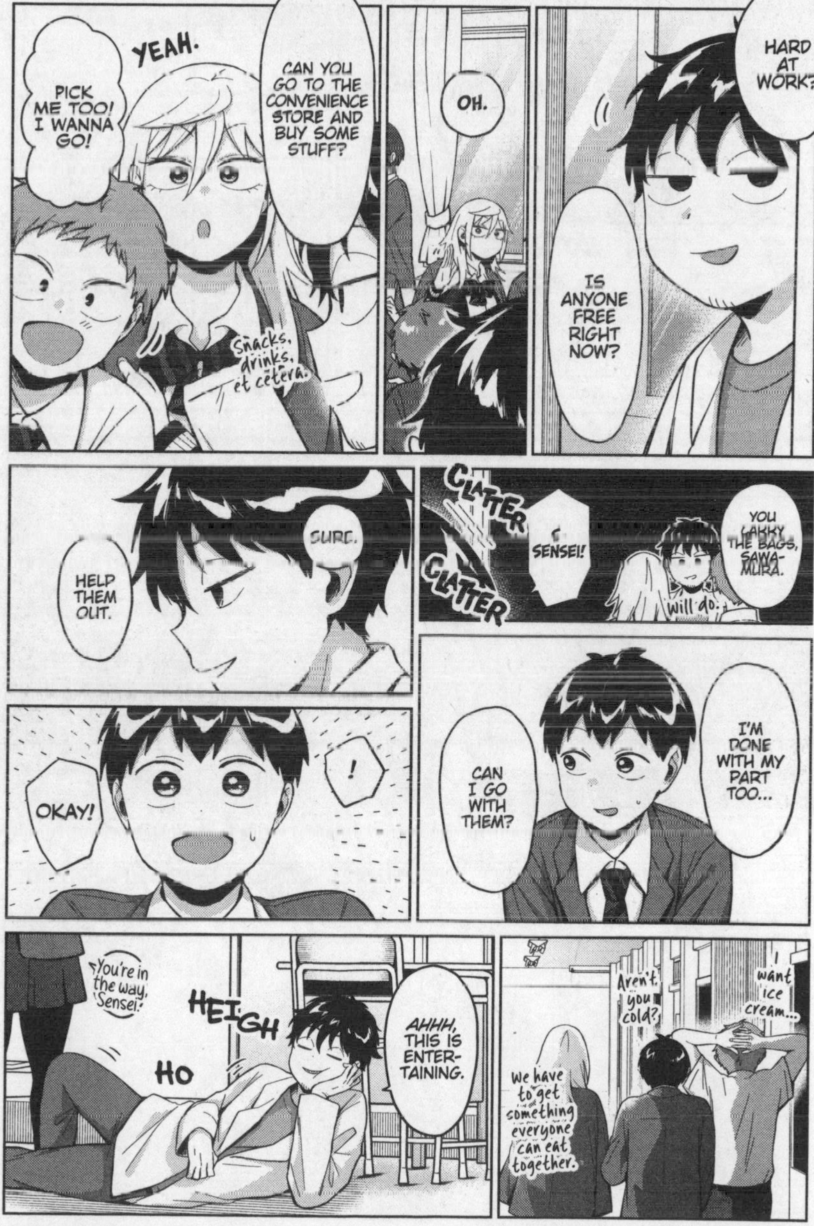
HARD AT WORK?
IS ANYONE FREE RIGHT NOW?
OH.
CAN YOU GO TO THE CONVENIENCE STORE AND BUY SOME STUFF?
YEAH.
PICK ME TOO! I WANNA GO!
Snacks, drinks, et cetera.
YOU CARRY THE BAGS, SAWAMURA.
SENSEI!
CLATTER
CLATTER
Will do.
SURE.
HELP THEM OUT.
I'M DONE WITH MY PART TOO...
CAN I GO WITH THEM?
!
OKAY!
I want ice cream...
Aren't you cold?
We have to get something everyone can eat together.
AHHH, THIS IS ENTERTAINING.
HEIGH
HO
You're in the way, Sensei!

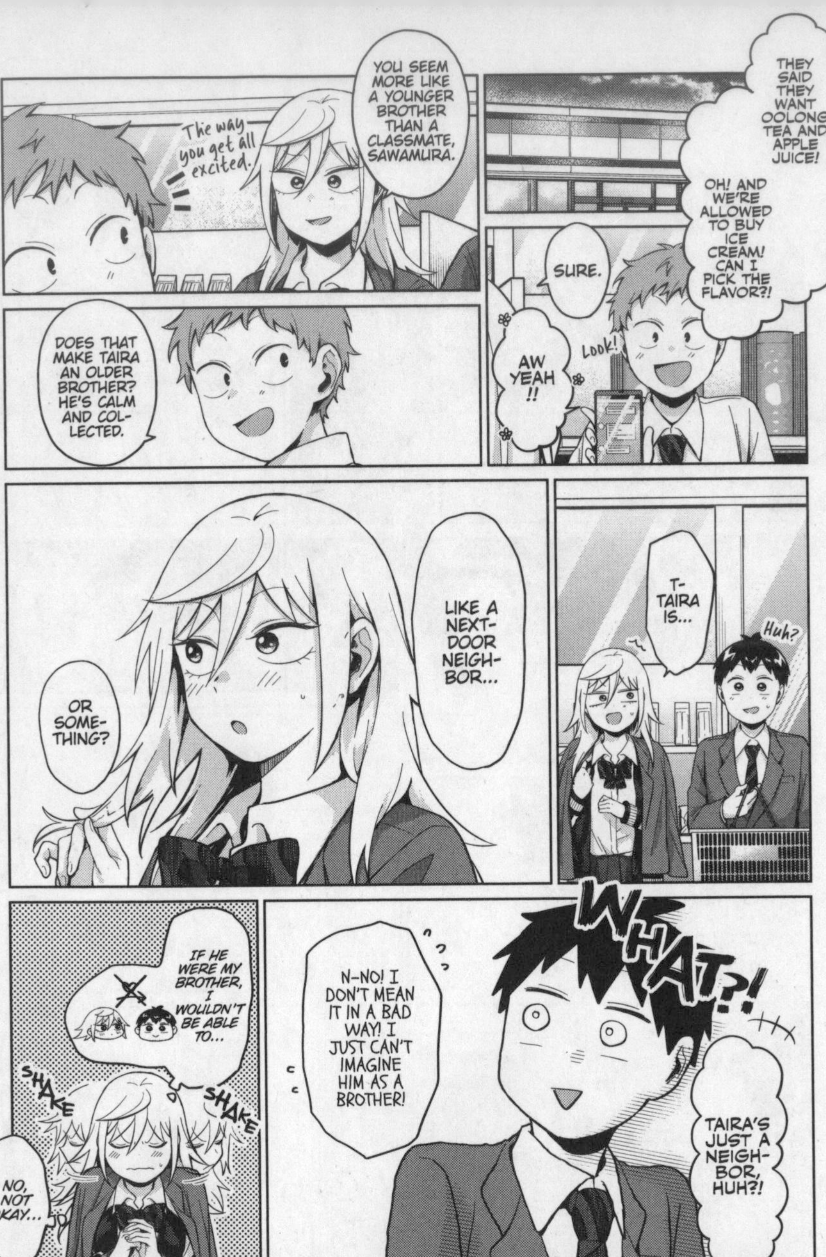
THEY SAID THEY WANT OOLONG TEA AND APPLE JUICE!
OH! AND WE'RE ALLOWED TO BUY ICE CREAM! CAN I PICK THE FLAVOR?!
SURE.
LOOK!
AW YEAH !!
YOU SEEM MORE LIKE A YOUNGER BROTHER THAN A CLASSMATE, SAWAMURA.
The way you get all excited.
DOES THAT MAKE TAIRA AN OLDER BROTHER? HE'S CALM AND COL-LECTED.
T-TAIRA IS...
Huh?
LIKE A NEXT-DOOR NEIGH-BOR...
OR SOME-THING?
WHAT?!
TAIRA'S JUST A NEIGH-BOR, HUH?!
N-NO! I DON'T MEAN IT IN A BAD WAY! I JUST CAN'T IMAGINE HIM AS A BROTHER!
IF HE WERE MY BROTHER, I WOULDN'T BE ABLE TO...
SHAKE
SHAKE
NO, NOT OKAY...

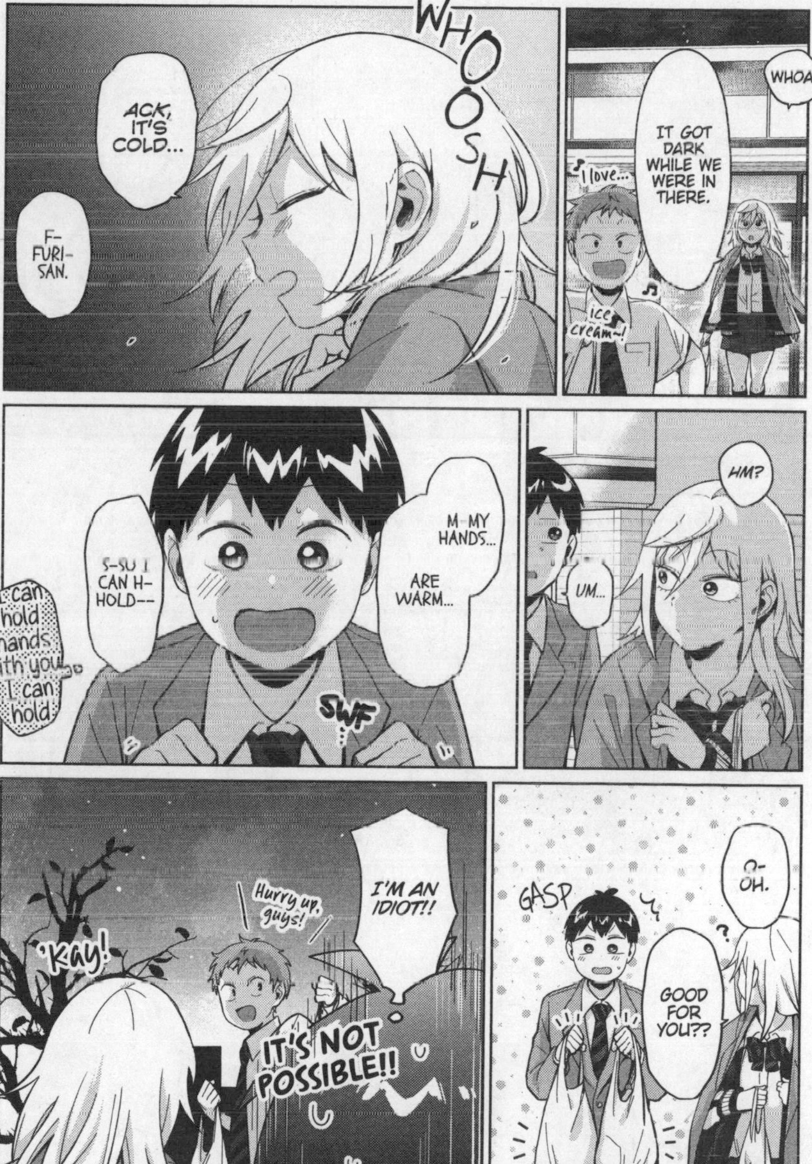
WHOA.
IT GOT DARK WHILE WE WERE IN THERE.
I love...
ice cream~!
WHOOSH
ACK, IT'S COLD...
F-FURI-SAN.
HM?
UM...
M-MY HANDS...
ARE WARM...
S-SO I CAN H-HOLD--
I can hold hands with you... I can hold
SWF
O-OH.
GOOD FOR YOU??
GASP
I'M AN IDIOT!!
Hurry up, guys!
'Kay!
IT'S NOT POSSIBLE!!

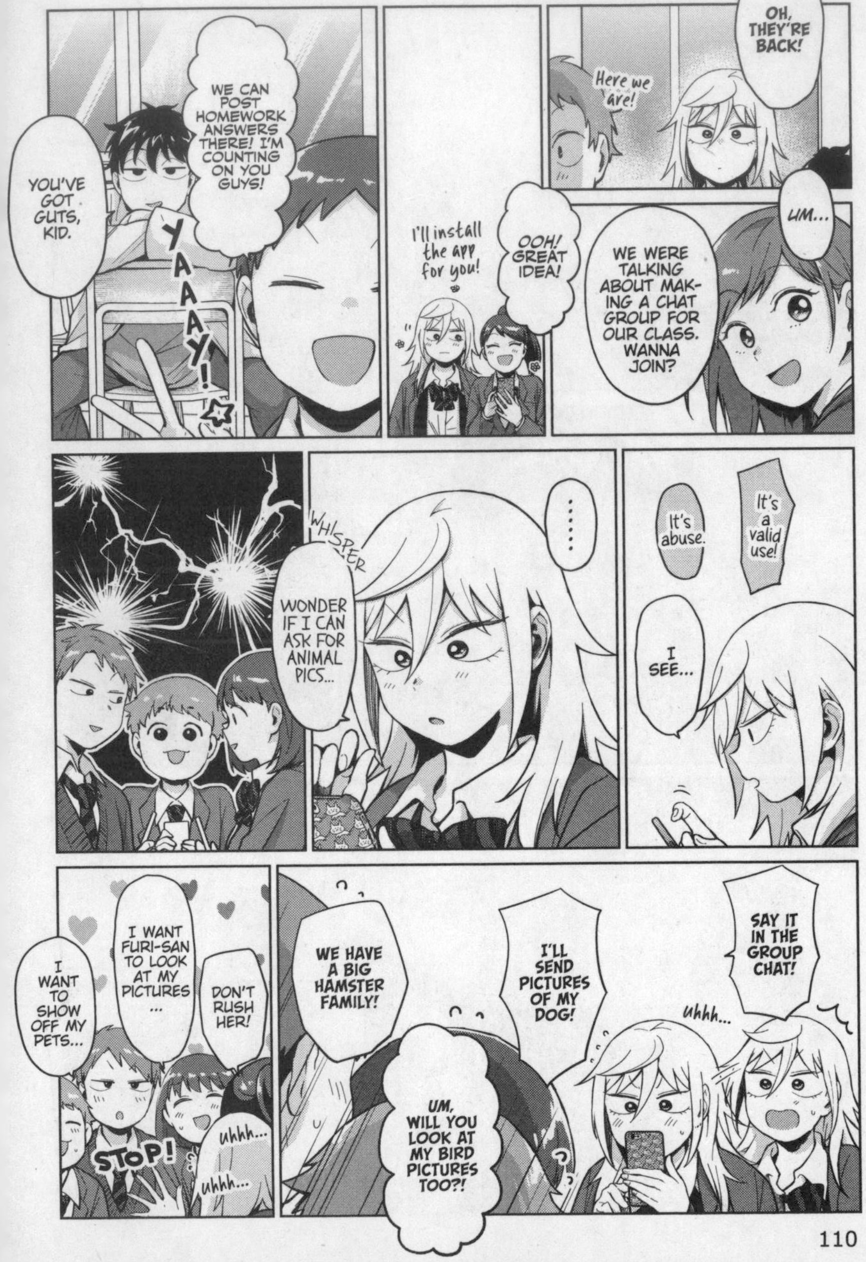
OH, THEY'RE BACK!
Here we are!
UM...
WE WERE TALKING ABOUT MAKING A CHAT GROUP FOR OUR CLASS. WANNA JOIN?
OOH! GREAT IDEA!
I'll install the app for you!
WE CAN POST HOMEWORK ANSWERS THERE! I'M COUNTING ON YOU GUYS!
YAAAAY!
YOU'VE GOT GUTS, KID.
It's a valid use!
It's abuse.
I SEE...
......
WHISPER
WONDER IF I CAN ASK FOR ANIMAL PICS...
SAY IT IN THE GROUP CHAT!
I'LL SEND PICTURES OF MY DOG!
WE HAVE A BIG HAMSTER FAMILY!
uhhh...
UM, WILL YOU LOOK AT MY BIRD PICTURES TOO?!
I WANT FURI-SAN TO LOOK AT MY PICTURES ...
DON'T RUSH HER!
I WANT TO SHOW OFF MY PETS...
uhhh...
STOP!
uhhh...

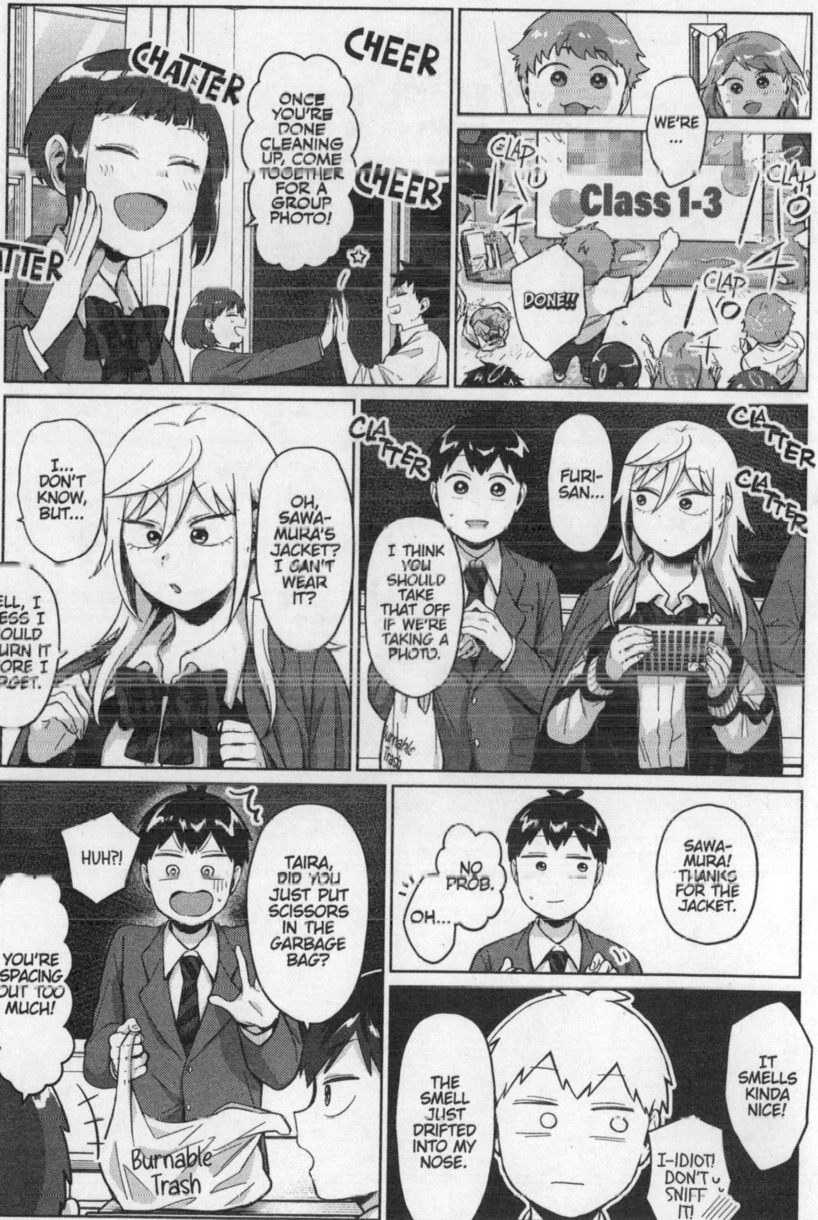
WE'RE ...
Class 1-3
CLAP
CLAP
DONE!!
CLAP
CHEER
ONCE YOU'RE DONE CLEANING UP, COME TOGETHER FOR A GROUP PHOTO!
CHATTER
CHEER
CHATTER
CLATTER
CLATTER
FURI-SAN...
CLATTER
I THINK YOU SHOULD TAKE THAT OFF IF WE'RE TAKING A PHOTO.
Burnable Trash
OH, SAWAMURA'S JACKET? I CAN'T WEAR IT?
I... DON'T KNOW, BUT...
WELL, I GUESS I SHOULD RETURN IT BEFORE I FORGET.
SAWAMURA! THANKS FOR THE JACKET.
NO PROB.
OH...
IT SMELLS KINDA NICE!
THE SMELL JUST DRIFTED INTO MY NOSE.
I-IDIOT! DON'T SNIFF IT!
TAIRA, DID YOU JUST PUT SCISSORS IN THE GARBAGE BAG?
HUH?!
YOU'RE SPACING OUT TOO MUCH!
Burnable Trash

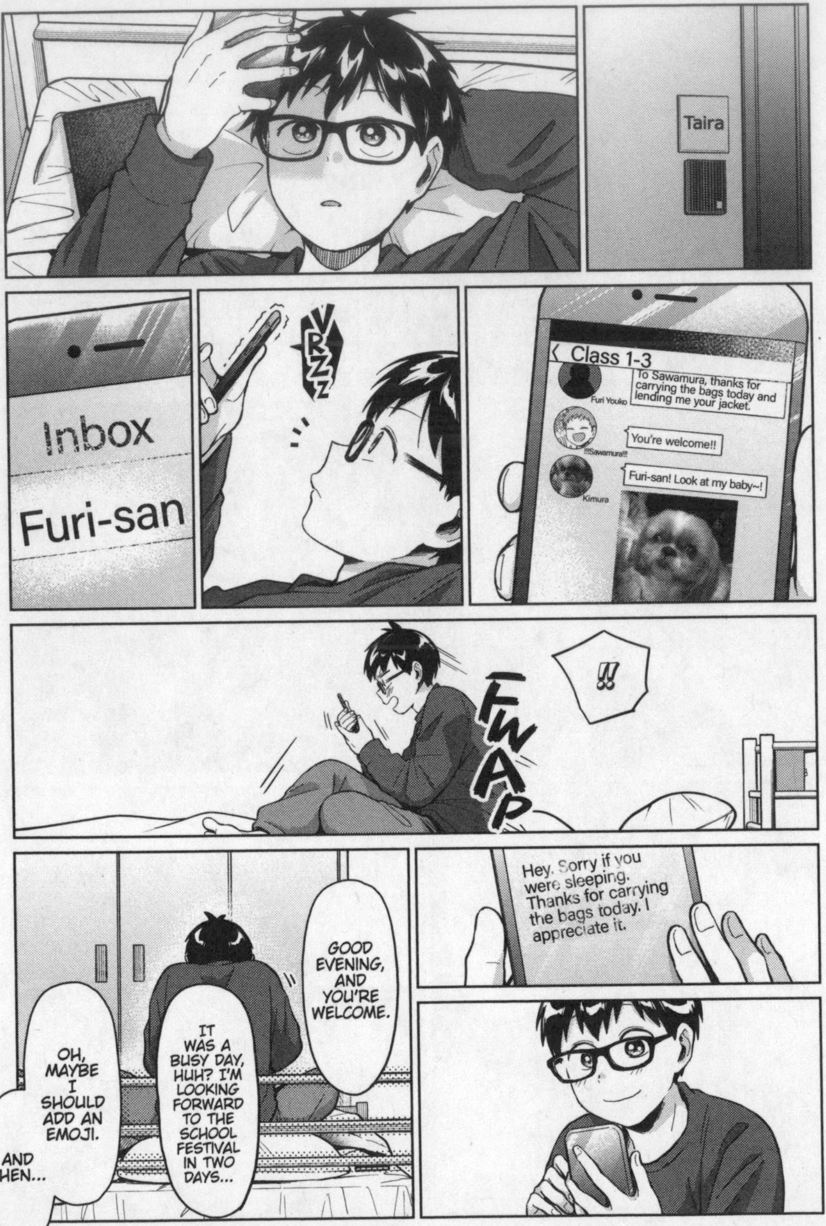
Taira
Class 1-3
To Sawamura, thanks for carrying the bags today and lending me your jacket.
Furi Youko
You're welcome!!
!!!Sawamura!!!
Furi-san! Look at my baby~!
Kimura
VRZZ
Inbox
Furi-san
!!
FWAP
Hey. Sorry if you were sleeping. Thanks for carrying the bags today. I appreciate it.
GOOD EVENING, AND YOU'RE WELCOME.
IT WAS A BUSY DAY, HUH? I'M LOOKING FORWARD TO THE SCHOOL FESTIVAL IN TWO DAYS...
OH, MAYBE I SHOULD ADD AN EMOJI.
AND THEN...

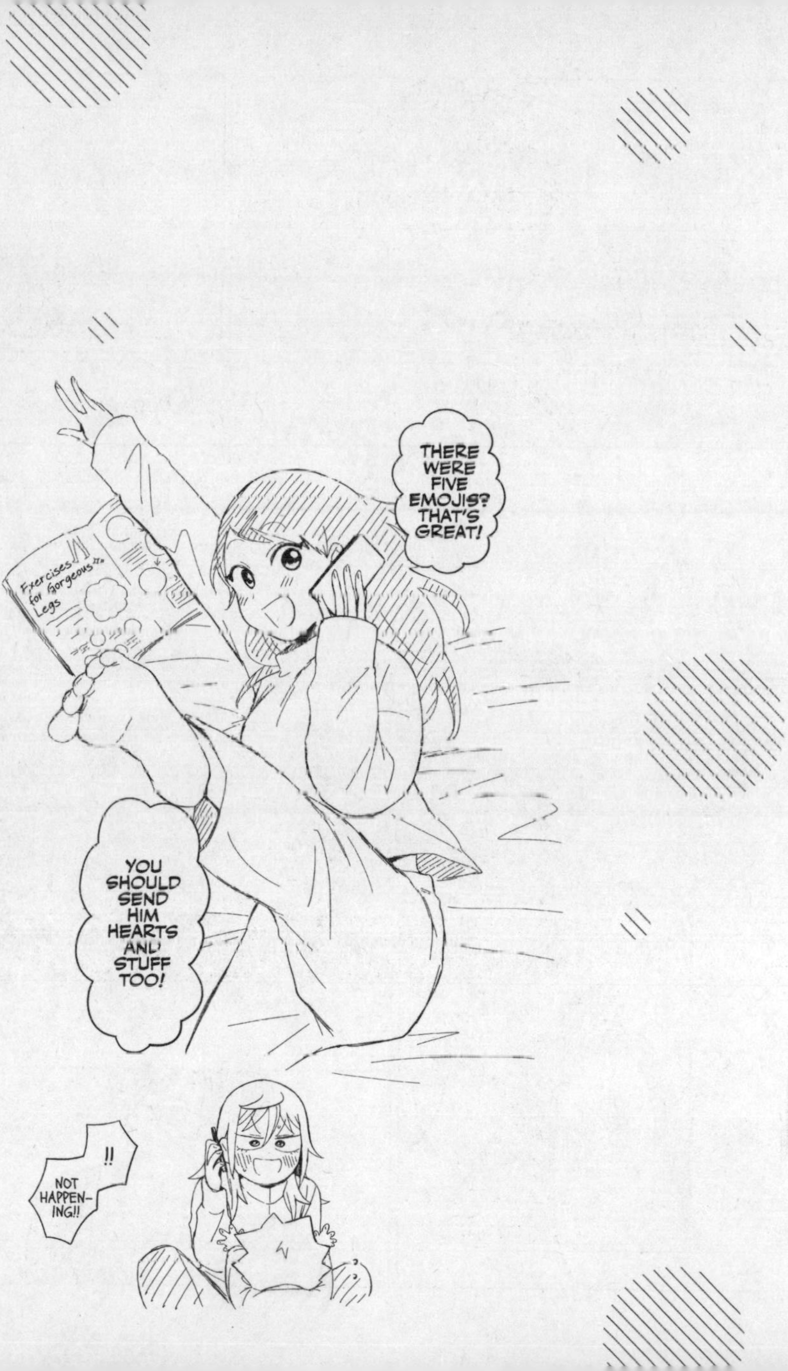
THERE WERE FIVE EMOJIS? THAT'S GREAT!
Exercises for Gorgeous Legs
YOU SHOULD SEND HIM HEARTS AND STUFF TOO!
!!
NOT HAPPEN-ING!!

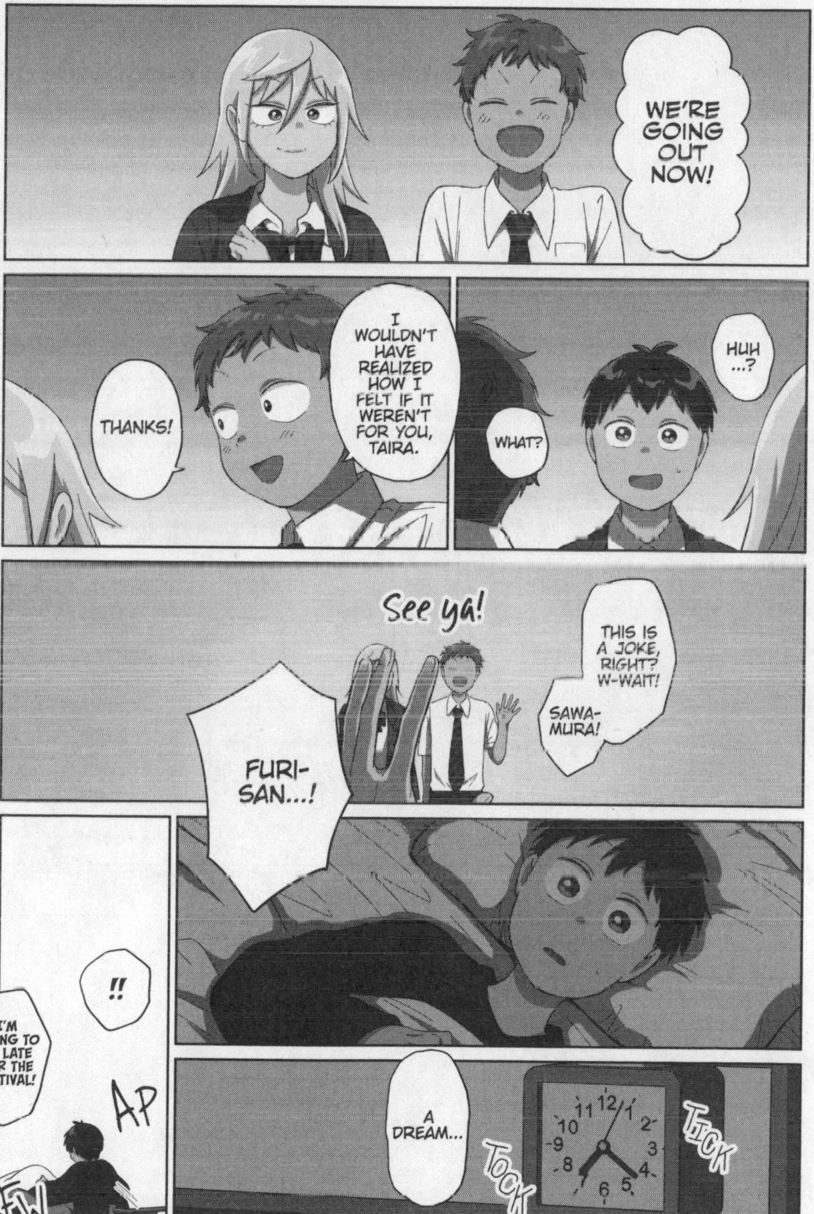
WE'RE GOING OUT NOW!
HUH ...?
WHAT?
I WOULDN'T HAVE REALIZED HOW I FELT IF IT WEREN'T FOR YOU, TAIRA.
THANKS!
See ya!
THIS IS A JOKE, RIGHT? W-WAIT!
SAWA-MURA!
FURI-SAN...!
TICK
TOCK
A DREAM...
!!
I'M GOING TO BE LATE FOR THE FESTIVAL!
AP
FW

Chapter 26

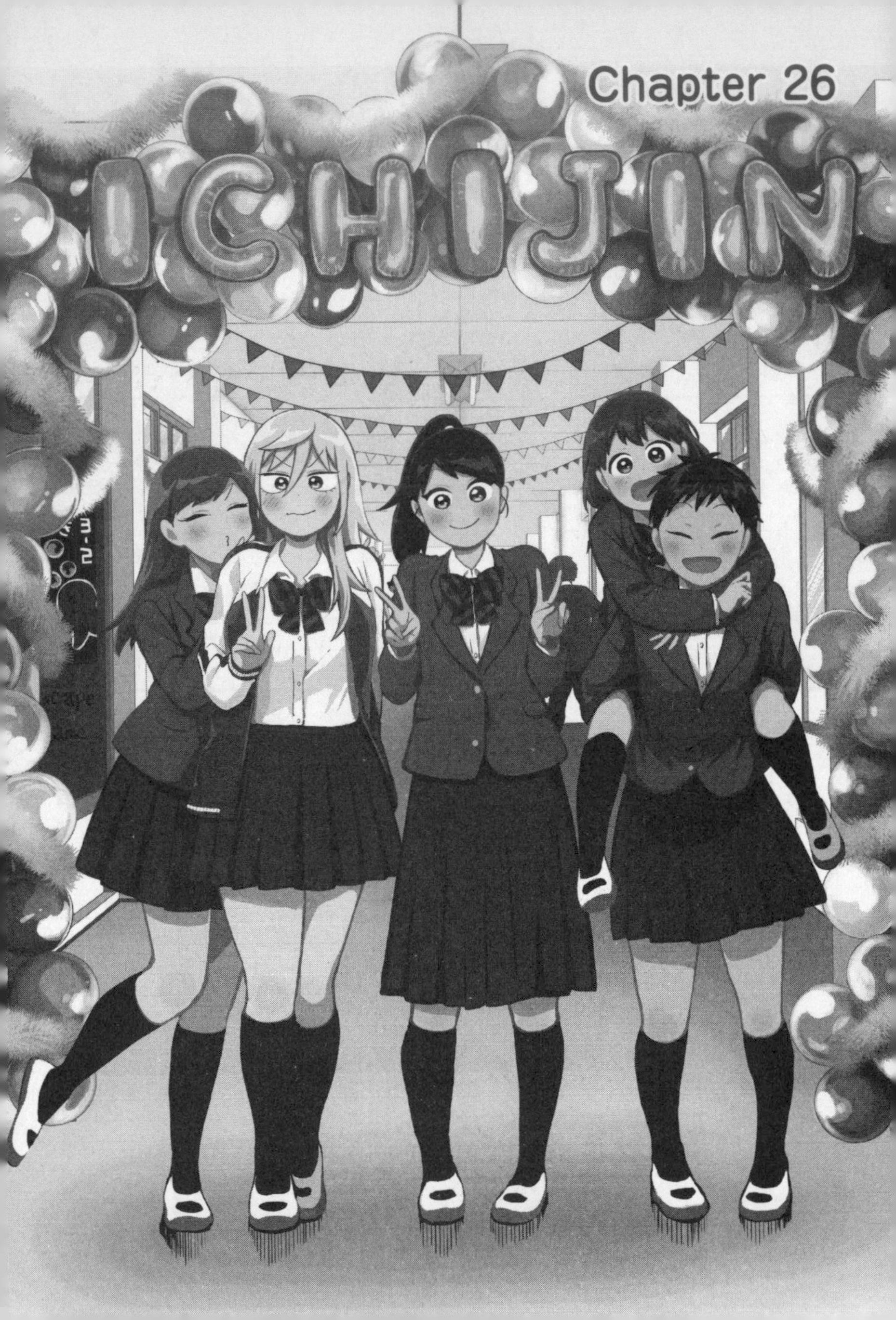
ICHIJIN
3-2

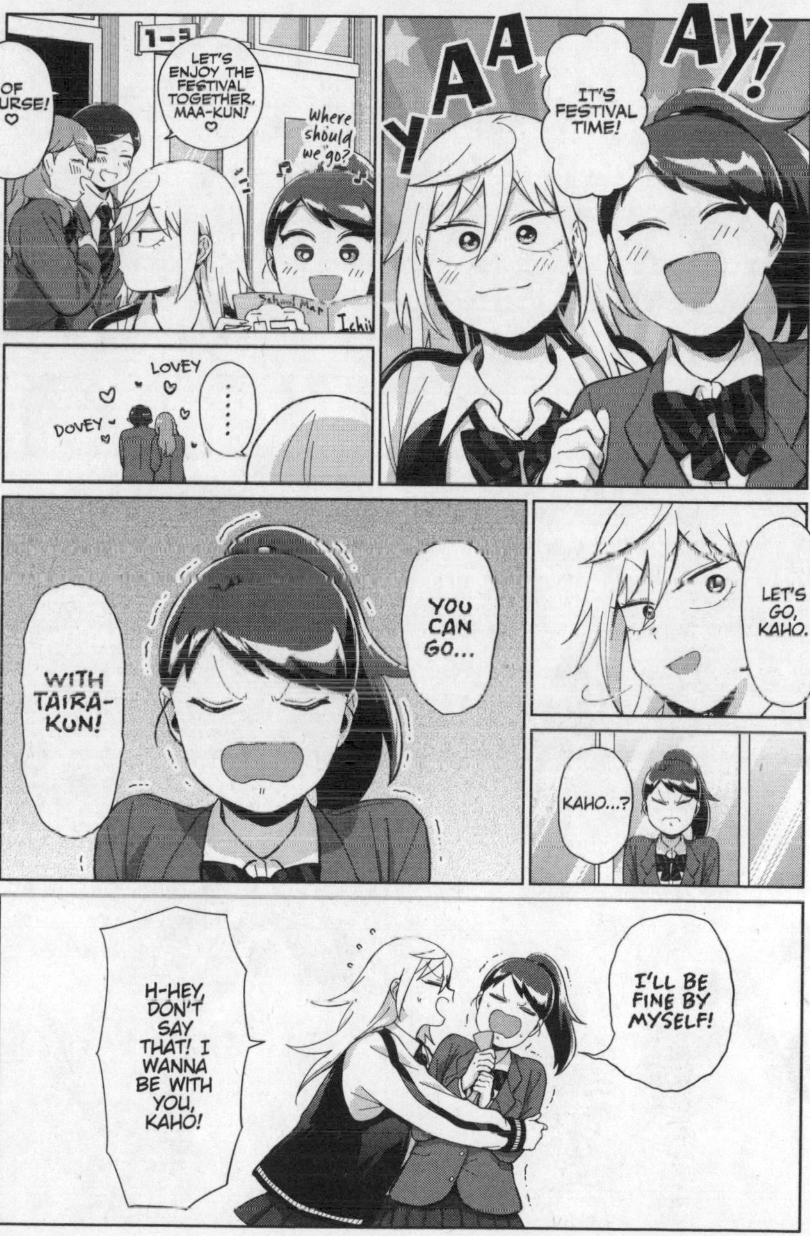

YAAAAY!
IT'S FESTIVAL TIME!
Where should we go?
LET'S ENJOY THE FESTIVAL TOGETHER, MAA-KUN! ♡
OF COURSE! ♡
School Map
Ichi
1-3
......
LOVEY
DOVEY
LET'S GO, KAHO.
KAHO...?
YOU CAN GO...
WITH TAIRA-KUN!
I'LL BE FINE BY MYSELF!
H-HEY, DON'T SAY THAT! I WANNA BE WITH YOU, KAHO!

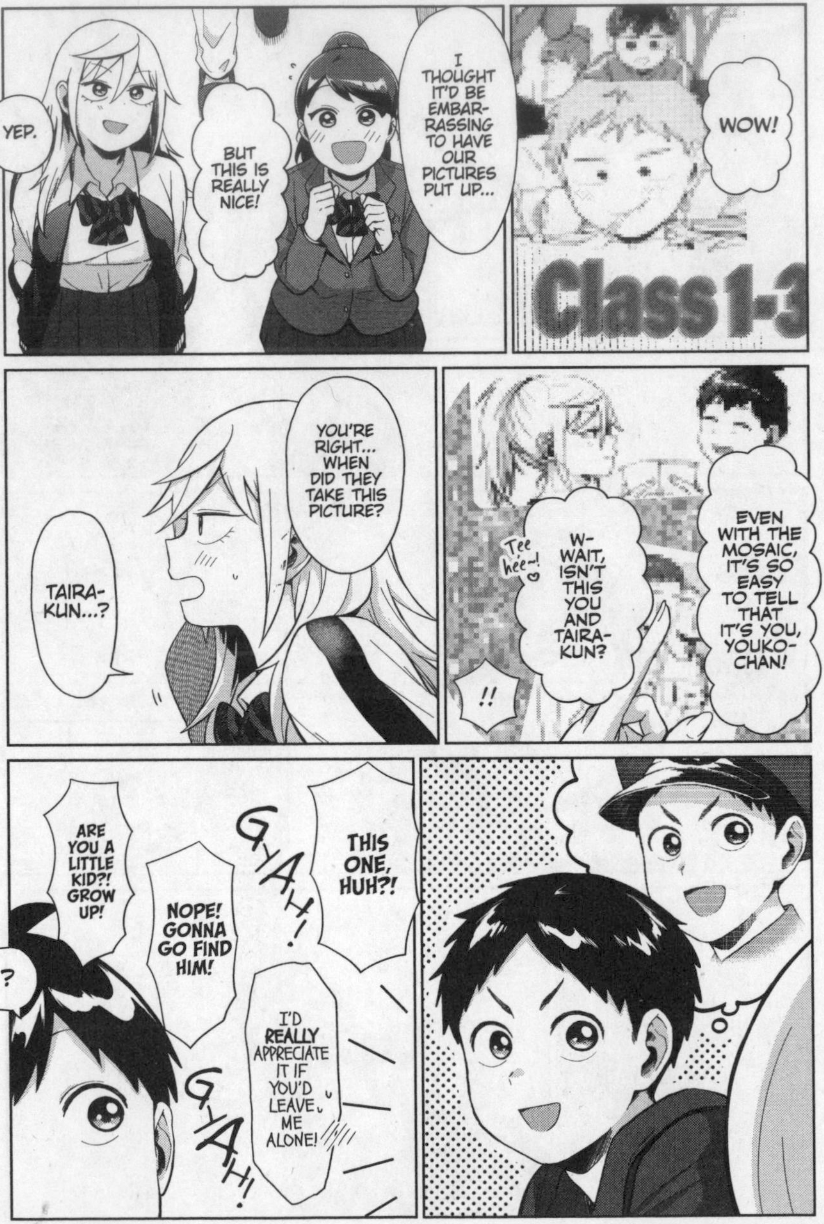
WOW!
Class 1-3
I THOUGHT IT'D BE EMBARRASSING TO HAVE OUR PICTURES PUT UP...
BUT THIS IS REALLY NICE!
YEP.
EVEN WITH THE MOSAIC, IT'S SO EASY TO TELL THAT IT'S YOU, YOUKO-CHAN!
W-WAIT, ISN'T THIS YOU AND TAIRA-KUN?
Tee hee~!
!!
YOU'RE RIGHT... WHEN DID THEY TAKE THIS PICTURE?
TAIRA-KUN...?
THIS ONE, HUH?!
GYAH!
NOPE! GONNA GO FIND HIM!
ARE YOU A LITTLE KID?! GROW UP!
I'D REALLY APPRECIATE IT IF YOU'D LEAVE ME ALONE!
GYAH!
?

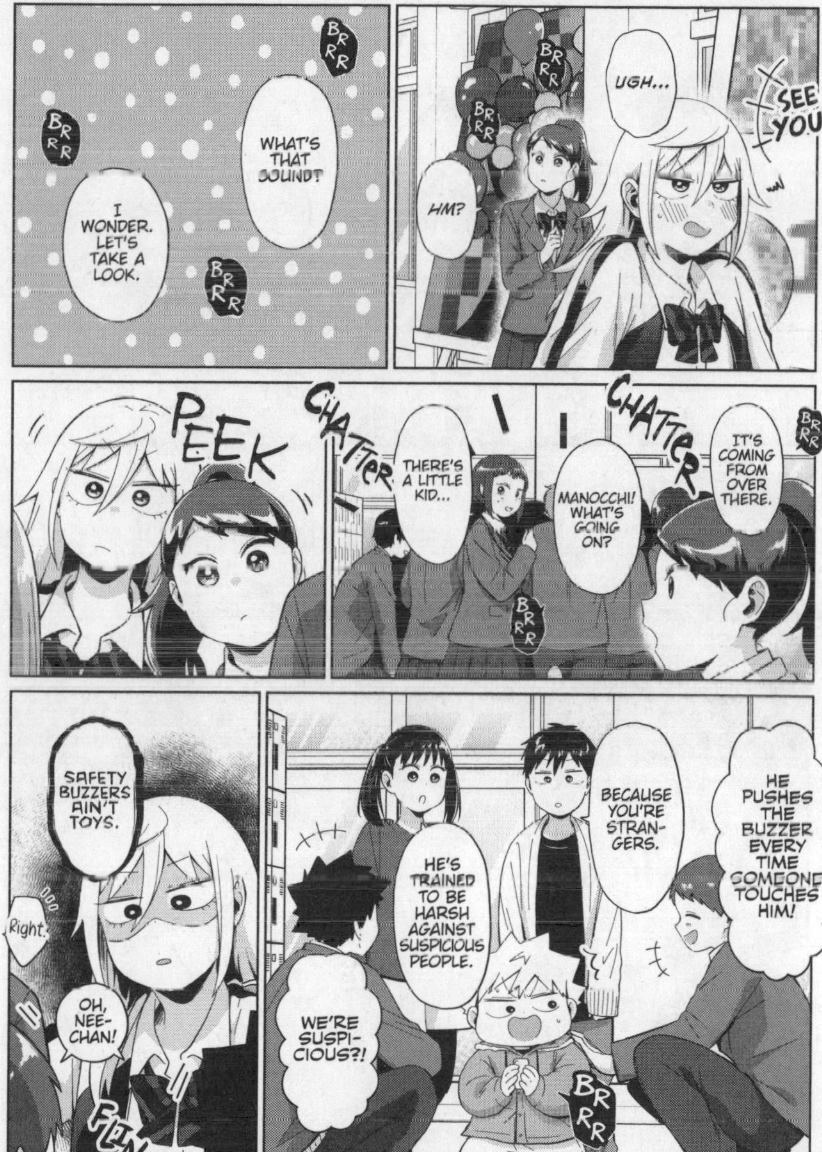
BRR
UGH...
SEE YOU!
BRR
HM?
BRR
WHAT'S THAT SOUND?
BRR
I WONDER. LET'S TAKE A LOOK.
BRR
BRR
IT'S COMING FROM OVER THERE.
CHATTER
MANOCCHI! WHAT'S GOING ON?
THERE'S A LITTLE KID...
BRR
CHATTER
PEEK
HE PUSHES THE BUZZER EVERY TIME SOMEONE TOUCHES HIM!
BECAUSE YOU'RE STRAN-GERS.
HE'S TRAINED TO BE HARSH AGAINST SUSPICIOUS PEOPLE.
WE'RE SUSPI-CIOUS?!
BRR
SAFETY BUZZERS AIN'T TOYS.
Right.
OH, NEE-CHAN!
FLINCH

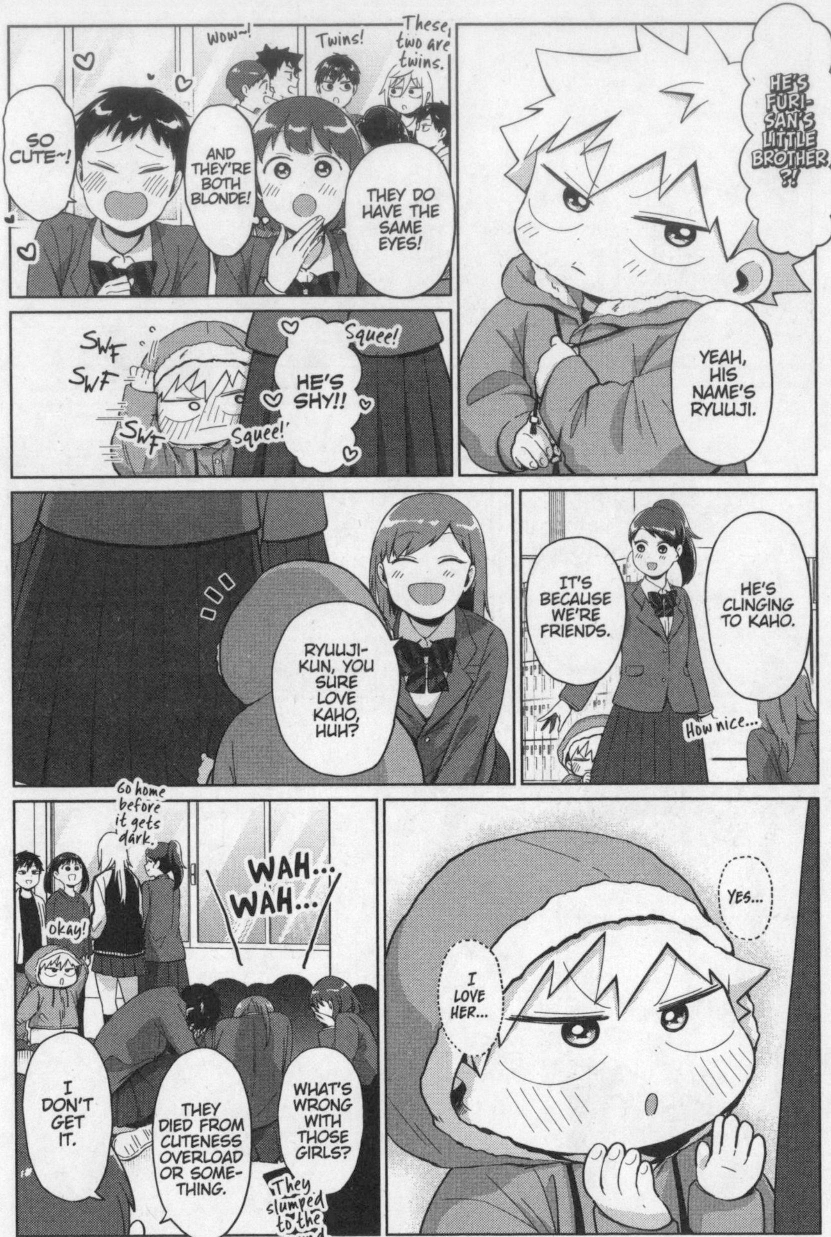
HE'S FURI-SAN'S LITTLE BROTHER?!
YEAH, HIS NAME'S RYUUJI.
These two are twins.
Twins!
THEY DO HAVE THE SAME EYES!
Wow~!
AND THEY'RE BOTH BLONDE!
SO CUTE~!
Squee!
HE'S SHY!!
Squee!
SWF
SWF
SWF
HE'S CLINGING TO KAHO.
IT'S BECAUSE WE'RE FRIENDS.
How nice...
RYUUJI-KUN, YOU SURE LOVE KAHO, HUH?
YES...
I LOVE HER...
WAH... WAH...
Go home before it gets dark.
WHAT'S WRONG WITH THOSE GIRLS?
They slumped to the ground.
THEY DIED FROM CUTENESS OVERLOAD OR SOME-THING.
okay!
I DON'T GET IT.

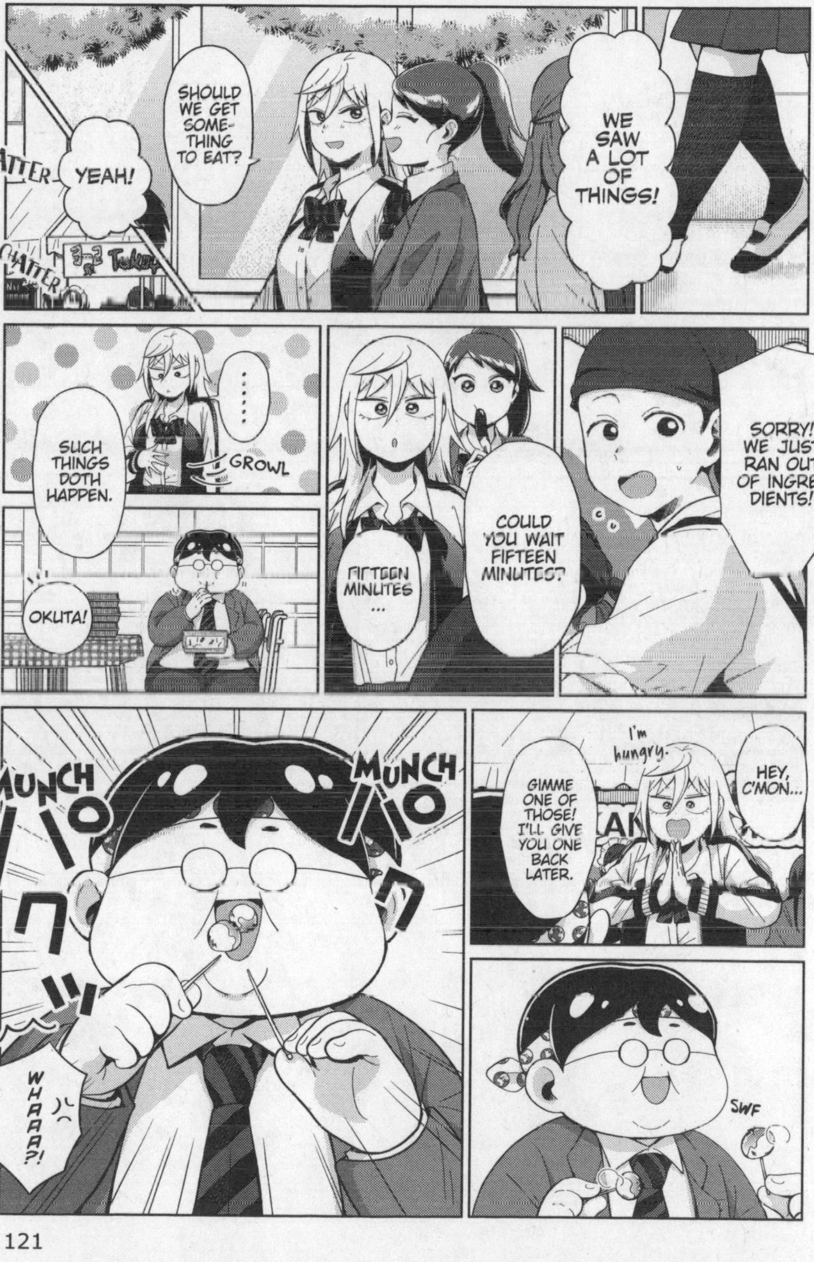
WE SAW A LOT OF THINGS!
SHOULD WE GET SOME-THING TO EAT?
YEAH!
CHATTER
CHATTER
SORRY! WE JUST RAN OUT OF INGRE-DIENTS!
COULD YOU WAIT FIFTEEN MINUTES?
FIFTEEN MINUTES ...
......
GROWL
SUCH THINGS DOTH HAPPEN.
OKUTA!
HEY, C'MON...
I'm hungry.
GIMME ONE OF THOSE! I'LL GIVE YOU ONE BACK LATER.
SWF
MUNCH
MUNCH
WHAAAA?!

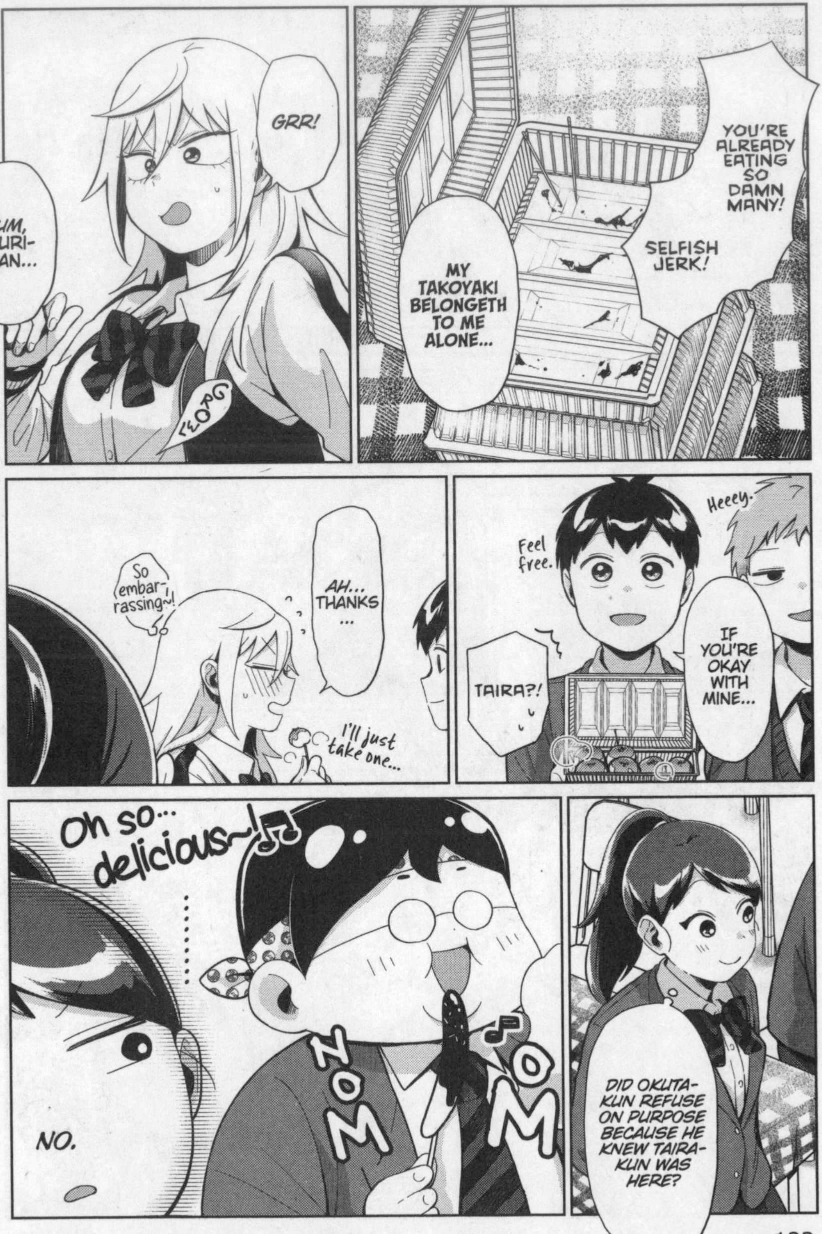
YOU'RE ALREADY EATING SO DAMN MANY!
SELFISH JERK!
MY TAKOYAKI BELONGETH TO ME ALONE...
GRR!
UM, FURI-SAN...
Heeey.
Feel free.
IF YOU'RE OKAY WITH MINE...
TAIRA?!
AH... THANKS...
So embarrassing~!
I'll just take one...
DID OKUTA-KUN REFUSE ON PURPOSE BECAUSE HE KNEW TAIRA-KUN WAS HERE?
Oh so... delicious~!
NOM
NOM
NO.

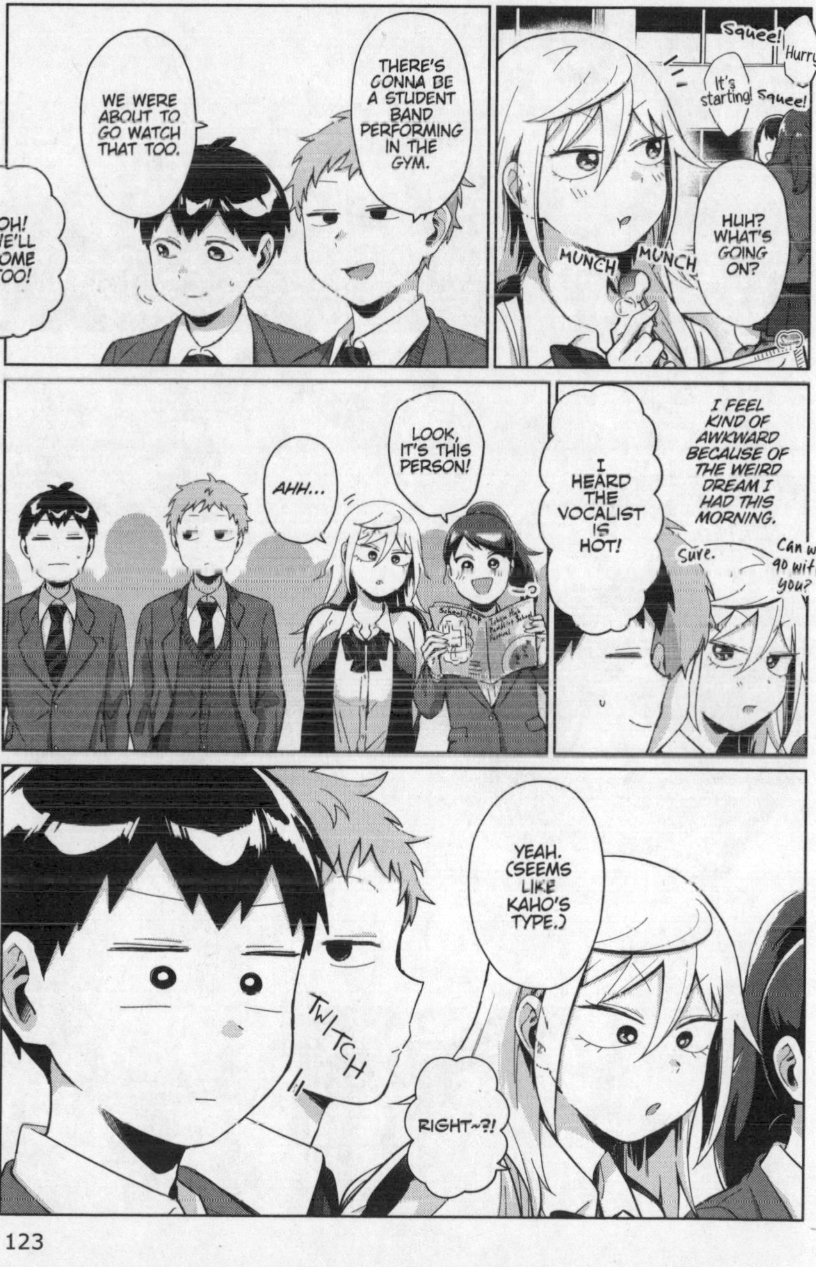
Squee!
Hurry!
It's starting!
Squee!
HUH? WHAT'S GOING ON?
MUNCH MUNCH
THERE'S GONNA BE A STUDENT BAND PERFORMING IN THE GYM.
WE WERE ABOUT TO GO WATCH THAT TOO.
OH! WE'LL COME TOO!
I FEEL KIND OF AWKWARD BECAUSE OF THE WEIRD DREAM I HAD THIS MORNING.
Can we go with you?
Sure.
I HEARD THE VOCALIST IS HOT!
LOOK, IT'S THIS PERSON!
AHH...
YEAH. (SEEMS LIKE KAHO'S TYPE.)
TWITCH
RIGHT~?!

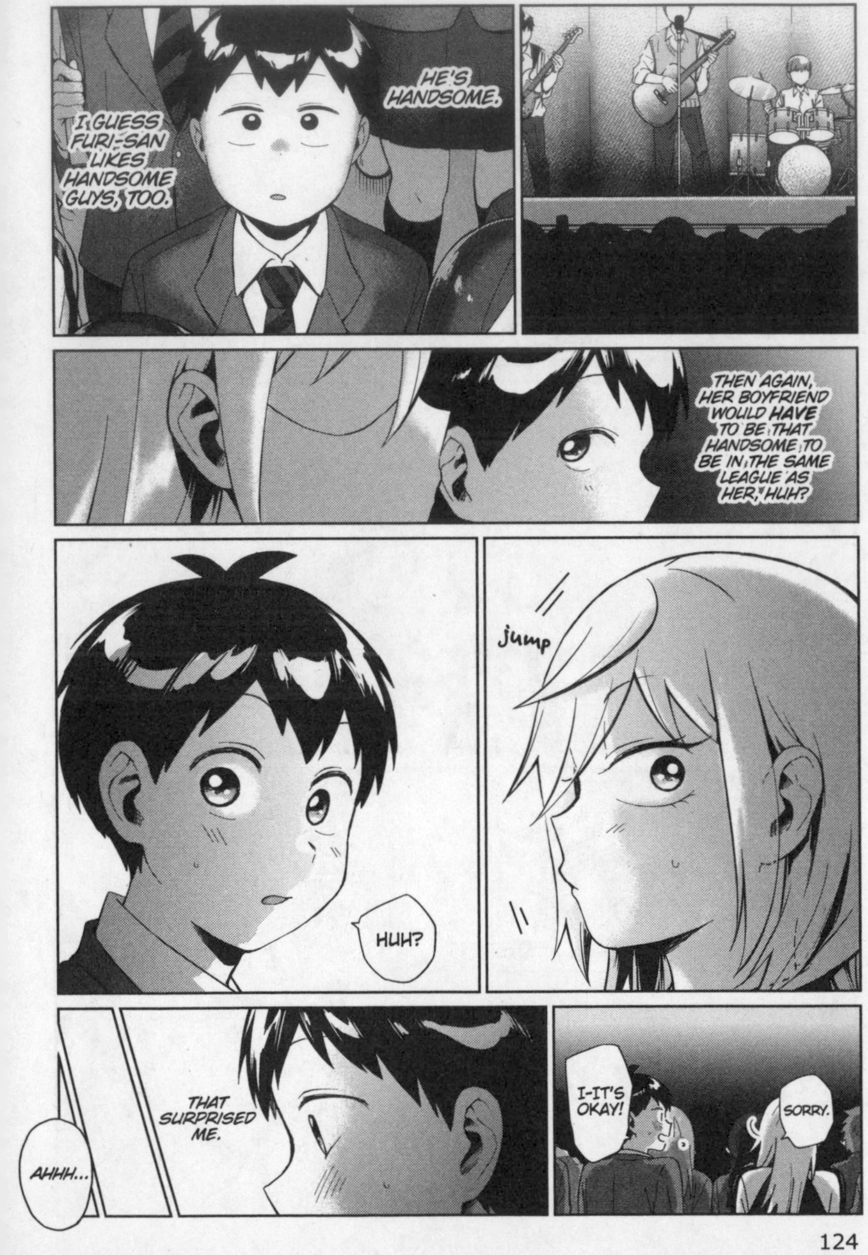
HE'S HANDSOME.
I GUESS FURI-SAN LIKES HANDSOME GUYS, TOO.
THEN AGAIN, HER BOYFRIEND WOULD **HAVE** TO BE THAT HANDSOME TO BE IN THE SAME LEAGUE AS HER, HUH?
jump
HUH?
SORRY.
I-IT'S OKAY!
THAT SURPRISED ME.
AHHH...

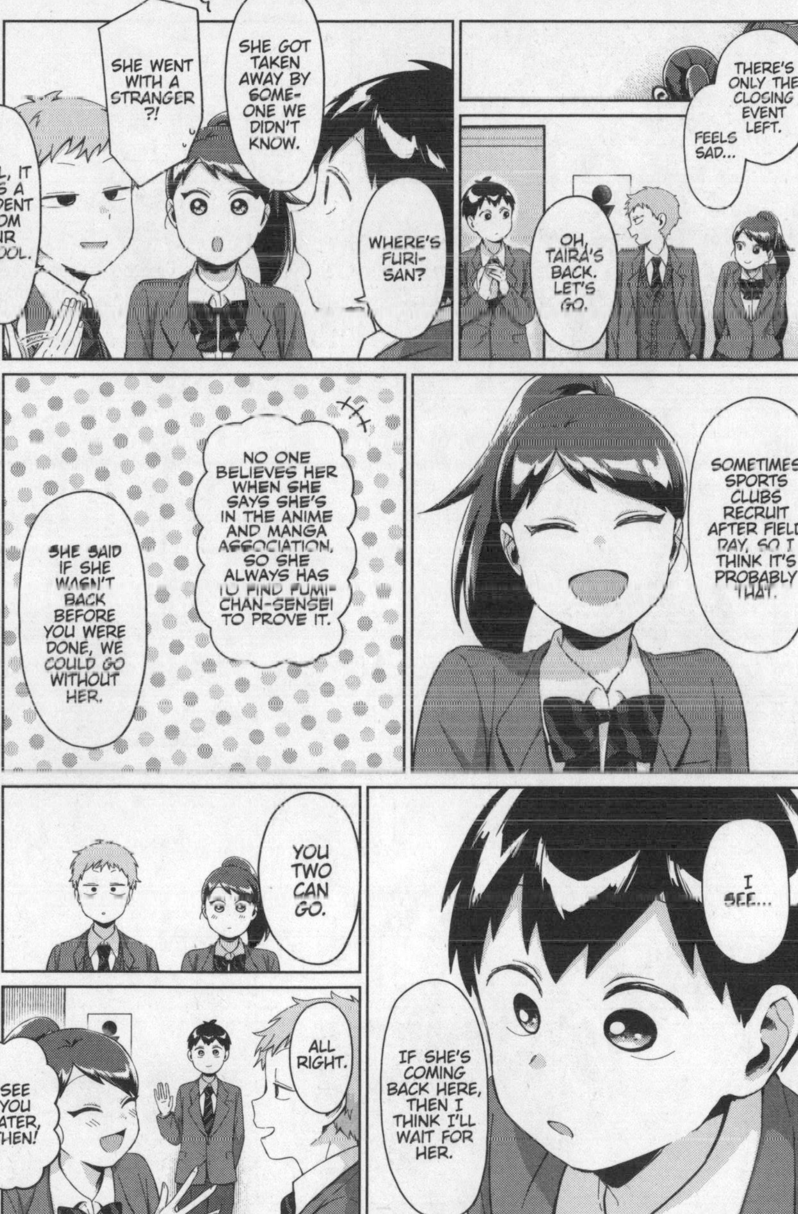
THERE'S ONLY THE CLOSING EVENT LEFT.
FEELS SAD...
OH, TAIRA'S BACK. LET'S GO.
WHERE'S FURI-SAN?
SHE GOT TAKEN AWAY BY SOME-ONE WE DIDN'T KNOW.
SHE WENT WITH A STRANGER ?!
CHILL, IT WAS A STUDENT FROM OUR SCHOOL.
SOMETIMES SPORTS CLUBS RECRUIT AFTER FIELD DAY, SO I THINK IT'S PROBABLY THAT.
NO ONE BELIEVES HER WHEN SHE SAYS SHE'S IN THE ANIME AND MANGA ASSOCIATION, SO SHE ALWAYS HAS TO FIND FUMI-CHAN-SENSEI TO PROVE IT.
SHE SAID IF SHE WASN'T BACK BEFORE YOU WERE DONE, WE COULD GO WITHOUT HER.
I SEE...
IF SHE'S COMING BACK HERE, THEN I THINK I'LL WAIT FOR HER.
YOU TWO CAN GO.
ALL RIGHT.
SEE YOU LATER, THEN!

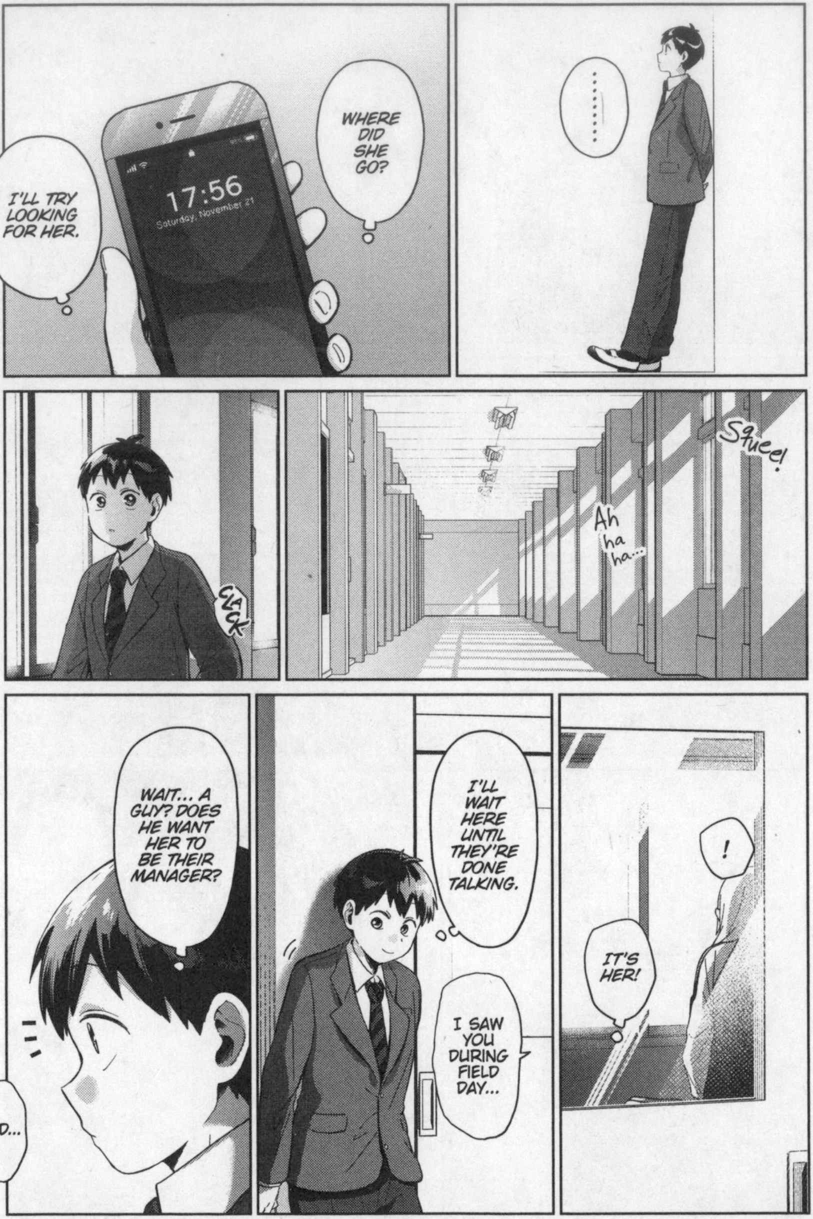
……
WHERE DID SHE GO?
17:56
Saturday, November 21
I'LL TRY LOOKING FOR HER.
Squee!
Ah ha ha...
CLACK
!
IT'S HER!
I'LL WAIT HERE UNTIL THEY'RE DONE TALKING.
I SAW YOU DURING FIELD DAY...
WAIT... A GUY? DOES HE WANT HER TO BE THEIR MANAGER?
AND...

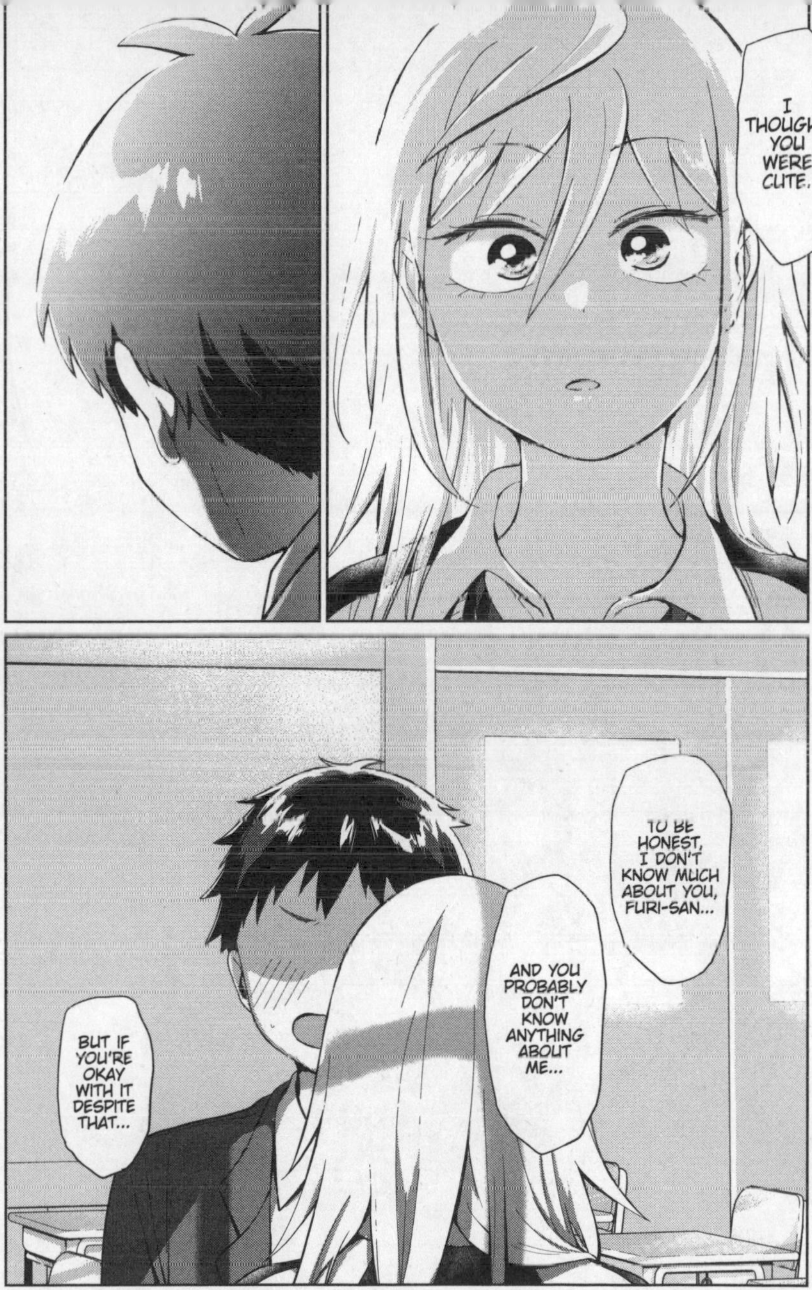
I THOUGHT YOU WERE CUTE.
TO BE HONEST, I DON'T KNOW MUCH ABOUT YOU, FURI-SAN...
AND YOU PROBABLY DON'T KNOW ANYTHING ABOUT ME...
BUT IF YOU'RE OKAY WITH IT DESPITE THAT...

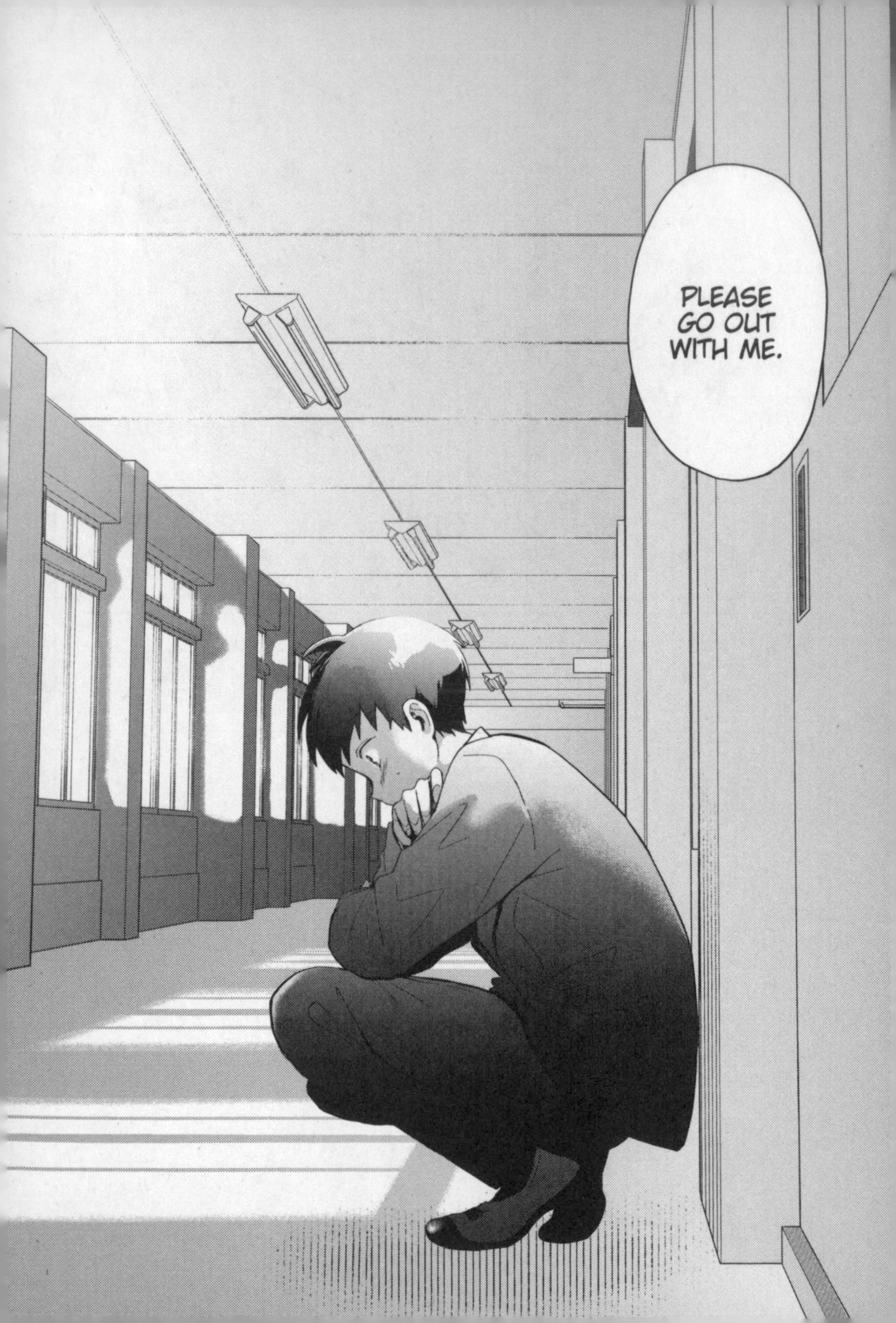
PLEASE GO OUT WITH ME.

Bonus Chapter (24.5) Jacket: Strongest Fighter in History

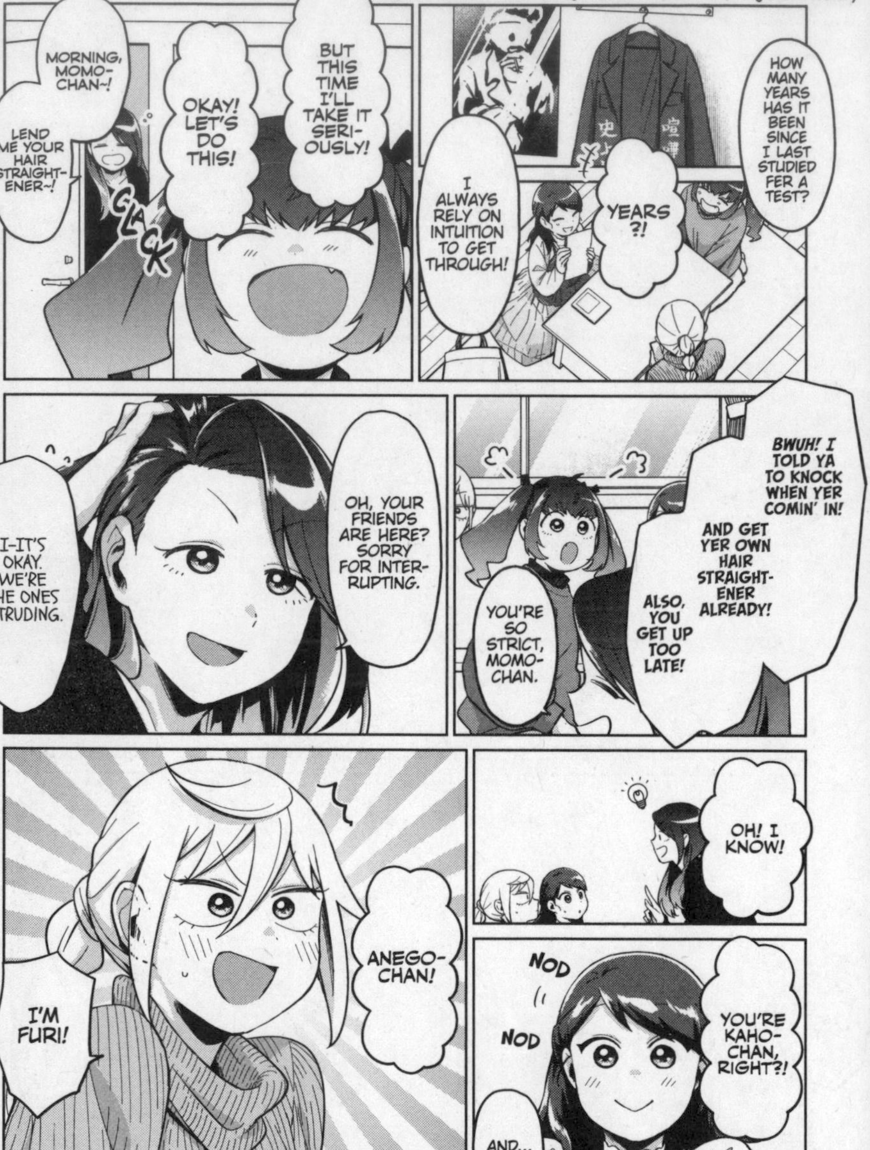

HOW MANY YEARS HAS IT BEEN SINCE I LAST STUDIED FER A TEST?
YEARS ?!
I ALWAYS RELY ON INTUITION TO GET THROUGH!
BUT THIS TIME I'LL TAKE IT SERI-OUSLY!
OKAY! LET'S DO THIS!
MORNING, MOMO-CHAN~!
LEND ME YOUR HAIR STRAIGHT-ENER~!
CLACK
BWUH! I TOLD YA TO KNOCK WHEN YER COMIN' IN!
AND GET YER OWN HAIR STRAIGHT-ENER ALREADY!
ALSO, YOU GET UP TOO LATE!
YOU'RE SO STRICT, MOMO-CHAN.
OH, YOUR FRIENDS ARE HERE? SORRY FOR INTER-RUPTING.
I-IT'S OKAY. WE'RE THE ONES INTRUDING.
OH! I KNOW!
YOU'RE KAHO-CHAN, RIGHT?!
NOD
NOD
AND...
ANEGO-CHAN!
I'M FURI!

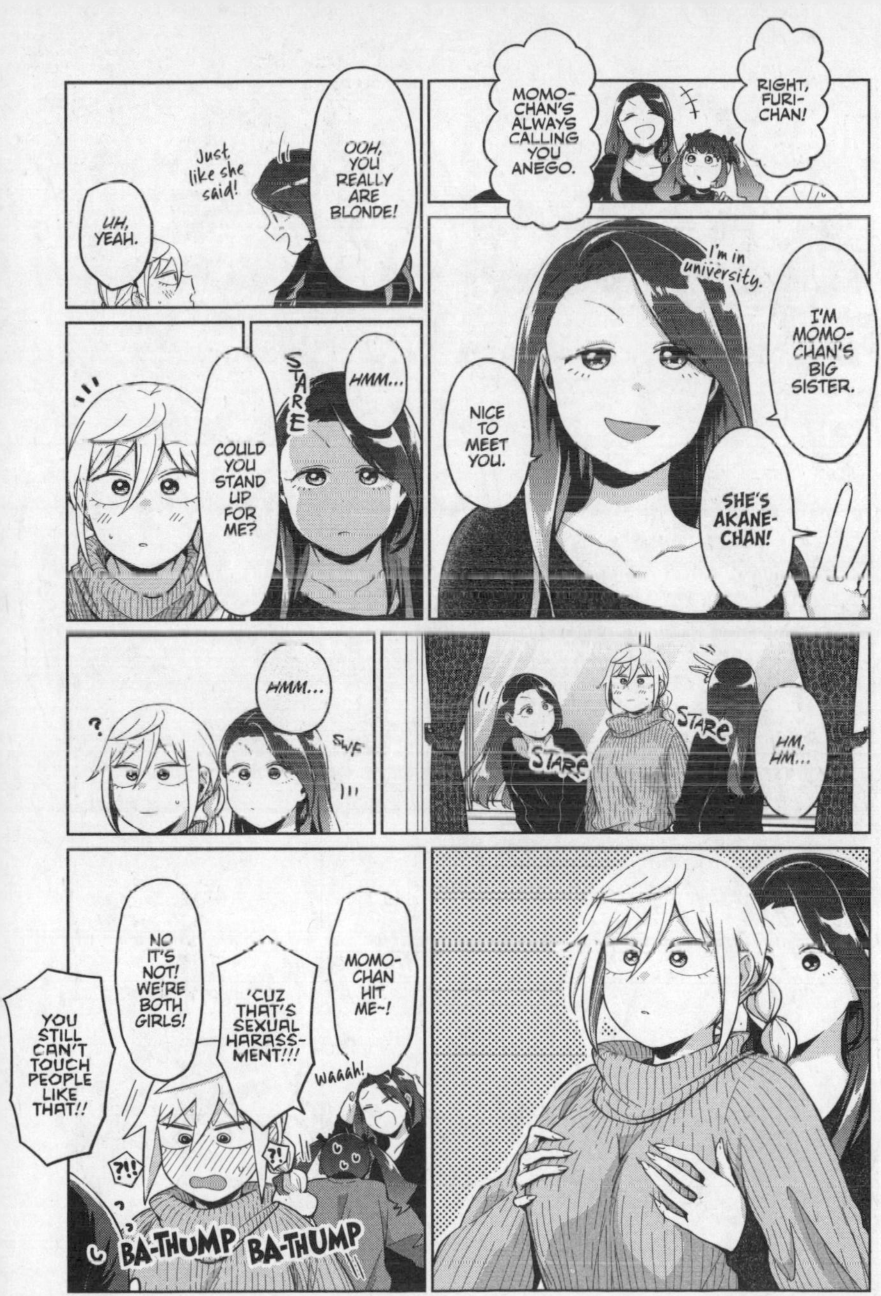
RIGHT, FURI-CHAN!
MOMO-CHAN'S ALWAYS CALLING YOU ANEGO.
OOH, YOU REALLY ARE BLONDE!
Just like she said!
UH, YEAH.
I'M MOMO-CHAN'S BIG SISTER.
I'm in university.
NICE TO MEET YOU.
SHE'S AKANE-CHAN!
HMM...
STARE
COULD YOU STAND UP FOR ME?
HM, HM...
STARE
STARE
HMM...
SWF
MOMO-CHAN HIT ME~!
Waaah!
'CUZ THAT'S SEXUAL HARASS-MENT!!!
NO IT'S NOT! WE'RE BOTH GIRLS!
YOU STILL CAN'T TOUCH PEOPLE LIKE THAT!!
?!
?!!
BA-THUMP BA-THUMP

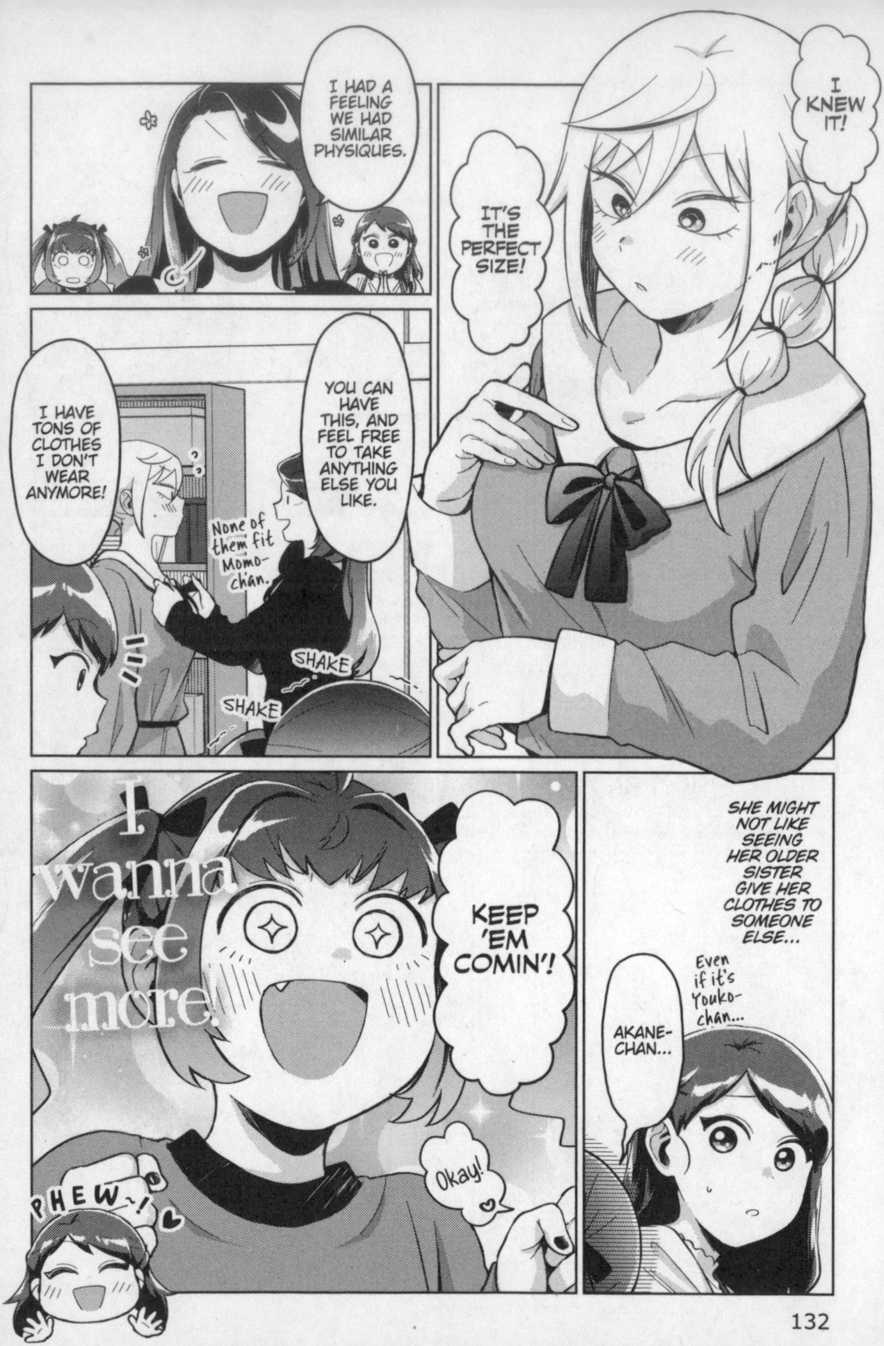
I KNEW IT!
IT'S THE PERFECT SIZE!
I HAD A FEELING WE HAD SIMILAR PHYSIQUES.
YOU CAN HAVE THIS, AND FEEL FREE TO TAKE ANYTHING ELSE YOU LIKE.
I HAVE TONS OF CLOTHES I DON'T WEAR ANYMORE!
None of them fit Momo-chan.
SHAKE
SHAKE
SHE MIGHT NOT LIKE SEEING HER OLDER SISTER GIVE HER CLOTHES TO SOMEONE ELSE...
Even if it's Youko-chan...
AKANE-CHAN...
KEEP 'EM COMIN'!
I wanna see more!
Okay!
PHEW~!

Jacket: Strongest Fighter in History

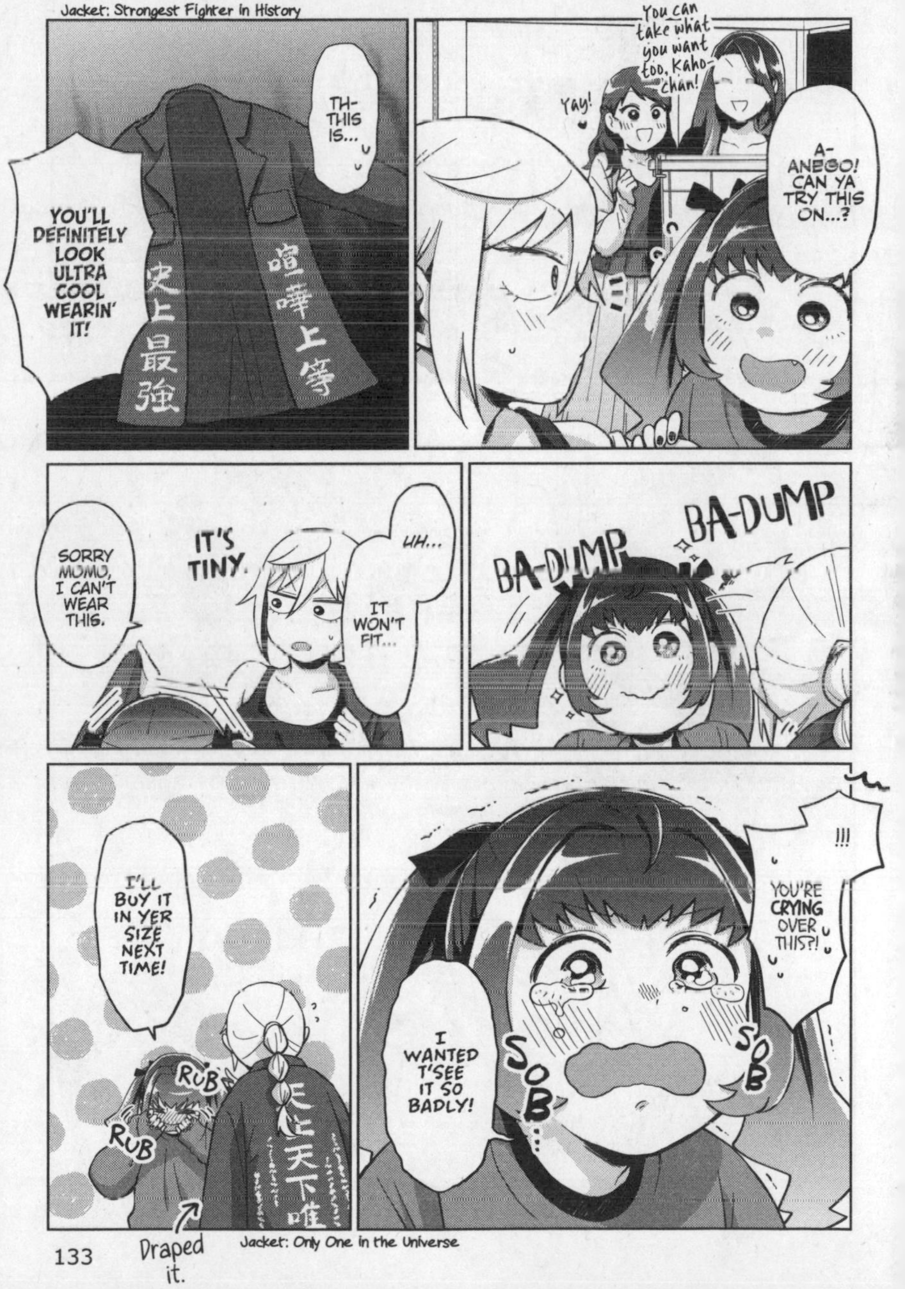

You can take what you want too, Kaho-chan!
Yay!
A-ANEGO! CAN YA TRY THIS ON...?
TH-THIS IS...
YOU'LL DEFINITELY LOOK ULTRA COOL WEARIN' IT!
喧嘩上等
史上最強
BA-DUMP
BA-DUMP
UH...
IT WON'T FIT...
IT'S TINY.
SORRY MOMO, I CAN'T WEAR THIS.
!!!
YOU'RE CRYING OVER THIS?!
I WANTED T'SEE IT SO BADLY!
SOB
SOB
SOB...
I'LL BUY IT IN YER SIZE NEXT TIME!
RUB
RUB
天上天下唯

Jacket: Only One in the Universe

Draped it.

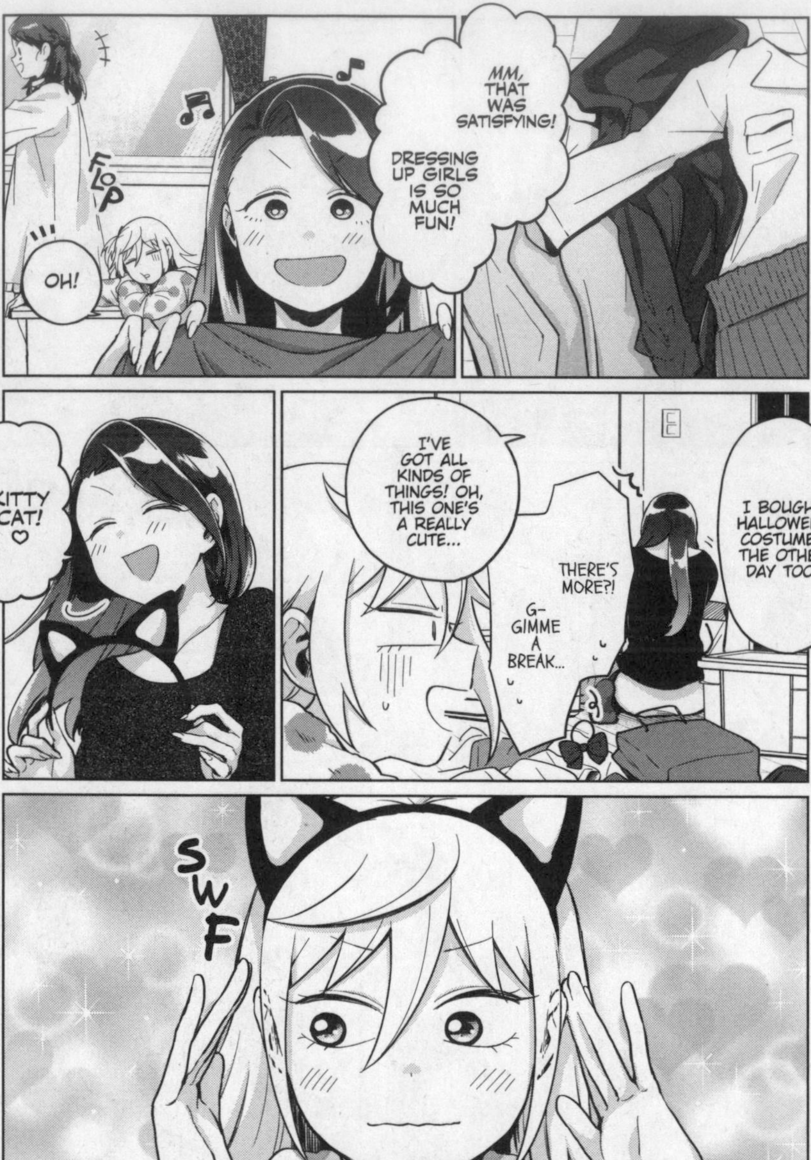
MM, THAT WAS SATISFYING!
DRESSING UP GIRLS IS SO MUCH FUN!
FLOP
OH!
I BOUGHT HALLOWEEN COSTUMES THE OTHER DAY TOO!
THERE'S MORE?!
G-GIMME A BREAK...
I'VE GOT ALL KINDS OF THINGS! OH, THIS ONE'S A REALLY CUTE...
KITTY CAT! ♡
SWF

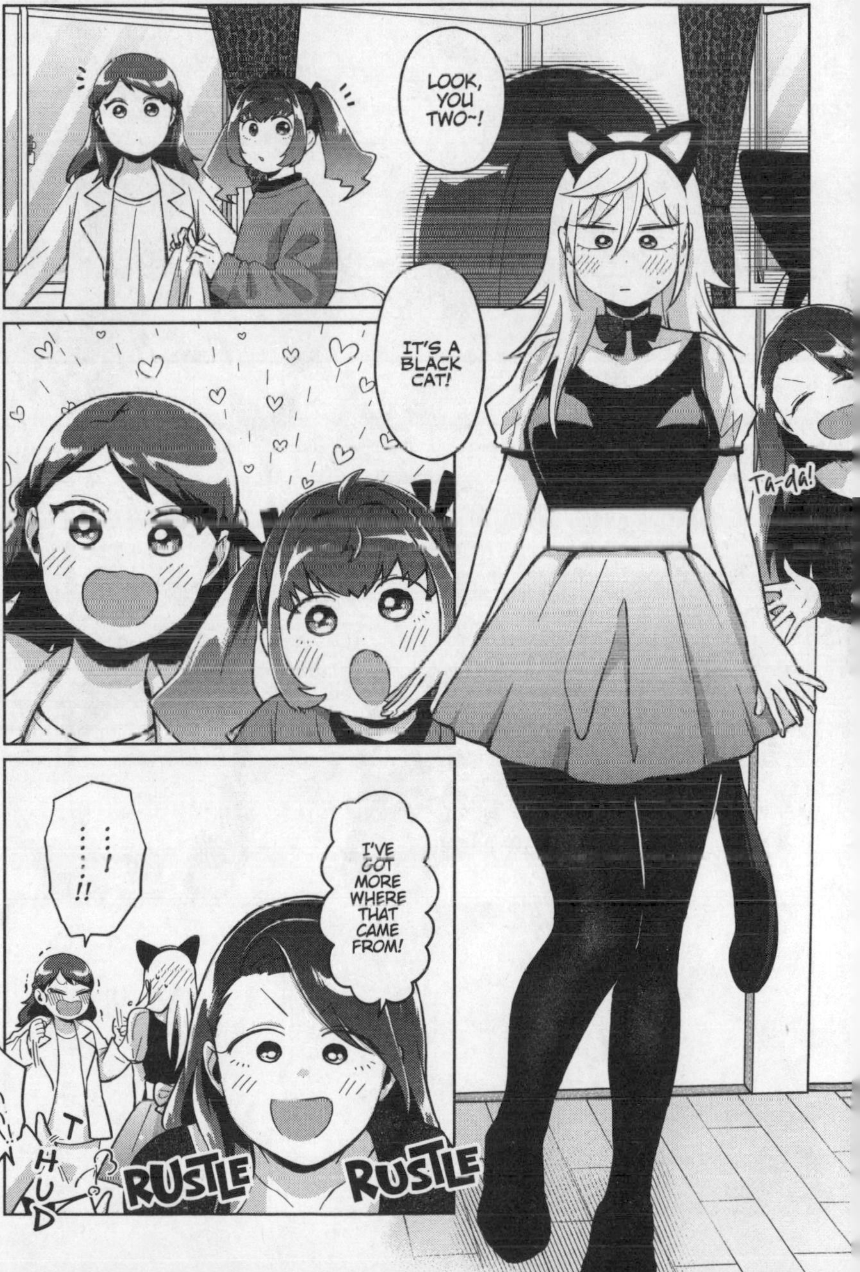
LOOK, YOU TWO~!
IT'S A BLACK CAT!
Ta-da!
I'VE GOT MORE WHERE THAT CAME FROM!
……! ……!!
Ahhh!!
THUD
RUSTLE RUSTLE

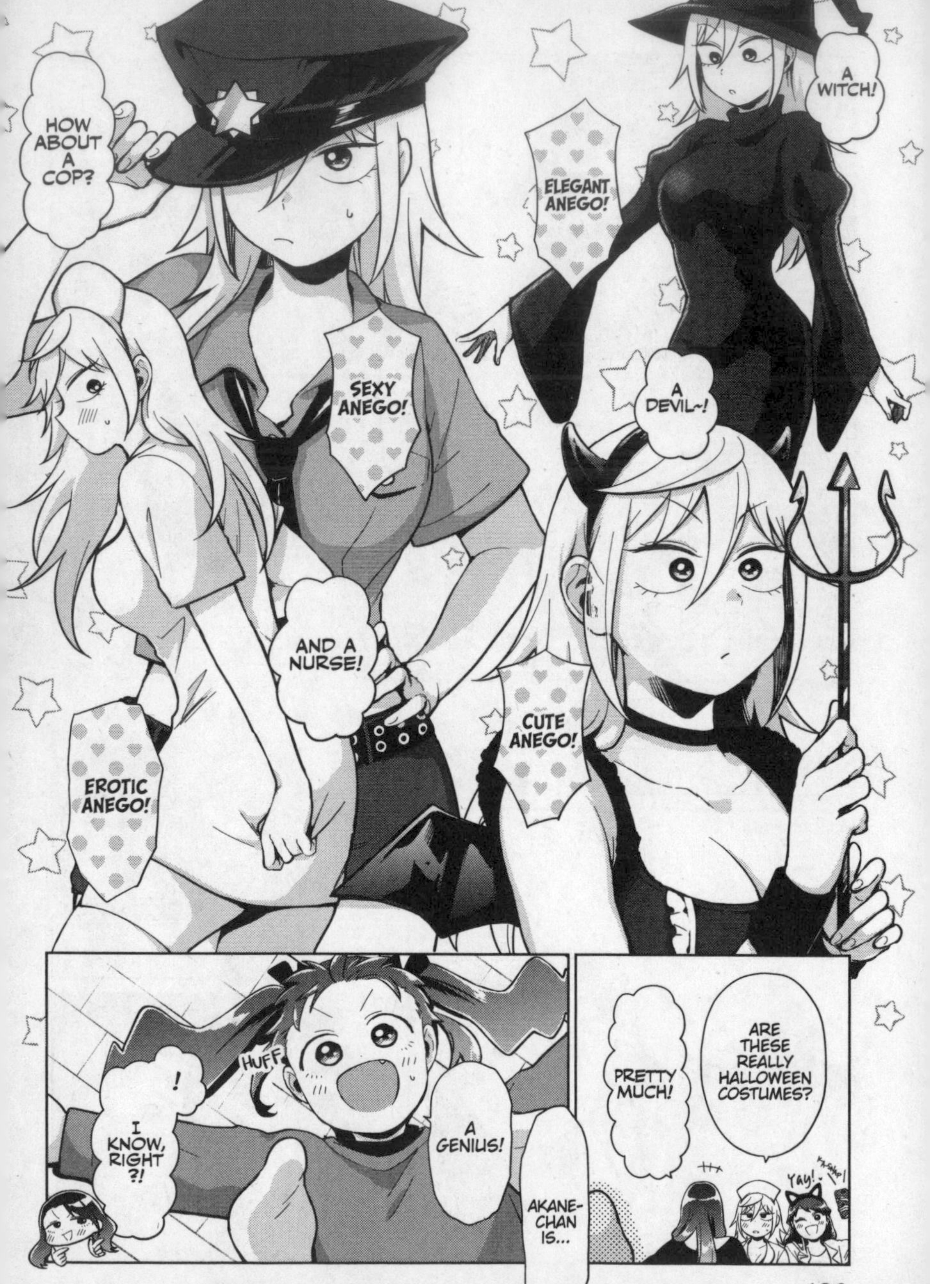
A WITCH!
ELEGANT ANEGO!
HOW ABOUT A COP?
A DEVIL~!
SEXY ANEGO!
AND A NURSE!
CUTE ANEGO!
EROTIC ANEGO!
ARE THESE REALLY HALLOWEEN COSTUMES?
PRETTY MUCH!
Yay!
AKANE-CHAN IS...
A GENIUS!
HUFF
!
I KNOW, RIGHT?!

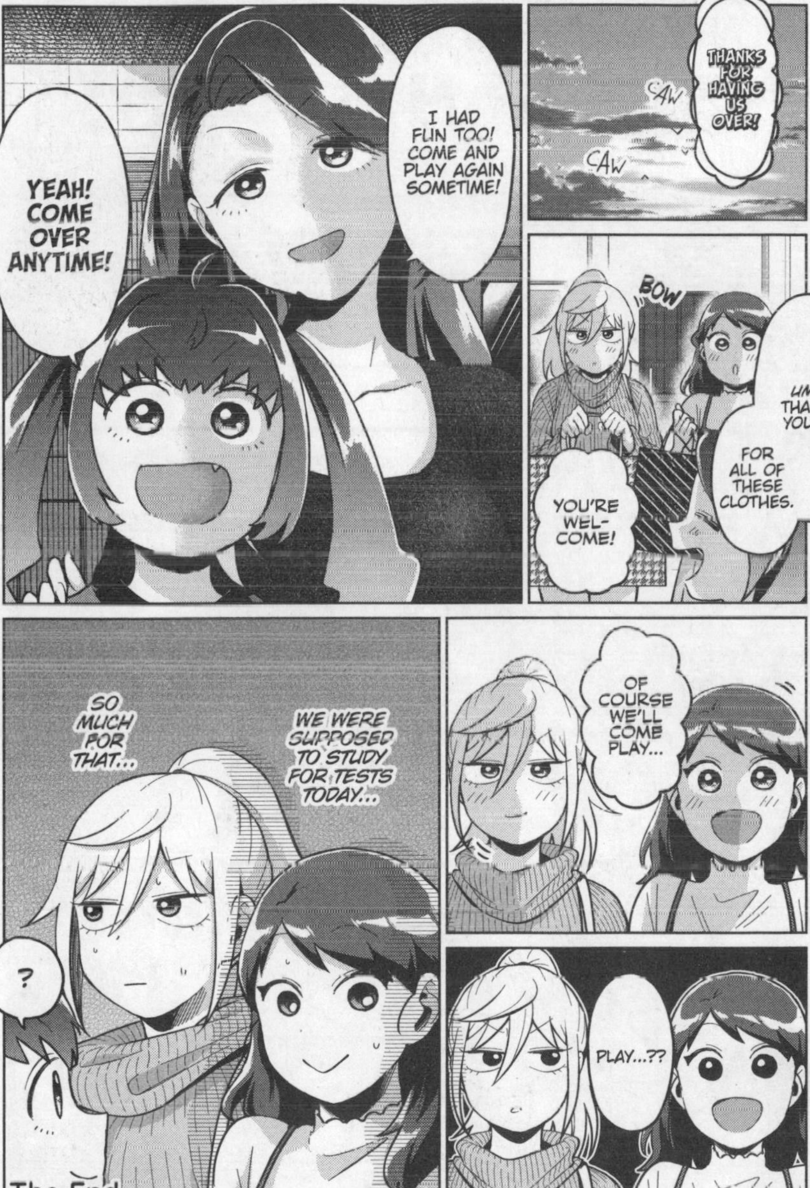
THANKS FOR HAVING US OVER!
CAW
CAW
BOW
UM, THANK YOU...
FOR ALL OF THESE CLOTHES.
YOU'RE WEL-COME!
I HAD FUN TOO! COME AND PLAY AGAIN SOMETIME!
YEAH! COME OVER ANYTIME!
OF COURSE WE'LL COME PLAY...
PLAY...??
WE WERE SUPPOSED TO STUDY FOR TESTS TODAY...
SO MUCH FOR THAT...
?
The End

SEVEN SEAS ENTERTAINMENT PRESENTS

NO MATTER WHAT YOU SAY, FURi-SAN is SCARY!

Vol. 3

story and art by SEIICHI KINOUE

TRANSLATION
Minna Lin

LETTERING
Carolina Hernández Mendoza

COVER AND LOGO DESIGN
H. Qi

PROOFREADER
Kurestin Armada

COPY EDITOR
Dawn Davis

EDITOR
K. McDonald

PRODUCTION DESIGNER
Christina McKenzie

PRODUCTION MANAGER
Lissa Pattillo

PREPRESS TECHNICIAN
Melanie Ujimori

PRINT MANAGER
Rhiannon Rasmussen-Silverstein

EDITOR-IN-CHIEF
Julie Davis

ASSOCIATE PUBLISHER
Adam Arnold

PUBLISHER
Jason DeAngelis

Seven Seas press and purchase enquiries can be sent to Marketing Manager Lianne Sentar at press@gomanga.com. Information regarding the distribution and purchase of digital editions is available from Digital Manager CK Russell at digital@gomanga.com.

ISBN: 978-1-63858-201-4
Printed in Canada
First Printing: April 2022
10 9 8 7 6 5 4 3 2 1

READING DIRECTIONS

This book reads from ***right to left***, Japanese style. If this is your first time reading manga, you start reading from the top right panel on each page and take it from there. If you get lost, just follow the numbered diagram here. It may seem backwards at first, but you'll get the hang of it! Have fun!!

1
2
3
4
5
6
7
8
9

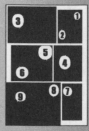